Bold in Battle

South African stories from the Second World War

Karen Horn

Helion & Company

For Nicola and Schalk, always in my heart

Helion & Company Limited
Unit 8 Amherst Business Centre
Budbrooke Road
Warwick
CV34 5WE
England
Tel. 01926 499619
Email: info@helion.co.uk
Website: www.helion.co.uk
X (formerly Twitter): @Helionbooks
Facebook: @HelionBooks
Visit our blog at helionbooks.wordpress.com

Published by Helion & Company 2025
Designed and typeset by Mach 3 Solutions (www.mach3solutions.co.uk)
Cover designed by Paul Hewitt, Battlefield Design (www.battlefield-design.co.uk)

Text © Karen Horn 2025
Illustrations © as individually credited

Every reasonable effort has been made to trace copyright holders and to obtain their permission for the use of copyright material. The author and publisher apologise for any errors or omissions in this work, and would be grateful if notified of any corrections that should be incorporated in future reprints or editions of this book.

ISBN 978-1-804518-10-6

British Library Cataloguing-in-Publication Data.
A catalogue record for this book is available from the British Library.

All rights reserved. No part of this publication may be reproduced, stored in a retrieval system, or transmitted, in any form, or by any means, electronic, mechanical, photocopying, recording or otherwise, without the express written consent of Helion & Company Limited.

For details of other military history titles published by Helion & Company Limited, contact the above address, or visit our website: http://www.helion.co.uk

We always welcome receiving book proposals from prospective authors.

Contents

Abbreviations		iv
Author's Note		vi
Introduction		viii
1	Uys Krige, War Correspondent	13
2	Lieutenant Derrick Norton in East Africa	34
3	Sydney Stuart and the 11th Field Ambulance	45
4	The Birch Brothers, *Die Middellandse Regiment*	52
5	Captain De Villiers Graaff	70
6	Fred Anthony Ernstzen of the Cape Corps	85
7	Chris Roux and the Transvaal Horse Artillery	97
8	Tom Mitchell and the Imperial Light Horse	114
9	Gerard Gafney and the Royal Natal Carbineers	122
10	Martin van Rooyen, the War Surveyor	143
11	Amalia Snyman, Rescuer of POWs	165
12	Constance Anne Nothard, Matron-in-Chief	184
Bibliography		198
Index		210

Abbreviations

BESL	British Commonwealth Ex-Services League
CBE	Commander of the Most Excellent Order of the British Empire
CCS	Casualty Clearing Station
CGS	Chief of the General Staff
DGMS	Director General Medical Services
DHQ	Division Headquarters
DMI	Director of Military Intelligence
DMR	*Die Middellandse Regiment*
GNR	*Guardia Nazionale Republicana*
HQ	Brigade Headquarters
HS	Hospital Ship
ILH	Imperial Light Horse
IO	Information Officer
MBE	Member of the Order of the British Empire
MC	Military Cross (officers)
MM	Military Medal (NCOs and rank and file)
NCO	Non-Commissioned Officer
NEAS	Non-European Army Services
NMR	Natal Mounted Rifles
NP	National Party
OB	*Ossewabrandwag*
OC	Officer Commanding/Commanding Officer
POW	Prisoner of war
RAF	Royal Air Force
RDLI	Royal Durban Light Infantry
RNC	Royal Natal Carbineers
SAA	South African Artillery
SAAF	South African Air Force
SAEC	Survey Company of the South Africa Engineer Corps
SAHA	South Africa Heavy Battery
SAMNS	South African Military Nursing Service
SAP	South African Party
SAS	Special Air Service
SG	Surgeon General
Sitrep	Situation Report

THA	Transvaal Horse Artillery
UDF	Union Defence Force
USAAF	United States Army Air Force
V.A.D.	Voluntary Aid Detachment

Author's Note

The content of this book came to me from the sons, daughters, grandsons and granddaughters of those who fought during the Second World War. When my first book, on South African prisoners of war (*In Enemy Hands*) appeared in 2015[1] people from all over began to share their families' war stories with me. I am grateful that they all trusted me with these memories and I hope I do them justice in this book.

Each chapter tells the story of an individual, and while readers will decide for themselves what the impact of war was on each of these men and women, there is no doubt that war changes us, whether it was a war in the past, or one raging in our time. Everyone is affected by war, sacrifices are made, however big or small. In reading about war, we become aware of the way humanity endures, inflicts cruelty and sorrow, triumphs or submit to defeat. The purpose of this book is not to analyse why South Africans chose to fight, or how they fought, it merely tells the story of what they saw, heard, felt, laughed and cried.

At any time, there are conflicts raging somewhere on the globe. Many books have been written about these conflicts and the methods, strategies, weapons and circumstances have been analysed in the finest detail. These books support current and future wars. Commanders, generals and colonels study them and learn lessons from the past, they improve their tactics for the next conflict. Mankind strives to improve the ways of killing and so wars become a feature of almost every generation and every world region.

Yet even when destruction is planned, created, or brought about by accident by those who seek glory and power, humanity survives, albeit with long-lasting scars. There will always be survivors, but the deadly cycle of war is set on repeat.

Bold in Battle offers a glance into the war experiences of a small number of individuals, and while the number is too small to be representative of the entire group of South African volunteer soldiers, their experiences go some way to provide insight into the many ways in which war touched the lives of those who lived through it. Most of the men and women in this book were born in South Africa, those who were not, made South Africa their home after the war. Some of them volunteered their services while others were dragged into battle against their will. Most survived.

For all of them, the war was a life-changing event, and one that they remembered with many emotions; sadness, humour, pride, grief, relief, frustration – the list of emotions is endless, yet for some, when the war revealed the unspeakable nature of

---

[1] *In Enemy Hands: South Africa's POWs in WWII* (Johannesburg: Jonathan Ball Publishers Pty, 2015).

man, there were no words. The individuals who share their war experiences in this book do so through their letters, memoirs, diaries and oral reminiscences.

As the author of this book, I confess that I have never experienced combat. I do not know what it is like to see friends fall in battle, or to hear the sound of artillery fire or to watch anti-aircraft guns take aim at bombers overhead. I have scars, but they are not battle scars. To do justice to those who told their stories of war, I let them speak for themselves, and as such, this is not a book about war, but a book about people.

I owe a debt of gratitude to all of those who trusted me with their families' war stories; they are Moray Norton, son of Derrick Norton; Sir De Villiers Graaff, grandson of Sir De Villiers Graaff; Zane Boltman, grandson of Frend Anthony Ernstzen; Chris Roux, grandson of Chris Roux and in–law family of the Birch brothers; Guy Gafney, grandson of Gerard Gafney; Marianne Cilliers, daughter of Martin van Rooyen; Charles Mitchell, son of Tom Mitchell; and Louis Eksteen and André Erwee, who shared Sydney Stuart's memoirs with me. The information for the chapter on Uys Krige came from the Special Collections Library at the University of Stellenbosch, and Matron Nothard's story came from the Department of Defence Archives in Pretoria. Last but not least, my thanks goes to William le Crerar[2] who first contacted me in 2016 and wrote to me about his mother-in-law, Amalia Snyman (née Tasciotti), and her remarkable story. I was lucky enough to talk with Amalia about her war experiences and she became the inspiration for this book.

My thanks also go to Duncan Rogers and everyone at Helion & Company who gave this book a chance to see the light, and to Jonathan Fennell who kindly read the manuscript and took the time to discuss it with me.

---

2   Unfortunately, William passed away in 2023.

Introduction

For a country on the southern tip of Africa, the Second World War presented a chance for it to participate in global events. Despite its relative geographic isolation, the Union of South Africa could, as part of the British Empire, take up the fight against Fascism, which at the time threatened liberty and democracy. One would of course only take up this battle if one believed that Fascism was indeed evil and that it was not acceptable for dictatorial leaders to suppress the free will of those working to better their own prospects. In the Union not everyone was convinced that the war against the fascist rulers was justified.

Jan Christian Smuts, former Boer War general and member of the Imperial War Cabinet during the First World War, believed that supporting Britain held more advantages than disadvantages for the country. The Prime Minister at the time, General J. B. M. Hertzog, did not want to take sides and stuck to his policy of defending the borders of the country, but nothing more. By remaining neutral, the physical distance between the Union and the Imperial powers would isolate and alienate its citizens from industrial, economic, and scientific progress, as well as from the enlightened worldview that was emerging in many Western nations.

Yet, Hertzog's followers believed, with the information they had at the time, that it was the right thing to do. After all, they argued, they were victims of a past war between the Afrikaners and the British, and they were adamant that they would go into the future looking backwards.

As an internationalist, however, Smuts looked beyond these national difficulties at the bigger picture. Smuts's part in the First World War and his role at the subsequent Treaty of Versailles in 1919, which brought that war to an end, confirmed to him that South Africa held a higher status than was perhaps the case. The treaty secured the Union's administration of the former German colony of German South-West Africa. Smuts also insisted that the League of Nations, the forerunner of the United Nations, be created to maintain world peace.

With the young country participating in these significant world events, Smuts was convinced that South Africa would continue in this role in future. As such, there was no doubt in his mind when the Second World War began in 1939, that South Africa had to support Britain in its fight against Fascism.[1] With Hertzog's supporters discussing the virtues of neutrality, Smuts outmanoeuvred them in a

---

1   Antonio Garcia and Ian van der Waag, *Botha, Smuts and the First World War* (Johannesburg: Jonathan Ball, 2024), pp.270–272.

parliamentary vote, took over as Prime Minister and threw in the fate of the country with that of Britain.²

Within the sensitive milieu of a country still trying to find its feet, Smuts knew that to call for conscription would serve only to provoke dissatisfaction, as was the case in 1914 when Afrikaners rebelled against South Africa's participation in the First World War. A continuous supply of willing volunteers, on the other hand, would need the support of the civilian population, and thus the campaign began to convince families to send their sons to battle.

To mitigate the tension between English and Afrikaans speaking South Africans, and between the pro-Smuts and anti-Smuts citizens, the Union Defence Force did not include language preferences in its documentation. In addition, the recruitment campaigns cleverly combined nostalgia and the newfangledness of up-to-the-minute war machines to draw in Afrikaners who were sceptical about the war.

The idea of going 'on commando', as men did during the South African War of 1899 to 1902, stirred sentimental emotions while the newly developed weaponry excited adventure-seeking young men. As was the case in Britain, the idea of war as sport played down the risks of battle and inspired many to join 'the team'. The art of propaganda was alive and well in South Africa.

In the end, however, harsh financial circumstances drove many Afrikaners to the recruitment offices and about half of those who volunteered, were Afrikaans speaking. Despite the political differences among the population, many young men volunteered to join the UDF and even Afrikaners, driven by harsh economic circumstances, found their way to the enlistment office.³ Some men had a strong sense of duty towards the British Empire – and in general the English-speaking part of the population signed up for war because they were loyal to the British Empire. A total of 342,792 men and women volunteered, each of their uniforms adorned with a red tab on the shoulder to set them apart from those who did not take the oath to serve in the war.⁴

As one historian reflected, the contribution was 'not massive' when compared to other Commonwealth countries and Dominions, but at least Smuts was able to demonstrate the country's loyalty to Britain.⁵ On the other hand, those who did not volunteer kept the economy going for the duration of the war. It was not for nothing that Smuts was known as '*Slim Jannie*'.⁶

---

2   F. L. Monama, 'The Second World War and South African Society, 1939 – 1945' in T. Potgieter and I. Liebenberg (eds) *Reflections on War Preparedness and Consequences* (Stellenbosch: Sun Press, 2012), p.48.
3   Albert Grundlingh, 'The King's Afrikaners? Enlistment and ethnic identity in the Union of South Africa's Defence Force during the Second World War', *Journal of African History* 40:1 (1999), pp.355–356, 360–361.
4   Many who were UDF members when the war started refused to take the oath. Ian van der Waag, *A Military History of Modern South Africa* (Cape Town: Jonathan Ball Publishers, 2015), p.175.
5   Keith Hancock quoted in Nasson, B. *South Africa at War 1939–1945* (Johannesburg: Jacana, 2012), p.11.
6   clever Jannie. G. Garland, 'The Strange disappearance of Jan Christiaan Smuts and What it can teach Americans', American Diplomacy (2010), https://americandiplomacy.web.unc.edu, accessed 18 April 2021.

The distance between the Union and the main theatre of war allowed life to continue on the home front in much the same way it did before Adolf Hitler's forces began to sow death and destruction across Europe. Many South Africans convinced themselves that the war was someone else's problem, after all, Europe was very far away from the tip of Africa. As is often the case though, some were not content to disagree with Smuts only in theory.

Among the fervent challengers were the *Ossewabrandwag*[7] (OB) movement. The paramilitary units of this organisation bore notable similarities with the Nazis. There were also the *Stormjaers*[8] and the *Terreurgroup*,[9] and their aim was to create as much chaos and unrest within the borders of the country as possible, and in so doing, limit the deployment of UDF volunteers against fascist forces, whether they were Italian or German in the African and European theatres of war.[10] Other anti-war organisations included the Greyshirts and the New Order, but the infighting and disagreements made them an annoying, but not overly dangerous, faction among those who did not stand with Smuts.[11]

The Union never saw bombing raids or hostile invasions as Europeans did when the Nazis seemed unstoppable during the first few years of the war. For the most part, South Africa's infrastructure development and food production continued as before, although with help from Italian prisoners of war from 1941 onwards.

It was up to British colonies to help supply food to the British Isles, but as merchant ships did not always get through the German U-boat lines, schemes such as the 'make do and mend' and the 'digging for victory' campaigns were launched in Britain. Housewives became very adept at mending clothes as new supplies were scarce and expensive – by the end of 1941 clothing prices had risen by 91 percent.[12] Flowerbeds were replaced by vegetable gardens as families tried to become self-sufficient. By 1941 women were also being drafted for war service and many became 'land girls,' working on farms to boost food production.[13]

It was not only basic shortages that changed daily lives, it was also the air-raid sirens that sent civilians scrambling to shelters while the Nazi bombs rained down on the British home front.[14] Sudden death at the hands of the enemy was as much a fear for those at home as it was for those on the battlefront. Mothers, wives, and daughters adapted to these difficult conditions as their sons, husbands, and fathers fought on the battlefields in Europe, Africa and the Far East.

---

7   Literally, Ox-wagon sentinel. The *Ossewabrandwag* was a right-wing Afrikaner nationalist organisation which was against South Africa's participation in the war.
8   Storm troops.
9   Terror group.
10 A.M. Fokkens, 'Afrikaner unrest within South Africa during the Second World War and the measures taken to suppress it,' *Journal for Contemporary History* 37:2 (2012), p.131.
11 Grundlingh, 'The King's Afrikaners?', p.353.
12 D. Todman, *Britain's War: Into Battle 1937–1941* (London: Penguin Random House, 2017), p.630.
13 S. K. Wing, *Our Longest Days a People's History of the Second World War* (London: Profile Books, 2008), p.64.
14 Todman, *Britain's War*, p.440.

In South Africa, the impact of the war was much milder when it came to shortages. In cases where particular food items or other supplies became scarce, specific marketing boards controlled the supply of those commodities. For many South Africans, however, the war hardly had an impact on their daily diet. With the large pay gap between the races, many black and unskilled workers were living on a type of ration anyway, eating only *mielie* meal,[15] as they could not afford food such as meat and vegetables. The lack of a national census, a result of racial segregation, also caused the government to resist implementing a formal rationing system. After all, if a large part of the population became aware that food were being exported while they had to make do with porridge, the Smuts government would have had another political problem on their hands.[16]

Critics argued that Smuts's government made too much of providing food for the war while the home front had to deal with shortages. Although those who felt aggrieved about Smuts's willingness to assist Britain probably knew very little about the sacrifices made in Britain. In the Union, the impact of war became evident only towards the end of 1941 when the government imposed rations on fuel. Food was still relatively plentiful, and although the government started to control prices, South African plates overflowed compared to those in Britain.[17]

Those who complained about conditions in the Union more often than not had an ulterior motive, many of them believed that Smuts's eagerness to participate in the war was misplaced. As ever, politics were volatile and the clashes between the anti-war and pro-war groups were egged on by the not-so-neutral newspapers. The closest the Union citizens came to experiencing first-hand the impact of battle was when the OB planned and carried out acts of sabotage.[18]

South African volunteers first saw combat in East Africa in 1940 and 1941. The task of the 1st South Africa Division was to occupy the Italian colonies there and to rid them of any influence that Benito Mussolini had hoped to retain. Victories against lacklustre Italian forces, the capture of thousands of prisoners of war, and the taking of 360,000 square miles proved significant for the 1st Division.[19] For them it was proof that they were capable in combat, morale was high as the commanders claimed the first victory over an Axis force.

With conquest fresh in their minds, the 1st Division joined the 2nd South Africa Division in Egypt as the Middle East Force under command of the British 8th Army prepared to start another phase of combat, one that would be fought in the deserts of North Africa. Libya, then known as Tripolitania and Cyrenaica, were Italian colonies on the Mediterranean Sea. To the west of Libya lay a French colony, Tunisia, and

---

15 Corn porridge.
16 Y. Albertyn, *Upsetting the Applecart: Government and Food control in the Union of South Africa during World War II c.1939–1948* (Thesis in fulfilment of Master of Arts, Stellenbosch University, 2014), pp.76–77.
17 B. Nasson, *South Africa at War 1939–1945* (Johannesburg: Jacana, 2012), pp.68–69.
18 A.M. Fokkens, 'Afrikaner unrest within South Africa during the Second World War and the measures taken to suppress it', *Journal for Contemporary History* 37:2 (2012), p.128.
19 Andrew Stewart, *The First Victory: The Second World War and the East African Campaign* (New Haven: Yale University Press, 2016), p.xii.

to the east lay Egypt, a British stronghold guarding the Suez Canal and control of the Mediterranean, both crucial passages for trade and war.

For Adolf Hitler, these factors were important enough for him to bring in one of his top men, *Generalleutnant* Erwin Rommel to help his Italian ally. The clash between the *Afrika Korps* and the British 8th Army was on a different scale and intensity to those fought in East Africa. For the South Africans, it would be especially significant in that they were involved in a major defeat and in an equally significant victory. The surrender of Tobruk by General H. B. Klopper led to almost 30,000 POWs taken by the Germans. A few months later, the victory at El Alamein would motivate the British Prime Minister, Sir Winston Churchill to say 'Now is not the end. It is not even the beginning of the end. But it is, perhaps, the end of the beginning.'[20]

As the call to 'Avenge Tobruk' went out across the Union, the 6th South Africa Armoured Division was getting ready to invade the Italian mainland along with British and American forces. Under command of Major General Evered Poole, the South Africans entered Rome on 5 June 1944,[21] the day before the D-Day landings took place in France. From Rome, the UDF forces moved northwards to arrive in Florence at the beginning of August. By 1945 they captured Bologna and were involved in the offensive at Monte Solo and Caprara.

On 2 May 1945 the Germans surrendered in Italy, followed a few days later by their complete surrender in Europe. The victories in Italy were not easily won, and the bitter battles there resulted in the 6th Division suffering 5,176 casualties, including 753 dead.[22]

---

20 W. S. Churchill, (ed.), *Never Give In! Winston Churchill's Speeches* (London: Bloomsbury, 2013), p.284.
21 Allied units entered Rome from 4 June onwards, some sources thus give 4 June as the date the city was taken. Other sources point to 5 June, by which time many more units had entered or passed through the city.
22 Apart from the casualties in the 6th Division, the South African Air Force lost 2,420 men in the Italian campaign. Ian van der Waag, *A Military History of Modern South Africa* (Cape Town: Jonathan Ball Publishers, 2015), p.210.

1

Uys Krige, War Correspondent

To say that anti-war sentiments ran high in the Union as the war began in 1939 is an understatement. From the day that Smuts beat Hertzog with seven votes to side with Britain, a war of propaganda began in the Union. As much as Smuts, now Prime Minister, craved the excitement of war, he also had to turn his attention to the Union's disgruntled citizens. Those who shared Smuts's view also realised that they were fighting two wars, one on the battlefield and one on the home front. While the UDF volunteers fought a physical war on the battlefront, the battle of opinion raged on the home front.

The Information Bureau therefore had work to do on both fronts. In July 1940, the methods by which the enemy would be attacked using propaganda was decided. The goal was to create dissention among enemy troops, stir up the populace so they would not give support to their own troops, to lower the morale and efficiency of enemy troops, and inciting enemy troops to desert or rebel against their authorities. Creating friction between the different Axis nations, was another aim, as was the goal to create awareness of the fallacies and dangers of Fascism.[1]

The work of the war correspondents and the Information Bureau was not only directed to propaganda amongst the enemy, but also amongst their fellow servicemen. The Defence Headquarters in Pretoria was of the opinion that, 'it is very evident that there are a number of men who may be regarded as disaffected, mainly amongst the Afrikaans section of the S.A. Forces, and the reason for the disaffection is almost entirely attributable to boredom.'[2] Apparently, English-speaking servicemen were not susceptible to boredom…

Early in 1941, another measure was taken when officers were appointed to each unit. These officers were known amongst the rank and file as 'welfare officers', but the military authorities referred to them as 'propaganda officers.' These officers, all with the rank of captain, were to pass on useful information gained from amongst the men in their unit to the Intelligence Officers. The Intelligence Officers were also the censor officers. To gain access to the information, the welfare officers were required to be men, 'of personality, energetic and keenly interested in the well-being of the men.'[3]

---

1 Department of Defence Archive (hereafter DOD): Press and Propaganda (hereafter PP) Box 39. *Appreciation on the prospects of attacking the enemy in Africa by means of propaganda* by J. E. Sacks 25 July 1940.
2 DOD PP Box 39. PR1/5/2/ D.H.Q to E.A. Force Headquarters, 8 November 1940.
3 DOD PP Box 39. PR1/2/1 2nd January 1941.

On the home front, the work of the Bureau of Information was critical. They had to reassure servicemen's families, while at the same time, convince those citizens who held anti-war and anti-Smuts views.

Although the war had hardly begun, at least as far as South Africa's participation was concerned, the Director of Military Operations and Intelligence was confident that the dissidents on the home front would not get the upper hand when he wrote in November 1940 that, 'schemes are being launched for countering subversive propaganda in the Union and an excellent team have been organised with every prospect of achieving big results.'[4]

Among those appointed as war correspondents for the Bureau, was Uys Krige. He, along with Conrad Norton, another correspondent, joined the volunteers in the East African campaign and later followed them to the Western Desert Campaign in North Africa, and finally on to Italy, where the 6th South Africa Brigade fought gruelling battles against determined Nazi forces.[5] Their despatches informed the Union citizens of victories and reassured them about setbacks, all the while maintaining the idea that the war was justified and that the Fascists were in fact the enemy. Their carefully worded pamphlets, strewn from aircrafts over every Italian colony reached countless Italians, informing them of 'the error of their ways.'

Uys Krige in uniform. (Photo: Uys Krige Collection, Special Collections, Stellenbosch University)

Looking at Uys Krige's pre-war years, however, it is unclear if his support for the war came from personal conviction. While living in Spain in 1934, Uys criticised Smuts and the British Empire, and in a letter, he sarcastically referred to Smuts as a, 'brave [and] genuine Boer [who is] the little golden haired herald to the British Empire, blowing up his bugle upon the crumbling walls…'[6] During an interview in 1944, however, he remembered that in Barcelona, he was:

> surrounded by Fascists, spies pretending to be communists, communists pretending to be Fascists, Nazis pretending to be anything. It was a boiling

---

4 DOD PP Box 39. PR1/5/2 29 November 1941.
5 J. Crwys-Williams, *A Country at War 1939–1945 The Mood of a Nation* (Rivonia: Ashanti Publishing, 1992), p.137.
6 Uys Krige quoted in J. C. Kannemeyer, *Die Goue Seun. Die Lewe en Werk van Uys Krige* (Cape Town: Tafelberg, 2002), p.244.

pot of intrigue, plot and counter-plot: and being very young and not politically minded, at the time, I had no idea what was going on. I found it all very bewildering and chaotic, but it was intensely interesting.[7]

The benefit of hindsight gave him perspective and the ability, a rare quality, to admit his own shortcomings.

Whatever Uys' views of Smuts before or after the war, his war experiences made it clear to him that personal differences and petty arguments diminished in the face of bigger issues, such as the threat presented by Fascism. Uys left Spain about six months before the civil war there broke out. Described by some historians as a revolution against nationalist forces, the country was plunged into a harsh dictatorship when Francisco Franco's forces defeated the Republicans.[8]

In an interview with Noreen Purdon of the South African Broadcasting Corporation's Mobile Recording Unit[9] in 1944, Uys stated that the Spanish war was a turning point in his life, and that when he returned to South Africa, he tried to create awareness among the general public of the, 'terrible tragedy of the Spanish people, but they remained, most of them, completely indifferent.'[10]

Having lived and worked among the Spanish people, then witnessing from afar how a civil war devastated that country must have been difficult for him. Like many young men it is likely that he believed he could make a difference. When South Africa entered the Second World War in 1939, it may be that Uys saw his work as war correspondent as another chance to take up his pen against indifference.

Shortly after Uys returned to South Africa in December 1935, he accepted a position at *Die Vaderland*.[11] Traditionally an Afrikaner Nationalist newspaper, it shifted its political stance when, in 1934, Hertzog and Smuts formed the United Party. It is more than likely that it was Smuts's broader interpretation of politics that brought about the change. However, the readership consisted of two groups, those who remained conservative in their outlook, and the more enlightened readers who, like Smuts, believed in realpolitik.[12] The consequence was that some viewed *Die Vaderland* as a mouthpiece paper of the South Africa Party, while others saw it as a nationalist paper.

It is not easy to pin down Uys's view on the shifting political landscape of the pre-war years. He also worked for the *Rand Daily Mail,* which was the polar opposite to *Die Vaderland,* and a paper that, along with other English language newspapers, was an important tool in the propaganda war that advocated for a

---

7   Stellenbosch University Special Collections (hereafter SuSP): 225.RO.6 (2): Uys Krige Interview with Noreen Purdon, 21 August 1944. Krige Collection.
8   B. Bolloten, *The Spanish Civil War Revolution and Counterrevolution* (Chapel Hill: University of North Carolina Press, 1991), pp.741–742.
9   R. Teer-Tomaselli, 'In Service of Empire: The South African Broadcasting Corporation during World War II', *Critical Arts South-North Cultural and Media Studies* 28:6 (2014), p.900.
10 SuSP, Uys Krige Interview with Noreen Purdon, 21 August 1944. Krige collection, 225.RO.6 (2).
11 Kannemeyer, *Die Goue Seun*, p.244.
12 Ian van der Waag and Tony Garcia, *Botha, Smuts, and the First World War* (Warwick: Helion & Co, 2024), p.xxi.

liberal outlook. When he joined *Die Vaderland,* Uys probably cared less about political ideology and more about an income as at this point the war was not a foregone conclusion.

When the war started, Uys and his brothers volunteered their services to the UDF. His work as war correspondent for the Bureau of Information started even before the first men crossed the borders of the Union. In May 1940, when German forces invaded The Netherlands, Uys wrote an article in which his mandate as correspondent stands out clearly; the aim of his writing was to sway public opinion towards support for Smuts and to justify South Africa's participation in the war. As many Afrikaners had ancestral links with the Dutch, Uys used the opportunity to vilify Nazi actions there, writing that, 'in the cover of darkness Germany, like the assassin that it is, invaded the quiet and peace-loving Netherlands. By attacking The Netherlands, Germany is also attacking us, the Afrikaner nation. They, the Dutch, are flesh of our flesh, blood of our blood.'[13]

Throughout the article, Uys emphasised Afrikaners' duty towards the Dutch by reminding them of the historical bond between the two countries. He pointed out examples of Dutch goodwill towards the Afrikaners during the 'Great Trek' and that they stood by the Afrikaners against the 'mighty overwhelming enemy' during the South African War. He conveniently neglected to mention that the 'mighty overwhelming enemy' of those times were the British, and the Afrikaners, if they heeded Uys's call, would be fighting alongside this erstwhile foe. Another fact that was usefully ignored, was that many Afrikaners also had German ancestry, and they still felt some kind of distant loyalty towards their Fatherland, as was evident by the Nazi-like organisations such as the OB, the *Stormjaers* and the *Terreurgroep.*

Uys's articles were all approved by the Information Bureau, and if found suitable, they were published in the Afrikaans press, including *Huisgenoot, De Gids, Die Brandwag, De Stem, Die Jongspan, Die Skrywerskring-jaarboek,* and *Die Weekblad.*[14] These newspapers were aimed at Afrikaners and the plan was that Uys's articles would go some way to change the readers' political outlook to one of pro-Smuts, if not pro-British.

The 1st South Africa Division was mobilised to the East African front in July 1940.[15] From then on, Uys and Conrad's task began in earnest. As soon as news of the first battles became known, the hesitant home front needed reassurance. Uys's written piece, 'Our Soldiers in Kenya', is one such example that would have stirred the patriotic emotions of any reader;

> You have all probably received or heard of letters from soldiers up here and felt sorry for them with all their grouses and tales of woe, but to be amongst them daily you will all agree that a more spirited crowd cannot be found.

13　Translated from Afrikaans. SuSP 225.RW.6. No. 147. 10/5/1940. Nazi Propaganda.
14　SuSp: 225.RW: Propaganda, Krige collection.
15　Gustav Bentz, "From El Wak to Sidi Rezegh: The Union Defence Force's First Experience of Battle in East and North Africa, 1940–1941". *Scientia Militaria* 40:3 (2012), p.181.

> The South Africans have made a wonderful impression and the red tabs[16] are very popular.
> Many amusing and other incidents which occur I would like to pass onto you.[17]

In the same article, Uys also wrote of a UDF soldier who boasted about the number of life-threatening battles he had been in before asking a British combatant,

> By the way where have you come from? "Only just from Dunkirk" his pal replied. Silence reigned for a while and on exchanging headgear they parted very much amused.[18]

The battles in Kenya were the UDF's first encounters with the enemy, and although they were significant in that theatre of war, they did not measure up in terms of numbers of casualties and the exigencies demanded from those who participated in the European theatre of war.

Dunkirk was a military loss for the Allied forces, but in Britain it is remembered as a victory, not only because 338,226 Allied soldiers were evacuated before the German forces reached them, but also because the home front participated in sending small privately owned boats to rescue 80,000 men. The evacuation took place between 27 May and 4 June 1940 and during that time, the Allies and the Germans fought a bitter battle that saw a number of British POWs shot by their captors.[19]

The South African press presented the public with daily updates on the situation and on 6 June the *Rand Daily Mail* acknowledged the setback with an optimistic tone, using the headline 'Hitler announces new offensive: Brave fighting of Allies praised.'[20] South Africa's participation in the war gains a new perspective when compared to the scale of the Dunkirk evacuation. With the 338,226 men evacuated from Dunkirk, and the 34,000 British taken prisoner, the total stood at 372,226, which was 29,434 more than the 342,792 UDF volunteers who fought in the entire war.[21]

With his anecdote, Uys most probably hoped to create a sense of solidarity and purpose, while at the same time he also implied that the UDF still had a long way to go if they were to make the same contribution as their British counterparts. As for the home front, Uys's piece left those in South Africa in no doubt that the war would demand more from all of them before it came to an end. Uys's story of the UDF soldier may or may not have been true, but it served the purpose of reminding the South African public that fighting the war would take courage, initiative and the

---

16   All South African volunteers who took the oath to serve outside the borders of the country, wore red tabs on their shoulders to set them apart from those who did not take the oath.
17   SuSP: 225.NB.OC.7: 'Our Soldiers in Kenya', Krige collection.
18   SuSP: 225.NB.OC.7: 'Our Soldiers in Kenya', Krige collection.
19   M. Gilbert, *Second World War* (London: Phoenix Giant, 1996), p.83
20   South African Press Association – Reuter. 'Hitler announces new offensive', *Rand Daily Mail*, 6 June 1940, p.11.
21   Ian van der Waag, *A Military History of Modern South Africa* (Cape Town: Jonathan Ball Publishers, 2015), p.175.

cooperation of the home front, just like the British home front did in helping to get many of the men off the beaches of Dunkirk.

With 'Our Soldiers in Kenya,' Uys continued to remind the home front of their responsibilities towards the UDF servicemen. Uys used humour and a light tone to draw the reader in, but throughout the text, he included ideas that held greater meaning. In one example, he noted that, 'on the more serious side, Mail day is the great occasion and friends and relatives cannot imagine how news from them is appreciated. Each letter received usually means two in reply...'[22]

To emphasise his point, Uys also endeavoured to drum up support for Smuts, deftly putting aside his earlier dislike of the man. Uys generalised in his writing and in 'Our Soldiers in Kenya,' he ignored the individual dissenters and wrote as if all servicemen agreed that they were 'naturally more than proud of the fact that we are South Africans but what really thrills us to the core is to hear the Imperial and East African troops regard the same man as their hero as we do – General Smuts. They usually ask numerous questions about, and want to hear all we can tell them, of him.'[23]

He ends the stirring article with a final reassurance; 'Whatever we have already done and are going to do, you may rest assured no matter what the task may be, it will be carried out with the same spirit and determination characteristic of our small nation and you at home will all be proud of us.'[24]

Uys's writing skill and talent is obvious from the article, but at the same time he must have been aware that he was no longer able to express his creativity in the way that the did before the war. By March 1941, the 1st South Africa Division had taken over a number of Italian positions and captured thousands of Italian combatants. Uys, enthused by the successes and convinced that he should be where the action was, intended to follow Major General Dan Pienaar's men to Addis Ababa. He was quickly reminded of his place in the military structure when he received a telegram:

No FN 1684.
FOR KRIGE FROM DIR INF [Director Information] STOP YOUR MESSAGES TWELFTH EIGHTEENTH MARCH REFER STOP MUST INSIST EITHER YOU OR NORTON REMAIN NAIROBI STOP DIXON KEARTLAND CAN PROCEED MOGADISHU TO CONTACT PIENAARS BRIGADE STOP HAVE CONSULTED LOCAL MILITARY AUTHORITIES THEIR ADVICE BEING NO PURPOSE SERVED FOR YOU AND CAMERAMAN REMAINING WITH FIRST DIVISION STOP UIOI [?] MAY BE UNABLE LEAVE CAPETOWN AS INTENDED APRIL THIRD OWING TO BUDGET ESTIMATES STOP BUT CONFERENCE URGENTLY NECESSARY TO DECIDE CHANGED LOCATION BUREAU ACTIVITIES STOP CONSIDER SAPA CORRESPONDENTS COVERING PIENAARS BRIGADE ADEQUATE THEREFORE YOUR PRESENCE NOT ESSENTIAL STOP MUST AGAIN OUTPOINT YOU

---

22 SuSP: 225.NB.OC.7: 'Our Soldiers in Kenya', Krige Collection.
23 SuSP: 225.NB.OC.7: 'Our Soldiers in Kenya', Krige Collection.
24 SuSP: 225.NB.OC.7: 'Our Soldiers in Kenya', Krige Collection.

NOT SPECIFICALLY WAR CORRESPONDENTS BUT BUREAU [of Information] REPRESENTATIVES STOP YOUR DUTY TO OBSERVE INSTRUCTIONS ONE OF YOU MUST REMAIN NAIROBI STOP ADVISE KEARTLAND AM STILL WAITING EXPLANATION HIS TELEGRAM STOP
20.3.41.
Public Relations Office
Force HQ
Nairobi[25]

The reminder that he and Norton were, 'not specifically war correspondents but Bureau representatives', must have been a blow to his desire to write freely. All articles written by staff of the Information Bureau went to the Military Intelligence for censorship and fact-checking, something that did not sit well with Uys.[26] In addition, men like Conrad and Uys were not news correspondents, and the task was not to write articles about 'hard news', but to write for the sake of morale.[27]

To follow Pienaar's Brigade would also have appealed to many adventurous young journalists, however, Uys and his counterpart were there to carry out a specific duty and they were not at liberty to write or do as they wished. With his instructions reiterated, Uys nevertheless reached Addis Ababa with the UDF troops – it must have been Conrad who remained in Nairobi.

Uys's description of the journey towards Addis Ababa through the Ethiopian highlands sounds more like romantic prose than a war correspondent's piece. The narrative is replete with accounts of effortless victories over small towns where, 'familiar white flags in the stinging heat' greet the men as they pass through. Although the mosquitos and the gnats irritated Uys while he wrote, he made the point that they were living an easy life in the bush, and he found cause to smile,

> …if I regard my little lamp, for then I think of the people in Johannesburg and Cape Town who pass their time in anti-air raid precaution practise, while we, only a hundred mile or so from Addis Ababa, can sit writing in lamp light and allow the lamps of our motor lorries to shine through the darkness like miniature lighthouses.[28]

The 'lighthouses', metaphorically speaking, were the UDF troops who were leading the way to liberation from their air-raid shelters, they would help lead the world, and the Union, from the dark to the light.

Despite the Union's distance from the main theatre of war, the threat of air raids became a possibility when South African cities fell within the range of Italian bombers taking off from Ethiopia. To counter this threat, the government

---

25 SuSP: 225.NB.OC (6/1): Bureau of Information to Uys Krige, Nairobi: Krige Collection.
26 DOD PP Box 63. Bureau of Information Complaints, 22 Aug 1940–7 January 1941.
27 DOD PP Box 63. Army publicity and propaganda. Nov. 26/40.
28 SuSP: 225. RW.39: 'Towards Addis Ababa', Krige Collection.

established the Civilian Protective Services in June 1940 for the home front.[29] For those well-informed Union citizens, it would have been obvious that when the UDF occupied Addis Ababa in April 1941, the bombing threat to the home front became a thing of the past.

In May 1941, the Duca di Aosta, the Viceroy of Italian East Africa, surrendered to the Allied forces.[30] However, Uys's work was not yet done, as many Italians were yet to be persuaded of the victory. Many Italians and Abyssinian fighters still offered resistance.[31] Among the documents in the Uys Krige Collection are examples of propaganda leaflets that the British and Commonwealth forces dropped on positions held by the Italians and their allies. The aim of these leaflets were to create confusion and sway public opinion, and in so doing, convince those who continued to resist, to accept defeat and surrender to the Allied forces.[32]

The Bureau of Information propaganda campaign also took advantage of the diversity of the population in East Africa, stating that, 'There is present such a varied mixture of peoples, religions, customs, interests and aspirations as to constitute a potential mine for the digging up of troubles that can all be directed to interfering with the war effort of the enemy.'[33]

The effectiveness of propaganda leaflets often relied on a combination of truth and rumour. If the target audience had difficulties in obtaining reliable war news in remote areas, they were more likely to resort to drawing their own conclusions, the leaflets often prodded them to think in the desired direction.

The enemy also had their own propaganda campaign, but in some cases, it was so far-fetched that the message held no value, as was the case when Nazi propaganda misjudged their allies in East Africa. Known for viciously effective propaganda, German informants planted stories of conflict between Afrikaners and British in South Africa. Uys saw these articles in the Addis Ababa press while talking to two Italian officers who had been taken prisoner after the fall of Mega in Ethiopia. One of the headlines stated, 'Arrest and immediate execution of Boer patriots.'[34]

In his account on the incident, which was meant for broadcast on 13 March 1941, Uys admitted that he fell for the story. He tried to refute the reports with a long explanation of the UDF's role in the East Africa Campaign, but the Italian officer smiled, shrugged his shoulders and uttered one word, 'Propaganda.'[35]

The tactics used by the Bureau of Information were less obvious and it cleverly played on fact while creating space for rumour to grow when they targeted the Somali soldiers as the UDF neared Mogadishu early in 1941:

---

29 F. L. Monama, 'Civil Defense and Protective Services in South Africa during World War Two, 1939–1945', *Historia* 64:2 (2019), p.84.
30 Kannemeyer, *Die Goue Seun*, p.316.
31 B. M. Scianna, 'Forging an Italian Hero? The late commemoration of Amedeo Guillet (1909 – 2010)', *European Review of History*, (2018), p.3.
32 F. L. Monama, 'South African Propaganda Agencies and the Battle for Public Opinion during the Second World War, 1939–1945', *Scientia Militaria* 44:1 (2016), p.146.
33 DOD PP Box 39. 'Appreciation on the prospects of attacking the enemy in Africa by means of propaganda' by J. E. Sacks, 25 July 1940.
34 Translated from Afrikaans.
35 SuSP: 225. RW.14: Nazi Propaganda, Krige Collection.

Somali Soldiers
Ask you officers why 150,000 Italian soldiers surrendered to the British in Libya rather than fight.
Ask your officers why thousands of your brothers in Somaliland refused to fight the British.
Ask you officers why your regiments are always on the withdrawal.
Ask your officers why their greatest General, Graziani, has now resigned.
Do not let them tell you these facts are not true – every word is true.
Come over to the victorious British, who are now on the attack. If you don't you will be taken prisoner or killed.[36]

Maresciallo d'Italia Rodolfo Graziani was the Commander-in-Chief of North Africa and the Governor General of Libya. In September 1940, he led a six-day offensive to invade Egypt with the Italian 10th Army, but a strong British offensive, Operation Compass, put a stop to his plans. Graziani resigned as Governor and returned to Italy. What the leaflet did not mention, was that Graziani was reluctant to invade Egypt in the first place. He knew that the Italian Army was not equipped for prolonged military encounters with the more mobile army of the British, however, for the Somalis, Libya and Egypt were far away, leaving them to speculate about what their fate may be when the UDF troops arrived on their doorstep.[37]

Graziani's defeat and his withdrawal from the war offered endless propaganda opportunities, and the Allies bombarded the Italians with this leaflet:

Italians!!
Why did Marshal Graziani, your greatest military leader, resign?
We will tell you!!

1. He was frustrated and let down by the inept Fascist officials.
2. This war against Britain was never wanted by our armies and generals, who were called upon to fight the Fascists.
3. He had to fight with old aeroplanes, poorly-armed tanks and bad ammunition.
4. His experience in Libya against the might of the British Empire showed him again how hopeless the struggle was.

You know how true these things are. One of the world's greatest soldiers has said he cannot go on. Other famous Italian leaders have also resigned.
With the example of these honoured Italians before you, how can you continue a futile struggle?
Surrender now and avoid useless bloodshed.[38]

---

36 SuSP: 225.NB.OC (4/3): Propaganda, 'Somali Soldiers', Krige collection.
37 S. Anglim, 'Callwell versus Graziani: how the British Army applied 'small wars' techniques in major operations in Africa and the Middle East, 1940–41' *Small Wars & Insurgencies*, 19:4 (2008), p.599.
38 SuSP: 225.NB.OC (4/2): 'Italians!!', Krige Collection.

The successes against Italian forces in Libya during 1940, and the simultaneous propaganda efforts in East Africa, combined to make victory over Mogadishu effortless, or indeed, an anti-climax. On 25 February 1941, Allied forces arrived to find that it had been declared an open city, with not one Italian soldier in sight.[39] Uys recalled how incredulous UDF troops found about 200 captive Italians in a holding pen that they had constructed themselves before compliantly locking themselves inside in anticipation of the South Africans' appearance.

In another case, an impatient UDF sergeant told an Italian officer to come back the next day. The Italian officer was trying to surrender his unit of 500 men.[40] Clearly, the South Africans did not see the Italians as a threat.

By March 1941, 160,000 Italians had become POW in East and North Africa, a result of military success on the part of British and Commonwealth forces, and to an indeterminable degree, a consequence of the propaganda campaign.[41] Following the British victory in Somalia, the same tactic, that of posing questions to soldiers who were either uninformed or open to rumour was used to convince even more Italians to surrender, as this leaflet shows:

> Italian soldiers!!
> Ask your commanding officers why 150,000 of your brother soldiers surrendered rather than fight the British in Cirenaica [sic].
> Ask your commanding officers why thousands of your brother soldiers did the same thing in Somaliland.
> Ask your commanding officers why there is a feeling of relief amongst the Italians of Magadiscio [sic] now that it has been occupied by the British.
> Ask your commanding officers why your battalions are now always on the withdrawal.
> Ask your commanding officers why you are continuing a hopeless struggle.
> Their answers, if true, will cause you to lay down your arms. By so doing you will protect your women and children.
> Avoid unnecessary bloodshed and surrender now before it is too late.[42]

While the Italians and Somalis were being targeted with propaganda, it was also necessary to remind the home front in South Africa of the work being done outside of its borders. In September 1941, Uys's piece on his work as a war correspondent was broadcast while he was on leave in the Union. Devoting the first three pages almost exclusively to descriptions of the natural beauty of East Africa and the privilege of serving with the UDF, he then turned his attention to the military censors. For someone in the employ of the Bureau of Information, Uys's criticism of the censors,

---

39 James Ambrose Brown, *The War of a Hundred Days Springboks in Somalia and Abyssinia* (Johannesburg: Ashanti, 1990), p.144.
40 Uys Krige, & Conrad Norton. *Veldtog vir Vryheid 'n Kort Oorsig van die Oorwinning van die Afrikasoldate in Oos-Afrika, 1940–1941* (Pretoria: Bureau of Information, 1941), p.36.
41 Bob Moore, & Kent Fedorowich. *The British Empire and its Italian Prisoners of War, 1940–1947* (Hampshire: Palgrave, 2002), p.111.
42 SuSP: 225.NB.OC (4/1): Krige Collection.

that they were more 'fickle' than women, is an interesting approach. Uys went on to say that the 'military machine' detested anything that resembled 'individuality, warm humanity or creativity.'[43] Clearly he had not forgiven the authorities who a few months earlier labelled him a Bureau representative, while he saw himself as an author.

Changing the topic to combat, he told the listeners that the fear of the unknown, like being led into an ambush, was far greater than that of the fear of the obvious, such as being blasted by cannon fire or taking cover during an air raid.[44]

Later the same month, Uys was back in Cairo, and he reported on that city's first air raid. He witnessed the bombing from his fourth floor balcony, and for once, his vivid description did not attempt to colour the event in overly positive tones. He concluded his report with the news that 39 people died during the attack.[45] The attack on Cairo took place on 16 September, but Uys's report was only broadcast 11 days later. What stands out from his report, was the fear that he felt upon being so close to the action.

Unlike Uys, Winston Churchill did not find anything frightening about the bombing of Cairo. A number of newspapers predicted that the Royal Air Force would bomb Rome, as the British Government had warned Germany and Italy of this in April of the same year. However, speaking in Parliament on 30 September, Churchill made his point, saying, 'People ask, for instance, "Why don't you bomb Rome? What is holding you back? Didn't you say you would bomb Rome if Cairo were bombed?" What is the answer? One answer is that Cairo has not yet been bombed. Only military posts on the outskirts have been bombed.'[46]

Churchill of course knew what he was talking about, after all, he had been in London during the Blitz, and large parts of the city lay in ruins, with about 30,000 civilian deaths and 51,000 serious casualties.[47] Uys would get a taste of this late in November, but not before he launched another brilliant propaganda offensive against the home front.

Broadcast on 11 October 1941, on the 42nd commemoration of the start of the South African War, Uys's piece on a 'General and a soldier', employed narrative strategies that would have softened the hearts of many former Boer Commando members as they recalled their heroic adventures of fighting against the British in the veld.

During the radio broadcast, Uys wanted to appeal to as many listeners as possible, so he described how he met a UDF general in Cairo, and later one of the rank-and-file men. The general was a 'total stranger' to Uys's unit, nevertheless, he welcomed them warmly, and invited them to swim in the Mediterranean, because 'it will do you good, wash off the dust and the cobwebs from your eyes…' The listeners of

---

43   SuSP: 225.RW.23: *'My werk as oorlogkorrespondent'* [My work as war correspondent], Krige Collection.
44   SuSP: 225.RW.23: *'My werk as oorlogkorrespondent'*, Krige Collection.
45   SuSP: 225.RW.16: *'Kairo se eerste Lugaanval'* [Cairo's first air raid], Krige Collection.
46   Hansard 1803–2005, *War Situation HC Deb 30 September 1941,* vol. 374 pp.509–551: The Prime Minister (Mr. Churchill) https://api.parliament.uk/historic-hansard/commons/1941/sep/30/war-situation, accessed 15 October 2020.
47   G. Field, 'Nights underground in darkest London the Blitz, 1940 – 1941', *Cercles* 17 (2007), p.183.

this radio programme also heard how this general created the Afrikaans word for 'mess' [*menasie*], firmly placing him in the elite Afrikaner group who stimulated the growth of the language. For Uys, however, it was important to stress that the general was able to win the trust of the ordinary men under his command. Addressing the men simply and spontaneously, the general spoke 'from his heart.'[48] In this way, his narrative evoked images of the South African War when Boer Generals and older members of the commandos comforted young men in the hours and minutes before battles took place.[49] Uys won the hearts of the young and old, as well as the officers' class and the young servicemen.

As members of the same family and of the same districts often found themselves in the same commando, camaraderie and common purpose sustained the men as they lived off the land and fought against an overwhelming British force.[50] The general in Uys's story, played the role of father figure, and he had the wisdom and leadership skills to carry out the difficult task at hand.

The other man in Uys's narrative was young and had no rank, but he made it clear that, just like the Afrikaners who fought for what they believed in 42 years before, this young soldier did the same, implying that the younger generation held the same values and beliefs as their forebears. Uys could not state his message more plainly:

> I am a pacifist, have always been one. I hate war, despise it. That is why I volunteered, why I participate in this war. I have grown tired of the people who trample peace in one country, who destroys one nation after the other; who not only threaten peace of the whole world, but peace for the future, of this century. Who misleads humanity that war is not a terribly abnormality but that it is something that is good and normal; that wants to imprint this idea on us; not that war is a crime against God and man, but the duty of every 'patriot', a virtue and praiseworthy. It has been many years that I have rejected Fascists who are convinced that the strongest persuasive methods are the club and the castor oil bottle, that the machine gun can effectively settle an argument and that by bombing women and children, the differences are settled in the best possible way … Since 1934 I have, along with thousands like me, warned, argued, pleaded and became angry… but our big bosses would not listen. When the Allies' eyes eventually opened in 1939, I had to join [the UDF], in this way remaining logical and true to my principles. And now, millions of us pacifists will continue to fight against those who choose war until at last they understand the madness, and what crime it is to reach for weapons.[51]

---

48 Translated from Afrikaans. SuSP: Krige Collection, 225.RW.12. *'n Generaal en 'n manskap*. [A General and a soldier]
49 Fransjohan Pretorius, *Life on Commando during the Anglo-Boer War 1899–1902* (Cape Town: Human & Rousseau, 1999), p.138.
50 Pretorius, *Life on Commando*, p.232.
51 Translated from Afrikaans. SuSP: 225.RW.12: *'n Generaal en 'n manskap*', Krige Collection.

Considering Uys's personal experience of emerging Fascism in Spain during the late 1930s, the young man of whom he wrote in this piece may have been the one looking back at him from the mirror. However, as the true identity of the young man remains a mystery, Uys nevertheless made the point that the volunteer's beliefs were commendable, and that he had the courage of his convictions. Uys's broadcast on the anniversary of the start of the South African War was excellent timing, but he was soon to experience the less romantic side of the war as the battles in Libya became more heated.

In November the 1st South Africa Division was given the task to advance towards Tobruk, but at Sidi Rezegh *Generalleutnant* Rommel's forces lay in wait for them. It was here that Uys's work as propaganda operative came to an abrupt end. Unlike the Italian forces in East Africa, the *Afrika Korps* were far more determined to fight, in addition, the quality and quantity of their weaponry was superior to that of the Italians, and to a certain extent to that of the British.[52]

Most importantly, Rommel, nicknamed 'the Desert Fox' by journalists, was a brilliant tactician. In this, their first encounter against the Germans, the South Africans did not know what hit them.

A solitary mosque marked the spot where the battle took place. Around the small white building, the featureless landscape offered no protection against flying bullets. Soldiers who stood up to view the area and make sense of events were spotted from afar by the fast-approaching *Afrika Korps* panzers. Those who lay down in the sand, were easily discernible by the low-flying German aircraft, strafing everything that moved.

A first for many South Africans was the nerve-shattering experience of an attack by the screaming Stuka bombers as they dived downwards towards the hapless men.

Over the space of the weekend of 21 to 23 November, German tanks mercilessly overran South African positions and equipment.[53] Writing after the war, Uys recalled that he initially did not grasp the seriousness of the situation. As he and Conrad were with the Brigade Headquarters (HQ), they did not see the devastation of the early days' fighting on the outskirts, but when the HQ itself came under attack, reality dawned.[54] Terrified, Uys and Conrad took cover in a bomb crater, believing that the same spot is never hit twice during a battle. As they were not combatants, the best they could do was to take cover and hope for the best.

German bombardments continued throughout the battle, but the 'diabolical' sound of nearby machine-gun fire left Uys weak with fear.[55] Later, he saw how a German tank simply drove over two South Africans when they refused to surrender, crushing them to death.[56] On the same day, Uys and Conrad were hauled out of their

---

52   Simon Gonsalves, 'The Italian Army in the Second World War: A Historiographical Analysis', *The Great Lakes Journal of Undergraduate History*, 5:1 (2017), p.18.
53   Van der Waag, *A Military History of Modern South Africa*, p.199.
54   SuSP: 225.RW: 'Die Slag van Sidi Rezegh' [The Battle of Sidi Rezegh], Krige Collection.
55   Uys Krige, 'Totensonntag', *Sout van die aarde* (Cape Town: HAUM, 1964), p.29.
56   Kannemeyer, *Die Goue Seun*, p.332.

hiding place and made to run, with hands held high, 'resembling awkward herons struggling to take flight', towards a holding pen.[57]

When the battle finally ended, the South Africa 5th Brigade was decimated, and thousands lay dead and wounded, while the remainder were captured. In the days following the battle, Uys's brother, Francois, arrived at the scene. As one of the war artists within the UDF, he recorded the aftermath with illustrations of British and German dead, horrified by the devastation that greeted him.[58]

While Francois recorded the destruction, his brother was on his way to a temporary POW camp near Benghazi on the Libyan coast. From there, he was transferred along with thousands of POWs to permanent camps in Italy. Bad luck followed Uys during the early days of his captivity. He had lost his rank card during the battle, and therefore had to walk, in the so-called thirst march, to Benghazi while other officers were transported by car. Once in Italy, he was held captive along with the rank and file in conditions that were very basic.[59] Men were sent out in labour parties, while officers were not required, or allowed, to work.

Although all camps had to adhere to the Geneva Convention regulations pertaining to conditions of captivity and treatment of POWs, men were often left half-starved before the Red Cross parcels arrived with much-needed sustenance.

It was seven months before Uys could confirm his officer status, and when he wrote to his wife following his transfer to an officers' camp, he told her of the relative luxuries that he experienced there; with a batman at his service, he no longer washed his own clothes or bedding. The batman also kept, 'his own little piece of the campground' clean.[60] In another letter, however, he complained bitterly of the fact that he did not get his own room and that he had to share with a bunch of *rooi offisiere*.[61]

Uys's wish for privacy was linked to his desire to write, as he found the experience of captivity detrimental to his creativity.[62] The camp conditions deprived him of the spark, 'everything is so grey... the same [captivity] is becoming an enormous waste of time!'[63] At other times, he felt more positive, and in an undated letter, he wrote to Lydia that he was, 'feeling splendid these days. Busy all day, writing a lot – short stories. Progress slow but sure. Have also done my 40th poem in captivity. So, at least I've done something...'[64] Ironically, Uys's captivity allowed him to do what the Information Bureau would not, he was able to express his creativity in his writing.

---

57 Translated from Afrikaans. Krige, 'Totensonntag', p.34.
58 A. Sinclair, 'Sidi Rezegh: Images of Death and Horror' Ditsong National Museum of Military History, https://ditsong.org.za/2020/07/23/sidi-rezegh-images-of-death-and-horror/, accessed 12 October 2020.
59 C. van Heyningen, & J. Berthoud. *Uys Krige* (New York: Twayne, 1966), p.37
60 Translated from Afrikaans. SuSP Krige Collection, 225.KF. 15(1). Letter from Uys Krige to Lydia Krige, 30 April 1943.
61 'Red Officers', i.e. English or British officers.
62 SuSP: 225.KF. 15(10): Letter from Uys Krige to Lydia Krige, no date. Krige Collection.
63 Translated from Afrikaans. SuSP: 225.KF. 15(1): Letter from Uys Krige to Lydia Krige, 30 April 1943, Krige Collection.
64 Uys Krige wrote this letter using the name George Kerr. He wrote most of his letters to his wife in Afrikaans, but the 'Kerr' letter was written in English. The letters signed with the name Krige, however, contains some of the same topics as those mentioned in the 'Kerr'

As Uys whiled away his time in a prison camp, Italian citizens, King Victor Emmanuel III and *Maresciallo d'Italia* Badoglio, a veteran of the East African campaign, grew increasingly frustrated with Benito Mussolini and his unyielding fascist dogma. On 25 July 1943, a plan was at last put into action and Mussolini was overthrown.

News of this event reached Allied prison camps all over Italy, and captives and captors waited in anticipation for freedom. On 3 September, the Italians and the Allies agreed on armistice terms. The consequences of the agreement were many, but in the short term POW camps were thrown open, and for a while, POWs roamed free. At the same time, German forces were mobilised to settle the score with their erstwhile ally and to round up the POWs and imprison them in German occupied territories.

Under the Badoglio government, a devastating war was about to start as the Allies, German forces, hard-line Italian Fascists and Italian partisans fought each other from the heel of Italy all the way to the northern border from September 1943, when Allied troops landed at Salerno,[65] until they could see the tips of the Alps in May 1945.[66]

Into this chaotic situation, Uys and three others escaped, taking their chances and hoping for freedom. The kindness of Italian peasants, and a good dose of luck, helped the escapees achieve their goal and they eventually reached British forces in the town of Salcito.[67]

Once back in South Africa, Uys had time to reflect on his captivity, and in an undated narrative, he wrote how many fellow POWs became adept at new skills because they were forced to look within for self-enrichment. He referred to this process as an 'excavation of yourself [which] undoubtedly helps you to realise some of the possibilities latent within you.' For Uys, a greater awareness of self and the fellow man was a way towards, 'greater understanding, a greater tolerance and also cooperation. So POW life is, in some respects, a training in citizenship.'[68] In this piece, his personal world view became evident. Perhaps his personal convictions and the aims of the Bureau of Information aligned perfectly for the first time as both were working to establish a greater sense of unity on the home front.

In his interview with Noreen Purdon in August 1944, however, Uys made it clear that he had done his share of 'self-excavation':

> Noreen Purdon: "I heard you say the other day everybody should be put in a concentration camp for at least a year – that it would do them the world

---

letter, including a monthly payment of £10 to his wife, and the 40 poems that Krige wrote while in captivity. POWs were limited to two letters and four postcards per month, and the use of an alias may have been Krige's attempt at sidestepping this restriction. SuSP: 225.KF. 15(12): Letter from 'George Kerr' to Lydia Krige, no date. Krige Collection.

65 W. S. Linsenmeyer, 'Italian Peace Feelers before the Fall of Mussolini', *Journal of Contemporary History* 16:4 (1981), p.650.
66 James Holland, *Italy's Sorrow A year of war 1944 – 45* (London: Harper Press, 2009), p.526.
67 Uys Krige, *The Way Out* (Cape Town: Maskew Miller, 1955), p.248.
68 SuSP: 225.RW.9: 'The Credit of POW life', Krige Collection.

of good, add years to their life. You aren't thinking of going in for another spell?"

Uys Krige: "Not on your life!"[69]

Soon after this interview, Uys left the Union again to join the South Africans in Europe. His departure was not without its difficulties. He left behind his pregnant wife, Lydia, and his young daughter. When it became known that Uys was leaving again, Lydia was, according to the Staff Officer, suffering from, or responsible for 'complications' resulting from 'nervous troubles … combined pregnancy.'[70] It seems Uys had been kept back in the Union as a result of Lydia's condition. Uys also had time to recover from the stresses and strains of his captivity and escape following Italy's armistice, but compassionate leave could only last so long, and Uys was back in Cairo by September 1944.[71]

By now Uys was now no longer a war correspondent with the Bureau of Information, but was appointed as Radio Observer in the Public Relations Unit of the UDF.[72] In January 1945, Uys and a fellow Radio Observer, Jacques Malan, were sent to the British Broadcasting Corporation for training. While in London, their observations of the Italian campaign were broadcast by the BBC and the South African radio service.[73]

Uys viewed the war in Italy from the perspective of a former POW and escapee in that country. The British 8th Army, under General Bernard Montgomery, along with the American 5th Army under Lieutenant General Mark Clark, made slow progress in Italy. When Uys took up his work for the radio unit, the South African 6th Division had also been fighting for some time.[74]

Struggling to cross numerous defensive lines, the difficult terrain and the determined fighting from the German forces made the Italian campaign a hellish encounter for everyone. Yet, each time the Allies broke through one of the defensive lines, they pushed the Germans further north out of Italy and towards Germany, bringing the war closer to home for Hitler. It was crucial for the Allies to make the right moves at the right time.

Montgomery, however, was cautious and insisted on ensuring that everything was in his favour before confronting the enemy. In one example, Montgomery delayed crossing the Sangro River because the weather was not favourable. Waiting for the construction of a bridge to take his army safely across, Montgomery was criticised for missing an important opportunity to move the 8th Army forward.[75]

---

69   SuSP: 225.RO.6 (2): Uys Krige Interview with Noreen Purdon, 21 August 1944, Krige collection.
70   DOD Personnel File P1330/1: OI – SAPR1/3/1/21, DCS – DMI, 12 September 1944.
71   DOD Personnel File (hereafter PF), Record of Service (hereafter RS), M. U. Krige, Record of Service.
72   DOD PF RS, M. U. Krige, Record of Service.
73   DOD PF RS, M. U. Krige, Record of Service.
74   James Bourhill, *Come back to Portofino Through Italy with the 6th South African Armoured Division* (Johannesburg: 30o South Publishers, 2011), p.93.
75   E. P. Hoyt, *Backwater War: The Allied Campaign in Italy, 1943–1945* (Westport: Praeger, 2002), p.96.

Uys Krige with his wife Lydia Lindeque and their daughter Eulalia. (Photo: Uys Krige Collection, Special Collections, Stellenbosch University)

Uys Krige with Vinecenzo Petrella in Italy. (Photo: Uys Krige Collection, Special Collections, Stellenbosch University)

For Uys, the slow progress of the 8th Army was no surprise. His undated piece on Montgomery's army placed emphasis on the difficult terrain and the relative ease with which the Germans were able to delay the movement of the Allies. Writing from his own experience as an escapee, Uys knew the terrain very well and he was able to write with a humble authority on the matter. He portrayed the mountains not as an obstacle, but as the enemy itself: 'it was the great natural enemy that always surrounded us, that always captured us, and always hindered our progress to the south – to freedom.'[76] Luckily for Uys and his fellow escapees, they found shelter with Vinecenzo Petrella who allowed them to hide in the cellar and avoid the German patrols in the area.[77]

He also made the point that the destruction of one bridge enabled the Germans to create sizeable obstacles for any army as it tried to find its way north over the mountains. In the same way, according to Uys,

> a few machine guns at the top of a mountain pass could hold back units for days … mortars at the top of a ravine could do enormous damage … a bridge over a gorge need only be destroyed to create an obstacle for the advancing army. And that is precisely what the Germans have been doing for months now.[78]

---

76 Translated from Afrikaans. SuSP: 225.RW.5: 'Wat die Agtste Leer mee te kampe het' [What the 8th Army has to contend with], Krige Collection.
77 Erika Terblanche, 'Uys Krige (1910 – 1987)', Litnet (2022), https://www.litnet.co.za/uys-krige-1910-1987/, accessed 22 January 2025.
78 Translated from Afrikaans. SuSP: 225.RW.5: 'Wat die Agtste Leer mee te kampe het' [What the 8th Army has to contend with], Krige Collection.

Uys even mentioned how, as an escapee, he witnessed how the Germans destroyed the bridges over the Sangro River. The fighting at Monte Casino and the Allies' occupation of Rome is not part of the narrative on Montgomery's progress, but by February 1945 he wrote again, this time about his experiences while with the American troops near Bologna.

Cleverly avoiding censorship of his work, Uys did not give away any details of how he and Jacques Malan, a fellow war correspondent, came to join the Americans. On the matter of the warm welcome they received from their American hosts, he was very specific. At this point, the war had been raging for more than five years, yet it was still necessary to let the home front know of the value of the UDF volunteer on the battlefront.

In his narrative, Uys speculated on the reason for the Americans' good treatment of two South African correspondents; was it because Clark spoke well of the 6th Division, or was it because the 6th Division now fell under the command of Clark and was part of the American 5th Army? Or, better yet, was it because the Americans now regarded the South Africans in a positive light because they had the opportunity to become acquainted with them? On the other hand, Uys wondered if perhaps it was the, 'inborn friendliness [of the American], his spontaneous tendency to make you feel at ease.'[79]

For Uys and Jacques, the feeling of belonging among the Americans was personified by the American war correspondent, 'McTique', who, from day one, practically 'adopted' the two of them. The use of the father figure in the narrative is reminiscent of Uys's 1941 story of the 'General and a soldier', yet in the 1945 version, 'McTique' tells how his life was saved by UDF volunteers:

> He was trapped [between two groups of German soldiers]. The Germans started shooting at [McTique] and his friends. What to do? Suddenly, like a miracle, rescue came; a truck full of soldiers, all wearing the red tab [of UDF volunteers] they fly from the truck like bees and take the lost American press party under their protection…[80]

The next day, another one of Uys's broadcasts extolled the virtues of, 'the bearer of an Afrikaans name famous in the annals of South African warfare, the commanding officer of one of our tank battalions in Italy.'[81] The officer, whose name was never mentioned, apparently had the ability to stand upright in his tank turret during a battle, shouting out orders in foul language, yet garnering the admiration of all his men as he had the ability to remember each face and each name. Not surprisingly, the officer was wounded several times, but his concern remained with the men, as was the case when he woke from a delirious state in a military hospital and ordered

---

79 Translated from Afrikaans. SuSP: 225.RW. 40(3/3). *Uit 'n oorlogkorrespondent se dagboek – nommer drie – Uys Krige*. Transmission: Wednesday, 7th February 1945, Krige Collection.
80 Translated from Afrikaans. SuSP: 225.RW. 40(3/3). *Uit 'n oorlogkorrespondent se dagboek – nommer drie – Uys Krige*. Transmission: Wednesday, 7th February 1945, Krige Collection.
81 SuSP: 225.RW. 40(3/2): Radio Trek No. 47. *Commanding Officer* by Capt Uys Krige. Transmission: Thursday, 8th February 1945, Krige Collection.

the nurse to bring his clothes as he wanted to re-join the battle: 'listen to the boys pasting 'em! They're my boys, mind…'[82]

For the third time, Uys employed the father figure in his writing, possibly to reassure the home front, to raise morale on the battlefront or to clarify the military system at work. The tank officer carried with him the values of many Afrikaners at home, the officer had one dream, 'to buy a farm after the war.'[83] With many of his men referring to him as 'Papa [Brits] his great gifts of leadership … his capacity to inspire his men with a supreme confidence in their own abilities' remained his priority.[84]

During the last weeks of the war in Europe, Uys carried out his task as Radio Observer, but at this late stage of the war, his last reports offered a fair balance between propaganda, reality and his own beliefs, a result of his experience of war and captivity and of witnessing the consequences of Fascism. In a broadcast on 29 March, Uys chose to ignore the 'world-shaking events of the past few days' and returned to the early days of the war when the 1st Division fought in Abyssinia.

In his report, Uys told of a Norwegian naval officer who, during the first years of the war, fought with his country's underground movement. For this man, and the rest of the underground, the UDF victories against the Italian forces in East Africa kept up their morale in their 'blackest hour' against the Nazis. In essence, the entire broadcast was a victory parade for the South African campaign, and Uys's aim became clear when he quoted the naval officer: 'Don't underestimate Abyssinia – it was a link, a small one, it is true, but a vital one in a long, long chain.'[85] He wanted to remind South Africans, and anyone who would listen, that the task of the volunteer servicemen in the UDF was a necessary one.

Those who volunteered their services to the UDF, regardless of their personal, political or financial motivations, were exposed to new ways of thinking as they interacted with different nationalities and races. When they returned to the Union after the war, they looked at the world with different eyes. Those who remained behind stayed the same because the South African home front was a safe place compared to Britain, France, The Netherlands or any other European country.

Many years after the war, Elie Wiesel, holocaust survivor and Nobel Prize winner, reminded the world that 'neutrality helps the oppressor, never the victim. Silence encourages the tormentor, not the tormented. Sometimes we must interfere…'[86] With the final paragraph of his broadcast of 29 March 1945, Uys pointed out that South Africa's 'interference' was of value, but that it also came at a cost:

---

82 SuSP: 225.RW. 40(3/2): Radio Trek No. 47. *Commanding Officer* by Capt Uys Krige. Transmission: Thursday, 8th February 1945, Krige Collection.
83 SuSP: 225.RW. 40(3/2): Radio Trek No. 47. *Commanding Officer* by Capt Uys Krige. Transmission: Thursday, 8th February 1945, Krige Collection.
84 SuSP: 225.RW. 40(3/2): Radio Trek No. 47. *Commanding Officer* by Capt Uys Krige. Transmission: Thursday, 8th February 1945, Krige Collection.
85 SuSP: 225.RW. 40(3/2): Radio Trek No. 54. *From a war correspondent's diary No. 9* by Capt Uys Krige. African Service: Thursday, 29 March 1945, Krige Collection.
86 Elie Wiesel, 'Acceptance speech for Nobel Peace Prize', (10 December 1986), https://www.nobelprize.org/mediaplayer/?id=2028, accessed 1 October 2020.

> Where I have harked back to Abyssinia to-night, I did so with no intention of magnifying the importance of the brief, hectic campaign. Perhaps I did so only to honour the memory of a number of men I once knew. They have been dead these past four years. They died at the beginning of a long, weary war. Now that that war is at last drawing to a close, it is fitting, I think, to remember them – and also to realise that their sacrifice is not unrelated to the victory that is at hand.[87]

While Uys reminisced about Abyssinia, the matter of Lydia remained a headache for the military authorities at home. They decided to investigate and Lydia was interviewed on 10 March. The report revealed a lot, and it did not make for easy reading, as these extracts reveal:

> Mrs Krige appears normal, but states she is in a highly nervous state having lived alone since Oct. 1944, and is afraid that unless her husband returns she will have a complete breakdown … Mrs Krige cannot sleep at night … in the course of the conversation it transpired that Captain Krige did not desire to join the Armed Forces, but was talked into it by Capt. Delius … Mrs. Krige alleges that Capt. Krige was promised that he would be away for only three months and would be recalled for the birth of the second child … Capt. Krige in his letters to Mrs Krige gives the impression that he is not doing any useful work and desires to get back home … his attitude seems to be that he is wasting his time in the Army … Krige alleges that whilst in Italy he did not work at all … Dr van Selm states Mrs Krige is very temperamental and could easily suffer a nervous breakdown … Mrs Krige during the conversation threatened to divorce her husband if he did not return … Capt Krige in one of his letters requests his wife to interview Col Malherbe the DMI [Director Military Intelligence] and to ask for his assistance in getting returned and released.[88]

On 11 June, Uys was released from service, but almost immediately it was cancelled when it was confirmed that he would stay on in the Middle East as Public Relations Official Observer.[89] Uys was finally demobilised on 4 June 1946.[90]

---

87 SuSP: 225.RW.40(3/7): Radio Trek No. 54. 'From a war correspondent's diary No. 9 by Capt Uys Krige. African Service: Thursday, 29 March 1945.' Krige Collection.
88 DOD Captain Krige U. – GSC (V) ATT. SAPR. 29 March 1945.
89 DOD No. 558849V T/Capt. M. U. Krige: GSC(V), 30 June 1945.
90 DOD PF RS, *Aansoek om Veldtogmedaljes (Oorlog 1939–45)* [Application for war medals (War 1939–45)]. Krige M. U.

2

Lieutenant Derrick Norton in East Africa

'The Ito's [Italians] really are a lot of rats and can't fight pussy.'[1] One would not ordinarily ascribe these words to a man who was known as kind and courteous, yet on 10 April 1941 he could think of no other way to express himself. Somewhere in East Africa, Lieutenant Derrick Norton of the Royal Natal Carbineers (RNC) was writing to Joan Gutridge in Pietermaritzburg, a girl he had had his eye on for some time. His bitterness towards the Italians was not unexpected, after all, they were enemies.

Yet things were not that simple. In his earlier letters, he described the Italians with a sense of patronising paternalism. His new-found resentment towards the 'rats' also influenced his hereto openhearted and humorous letters to Joan. Somehow something changed his mind about the 'docile' Italians.[2]

Derrick grew up in Pietermaritzburg, a town that was named after two Voortrekker[3] leaders, Piet Retief and Gerrit Maritz. However, by the time the Second World War started, it had become known as a city influenced primarily by its British colonial past. For example, Derrick attended Merchiston Preparatory School which had been established in 1892 and adopted the name and motto of Merchiston Castle School in Scotland.[4]

Pietermaritzburg was also home to the RNC, a regiment that had fought against the Zulu nation in 1879 and then against the two Boer Republics from 1899 to 1902. When the First World War broke out in 1914, however, the Carbineers' loyalty lay with the Union of South Africa, and this was also the case in 1939 when the Second World War began.[5] The loyalty among the men of the regiment was based on 85 years of tradition. They became friends while they were still boys parading playfully on their school grounds. The strong sense of comradeship became a vital component of survival once the men had donned their uniforms and set off towards the battlefields of the Second World War.

---

1 Personal correspondence, Derrick Norton to Joan Gutridge, 10 April 1941.
2 Karen Horn, *Prisoners of Jan Smuts: Italian Prisoners of War in South Africa in WWII* (Cape Town: Jonathan Ball Publishers, 2024), p.71.
3 The Voortrekkers were Dutch speaking farmers who moved inland in 1838 to rid themselves of British control in the Cape Colony.
4 Merchiston Preparatory School, *Our Story*. https://www.merchiston.co.za/our-history/ 12 November 2019. https://www.merchiston.co.za/our-history/ 12 November 2019.
5 Mark Coghlan, '2005 The Natal Carbineers – 150th Anniversary. A glimpse of some new Battle Honours,' *Military History Journal*, 13 (3). http://samilitaryhistory.org/vol133mc.html 12 November 2019.

Derrick volunteered for service in the UDF and joined the RNC, as did many other English-speaking young men in the town. He was part of C Company, which was made up of volunteers who came from surrounding farms and countryside. By all accounts, and perhaps as a result of their physical work in the open air, these men were, on average, larger than those in A and B Companies.[6] Many also considered them to be more mature.

Derrick was good match with C Company. He was a keen sportsman and was selected to play rugby on the Currie Cup team for Natal in 1939. With the war putting a stop to his rugby career, Derrick must have had lots of unspent energy for war service. For most young men who lined up on the parade grounds, however, fear and bravado were close companions as they faced an uncertain future.

Derrick left Pietermaritzburg in May 1940 and travelled with his regiment to Premier Mine near Pretoria. Derrick's regiment was one of three infantry battalions in the 1st South Africa Infantry Brigade under General Dan Pienaar.[7] On 21 May 1940, the RNC arrived at their training ground near Pretoria, where the men received training to get acquainted with the techniques of handling weaponry in battle.[8]

Almost immediately, letters began arriving in Joan Gutridge's post box. In one of his first letters to Joan, Derrick explained that any thought of going on leave had been abandoned. Leave became a topic of their letters that would become all too familiar to both of them:

> I am afraid that all our hopes of getting some home leave have been dashed to the ground. Hard as it surely is, I feel sure that, as always we can take it. It is very hard to try and analyse our feelings. We want to get home, more than anything else we want that. But what is more when we get home we want to stay there, so maybe our not getting back now is a blessing in disguise. I sincerely hope so and we shall see. Enough of that![9]

The two had been friends in Pietermaritzburg since school days, and in all of his correspondence, Derrick's affection for Joan is obvious. He closed each letter with an expression of love, ranging from, 'cheerio old thing, much love, yours, Derrick' to 'give my love to your Mum Dad and Barry but don't forget to keep some for yourself.' Although the wording of his salutations changed slightly from one letter to the next, the meaning and intention remained constant throughout his slog through the mud of East Africa to the dry desert of North Africa. Officially, Derrick and Joan were not a couple at the time, yet the letters and the war events would bring them closer.

Remarkably there is no evidence of official military censorship in any of Derrick's letters. Servicemen were not allowed to include any information on troop strengths,

---

6   Gustav Bentz, 2013. *Fighting Springboks C Company, Royal Natal Carbineers: From Premier Mine to Po Valley, 1939 – 1945*. Master's dissertation, Stellenbosch University, pp.20–21.
7   James Ambrose Brown, *The War of a Hundred Days. Springboks in Somalia and Abyssinia 1940–41*. (Johannesburg, Ashanti, 1990), p.50.
8   Gustav Bentz, 2013. *Fighting Springboks C Company*, p.24.
9   Personal correspondence, Derrick Norton to Joan Gutridge, 25 May 1940.

location, movements, armament, or any other information that could potentially give the enemy a strategic advantage. In this way military authorities also hoped to protect the public from the stark realities of war and in so doing, keep home front morale positive. The government also imposed restrictions on the printing of subversive materials, the spreading of rumours and inciting public violence.[10]

Being aware of the restrictions, Derrick was careful to avoid forbidden topics when he wrote to Joan. In more than one instance, Joan would have had to make assumptions and comparisons based on what she read in his letters and what she read in the newspapers.

Following a few months' training, Derrick and his regiment were moved up to East Africa. Their task was to expel the Italian forces from Italy's African colonies. The East African campaign presented many challenges to the UDF. Muddy and mountainous terrain made it difficult for the troops to advance at speed, while the lack of clean water caused disease. Their Italian adversaries were often the least of their concern as the UDF trucks trundled along the near-impassable roads. From Derrick's early letters, it would seem that the South Africans did not expect much resistance from the Italian forces – or perhaps they were overly self-assured and optimistic as many young men often are. On 12 December 1940, Derrick wrote:

> I am afraid that I have not kept to the bargain of writing more often but honestly we have been terribly busy lately and I am a bit lazy at the best of times so please don't think that I have cracked up … hasn't the news been grand lately – we have a wireless in these parts now and get the news pretty often now. I think we are getting well on top now … what a wealth of experience we have gained up here Joan. We will all have changed when we get back and most of us for the better. It is an experience which except for the sordid side of it I will have greatly enjoyed, even the hard times. All will be well that ends well and this will … the busier we are the less news there is…[11]

Derrick wrote this before the RNC experienced any significant combat action, and his reference to good news must have been about the battles in Libya and Egypt. The Italians advanced into Egypt as far as Sidi Barani, but they were quickly driven back into Libya by British forces in December 1940.[12]

In East Africa, Derrick and his regiment was preparing to take the small town of El Buro Hachi, near El Wak. On 12 December, the same day that he wrote to Joan, Derrick and the other commanding officers, were informed what their role would be in the following days.[13] In anticipation of his first battle, Derrick may have written

---

10 F. L. Monama, 2014. 'Wartime Propaganda in the Union of South Africa, 1939 – 1945.' PhD dissertation. Stellenbosch University, pp.68–71.
11 Personal correspondence, Derrick Norton to Joan Gutridge, 12 December 1940.
12 C. Jacobs, 'The War in North Africa, 1940–43. An Overview of the contribution of the Union of South Africa', South African Military History Society, http://samilitaryhistory.org/lectures/nafrica.html, accessed 21 August 2024.
13 Gustav Bentz, 2013. *Fighting Springboks C Company*, p.43.

the words, 'all will be well that ends well and this will', comforting not only Joan, but also reassuring himself. By 14 December, the RNC had achieved its objective of taking El Buro Hachi, and on 16 December the battle of El Wak took place. The RNC and the Gold Coast Battery participated in this battle that was, apparently, planned for Dingaans Day[14] to boost the morale of the men.

In line with the atmosphere of the day, the troops sang a Zulu war song as they approach El Wak. By all accounts, the sight of the RNC approaching with their bayonets fixed and singing at the top of their voices, completely disheartened the Italians. Before the day was over, the battle was done. For the RNC and the Gold Coast men it was their first experience of combat, and the first victory of the Allies during the Second World War.[15]

Derrick waited until January 1941 before he wrote his next letter. Thinking that Joan may have been worried about him, he tried to put her mind at ease, stating that, 'Yes I am still alive and this time I really have a reason … I expect you people heard all sorts of rumours after our bit of a show but we are quite OK.'[16]

However, all was not 'OK', the RNC experienced its first casualties of the war in the days before Derrick wrote to Joan. Perhaps to take his mind off the loss of the regiment's men, Derrick described his two weeks' leave, and explained how he enjoyed some 'quiet time … because that is what I needed more than anything else.' This is in contrast with what the rest of the RNC experienced at that time. Derrick may have been economical with the truth as according to various other sources, the men enjoyed what seemed a fairly raucous Christmas, followed by the occupation of a number of small towns in early January 1941.[17]

Derrick's next letter of 10 February 1941 was one of optimism and enthusiasm, and in this case, it is possible to verify the facts that he alludes to as the RNC was at that time advancing towards the Juba River, easily taking over Italian occupied territories as they went along. His tone is once again optimistic as he enthusiastically wrote what he had seen: 'The news has been grand lately – it always is these days. I don't think the Ito's are going to last much longer. We are all dying to get at them as we can clean them up on any day of the week. Excuse the slangy expressions…'[18]

The next day he continued writing his letter, writing 'so sorry I had to stop yesterday but we really are terribly busy at the moment. We are in Ito country and are very busy mucking about.'[19]

The UDF had experienced one success after another. During February, they took Kismayu from where the Italians withdrew without putting up a fight.[20] The Juba River runs into the sea just north of Kismayu, but further inland the crossing of the river was crucial to carry out the strategy of the Allied forces. Somalia, part of the

---

14   It is ironic that the RNC sang Zulu war songs as they charged El Wak as Dingaan's Day, also known as the Day of the Vow, celebrated a Voortrekker victory over the Zulus on 16 December 1838.
15   Stewart, *The First Victory*, p.117.
16   Personal correspondence, Derrick Norton to Joan Gutridge, 15 January 1941.
17   Stewart, *The First Victory*, p.44.
18   Personal correspondence, Derrick Norton to Joan Gutridge, 10 February 1941.
19   Personal correspondence, Derrick Norton to Joan Gutridge, 11 February 1941.
20   Stewart, *The First Victory*, pp.131–133.

Italian Somaliland at the time, was the objective of the forces moving from Kenya. The Juba River presented an obstacle in that it served as a natural defensive line to the interior of Somalia. For some UDF men the crossing of the river presented few difficulties, while others spent valuable hours constructing bridges.

The experiences of the men also varied considerably, for some it was one of horror. One man recalled, for instance, that when his unit crossed the Juba River, they had to bury the bodies of their enemies in a mass grave. For him, the 'appalling jumble of arms and legs'[21] were his first encounter with death in the war, and a memory that would stay with him for a long time.

Derrick did not mention any such events in his letters to Joan, perhaps because he did not experience any, or perhaps because he wanted to shield her from the reality of war. Whatever the case may have been, the RNC's 'mucking about' was to come to an end soon after, as it was only a week or two later that they encountered a more sinister side of combat.

Early on the morning of 22 February 1941, the RNC and the Armoured Car unit attacked a Colonial Infantry unit near Cansuma at Bel Mamo. They then moved on rapidly towards Gelib,[22] reaching the outskirts of the town by 09:00. Heavy shelling and confusion among the different units stopped the RNC from crossing over the Juba to Gelib, a mere 6 kilometres from the river. By midday, C Section experienced more shelling while the other sections managed to cross the Juba.

In the afternoon, Derrick was patrolling the area when his platoon was approached by an Italian officer with a white flag. As Derrick went forward to discuss surrender, the officer fell to the ground and his men opened fire on the RNC platoon, killing 14 Carbineers. One of them was Platoon Sergeant B. Blomeyer, a good friend of Derrick.[23] This became known as the 'white flag' incident of Gelib.

As the enemy forces fired on the defenceless UDF men, Derrick sprinted across the firing line to reach the mortar crew. This enabled him to keep the enemy at a distance and effectively save the lives of the remaining men of his unit. By some accounts the men were 'shaken, saddened [and] depressed' following this incident. It is no wonder that historians referred to the men as 'bitter', following this experience.[24] Whether they were shaken, saddened, depressed or bitter, they were certainly no longer naïve.

Derrick was later awarded the Military Cross for his actions at Gelib, and his conduct was described as 'his personal example in a situation fraught with the greatest danger preserved unblemished the morale of his platoon, which carried the fight to the enemy until such time as assistance arrived…'[25]

21　James Ambrose Brown, *Retreat to victory A Springbok's Diary in North Africa: Gazala to El Alamein 1942* (Johannesburg: Ashanti, 1991), p.102.
22　Also known as Jelib or Jilib.
23　Neil Orpen, 'East African and Abyssinian campaigns', South African Force World War II, vol. 1 (1969), HyperWar: East African and Abyssinian Campaigns [Chapter 15] (ibiblio.org), accessed 9 February 2021.
24　Brown, *The War of a Hundred Days*, p.142.
25　A copy of Army Form W.3121 is included in the collection of letters, it provides details on Derrick Norton's conduct during the 'white flag' incident and recommended him for

On Sunday, 23 February, the day after the incident, Derrick hastily composed a letter to Joan saying that he had 'about two minutes to spare so please excuse the scribble … I am still OK and doing fine – will see you at home soon.… Don't worry about us and don't expect letters as we really never get a chance to write.'[26]

He included a photograph of Sergeant Blomeyer in the letter.

Two weeks later, on 9 March 1941, Derrick again alluded to the 'white flag' incident:

> Well now to get on to the news from up this end. It's not all pleasant. You probably have seen the bad news and I don't want to talk about it – we are all trying to forget about it. A lot of us were very lucky but let's not talk about it.
>
> Otherwise things have been going well here. The Ito's are not proving to be fighters at all and give in before the fight really starts. They are a cheeky lot of devils too and if I had anything to do with them I would give them all a damn good hiding first to teach them how to behave…
>
> We have caught thousands of prisoners – we are tired of the sight of them running around with white flags. It is part of the Ito army issue[27] – of that we are quite certain … write again soon and don't worry if you don't hear from me, there is still work to be done up here and we may have to do it.[28]

Although he did not directly refer to the event that killed his friend and several of his fellow servicemen, it is clear that he felt betrayed by the Italians who displayed a flagrant disregard for the rules of war. It was also clear that he had realised that war entailed more than 'mucking about' in the bush. For him, the Italians had been confirmed as an unworthy enemy, a view shared by many UDF men and a narrative that had persisted over time and had been cemented in myth.

Italian soldiers had long been described as docile and passive, unwilling fighters in a war that had been thrust upon them by their dictatorial leader. As with all myths, the belief has been challenged in more recent histories, yet as is the case with all nations, the Italian Army had among its ranks those who were not convinced of the merits of war.

Negative perceptions about the Italian forces were not unique to the Allied forces. *Generalleutnant* Erwin Rommel, for instance, who reluctantly cooperated with Italian forces in North Africa, was convinced that the Italian commanders did not have the skill to operate successfully in desert conditions. Additionally, the relationships between the Italian rank and file and their officers were strained and obstructive, further worsening the Italian success rate on the battlefield and adding to the idea of cowardice among Italian troops.[29]

---

the Military Cross. The form was signed by Lieutenant General Sir Archibald Wavell, Commander-in-Chief, Middle East.
26 Personal correspondence, Derrick Norton to Joan Gutridge, 23 February 1941.
27 A common slang word for 'Italians' during the war.
28 Personal correspondence, Derrick Norton to Joan Gutridge, 9 March 1941.
29 D. Petracarro, 'The Italian Army in Africa 1940–1943: An Attempt at Historical Perspective', *War & Society*, 9:2 (1991), pp.103–127.

For propaganda purposes, these views found manifestation in the contemporary press. In Parliament, the Italians and their willingness to fight became a topic of discussion as reported in the weekly newsletter for the week ending 22 February 1941. The 'story of the week' was about the dangers that the Italian forces faced in Africa. The liaison officer told everyone, 'In a cheerful vein … that the Italians not only have to face our bullets as they come towards them, but they have to face them again for the second time when, fleeing, they overtake the bullets.'[30]

Although the letters that Derrick wrote after February 1941 reflected a negative tone, his sense of purpose became more evident. It is unlikely that Derrick intentionally wrote for the sake of keeping up morale, yet he seemed to have become more determined when it came to issues of warfare. However, the fact that the Carbineers were 'tired of the sight of [Italians]' was undeniable. When Derrick wrote these letters to Joan, they were in the process of capturing as many as 14,000 enemy troops. By the end of July, the number had risen to more than 75,000 prisoners, placing the UDF contingents in East Africa under great strain as all of these captives had to be fed and accommodated.[31]

Ever conscious of the military censors, Derrick never related his version of the events at Gelib in any of his letters to Joan. However, those at home did not display the same concern for restrictions. When the news of the white flag incident reached the Union, self-censorship, objectivity and even accuracy was forgotten.

The pro-war section on the home front enjoyed stories of heroism and those who knew Derrick were delighted about his medal. Towards the end of March, a friend of the Norton family heard about the incident by word of mouth, and she immediately wrote to Derrick's father to tell him about it. While her letter reveals that the facts had become distorted by the time the news reached her, it is clear that the events at Gelib served only to increase her negativity towards the enemy:

> Do you remember a little while ago we read in the papers of a batch of Italians holding up a white flag & one of our officers & some men were sent to take them prisoner – when they got up to the Italians, the officer who was holding the white flag flung himself on to the ground & shouted an order to his men to fire on our men – our officer was Derrick – this soldier says Derrick immediately ordered his men to fire & pulled out his revolver & let them have it too – the devils … their damned coward of an officer was a German! He got away, but they found him soon after, crawling along, riddled with bullets, and as this man told Van with his guts dragging on the ground – he died a short while later, & I am glad to say he suffered intense agony – I don't think I am wicked to say I am glad he suffered … we don't know if you had heard it was Derrick, so I thought I would let you know

---

30 DOD PP: Weekly Newsletter No. 67. Week ending 22nd February 1941.
31 Moore and Fedorowich, *The British Empire and its Italian Prisoners of War,* p.20. This number include all Axis POWs taken in East Africa and consists of 49 258 Italian and 26 179 African prisoners.

– poor little Derrick. I still think of them as our happy little boys … life is the devil these days, but we still can smile.[32]

Obviously, she would not let facts stand in the way of positive home front morale.

Derrick's next letter to Joan was written on 14 March 1941 and by this time his tone had become more upbeat. No doubt, a short break had helped lift his spirits. As always, though, military censors were in the back of his mind.

> I am glad your holiday was a good one – it makes a difference when one has a damn jolly holiday what, what!! Anyway I am going to try and make this a long letter. Don't blame me if it is disjointed as I am writing it in spasms. I am in the middle of two jobs one is writing to you and the other is (?*!!**) censored. We have had a grand rest, swimming in the sea almost every day for a complete fortnight now. It has been wonderful fun and we have all recovered magnificently – all fit and ready to give the Ito's another bang. The place we were at was quite a decent place and the best by far…[33]

However, he also mentioned that any hope of home leave had been dashed as they were told that it would be impossible to leave East Africa at that time. Derrick must have been referring to the fact that on 11 March the Carbineers were told that they were to go for retraining and afterwards would be continuing the advance towards Mogadishu.[34] Although he stated that he did 'not mind as long as [they were] bringing the war closer to its end', his sentiment was in contrast with almost all his previous letters in which he wrote about how much he missed home, and his wish to 'give the Ito's another bang' may just as well have been an effort to keep up morale, for his own sake and for Joan's, as he had done in many a previous letter.

By the time Derrick and the Carbineers reached Cairo, he seemed to have had time to reflect on the white flag incident, and on 8 July 1941 he wrote to Joan about how much time had passed since he left South Africa. There was no way for him to know how long it would be before he would be back in the country. However, he must have realised that the war would not be over as soon as he had hoped, and he speculated that by the time he got back home, he would be too old to continue with his rugby career.

> I am afraid that I too will be a spectator. I will be too old to play! You really don't know how we long to get home. It all seems so far away now. It seems years and years since we left the quay at Durban, it is only a dim memory now, the life we had at home seems an impossible dream. Good heavens it looks as if I am getting sort of sentimental, excuse me!! One can't do that sort of thing here.[35]

---

32   Personal correspondence, anonymous to Norton family, March 1941.
33   Personal correspondence, Derrick Norton to Joan Gutridge, 14 March 1941.
34   Bentz, *Fighting Springboks C Company*, p.48.
35   Personal correspondence, Derrick Norton to Joan Gutridge, 8 July 1941.

From Cairo, Derrick's letters continued to show his reflective mood, although a wry sense of humour is also evident. On 12 July 1941, he again alluded to the white flag incident by including a photograph which was taken of a group of UDF soldiers shortly after a battle in Kenya. Some of those in the photo were killed at Gelib. By this time though, Derrick was relieved to be out of East Africa. For him the campaign was not one of easy victories, as some had subsequently described it, but one that left him disillusioned, dirty, thirsty and tired. He was glad to leave behind the mud of Africa for the dust of the desert.

It was only now that news of his Military Cross had spread and he started receiving letters of congratulations. One was from Joan, written on 24 July 1941.

> We were all awakened as soon as the paper arrived this morning with Daddy shouting "Derrick has been awarded the MC." Sincerest congratulations my boy we are all very proud of you especially me. I would just like to give you a big hug and a kiss. I think it's absolutely marvellous Derrick, honestly I just walk around with an incessant smile on my face! Just as well I am not your wife, if I was I don't think I would be speaking to my neighbours to-day!!?!! ... Gosh we were a funny little couple weren't we? Do you remember that dance we went to in the town hall? You took Elma and I went with Nick and we forgot we had partners at all and only looked at each other!!! The others thought we were a bit crazy I think, but we couldn't worry then could we, we might as well had gone to the dance by ourselves for all the notice we took of them!!³⁶

This was one of the very few letters written by Joan that survived the war. Derrick kept it with him throughout the war until he returned home, a much longer time that he could have guessed. Its contents were evidently of great value to him.

Perhaps Joan was buoyed by Derrick's award, or perhaps the rumours in Pietermaritzburg were being spread thick and fast, because by August 1941 she was under the impression that Derrick and the rest of the Carbineers were on their way to the Union for home leave. Rumours about home leave also circulated among the men 'up north',³⁷ but by October 1941 Derrick had become despondent.

> The old home leave question is not going nearly as well as it promised at first and I am now being very pessimistic about it again and don't expect to get home for quite a long while. It is a damn shame about this leave one minute our hopes are on top of the world and the next they have sunk far below zero. I don't really know whether I do want to go home now – what I mean is this – I should hate to go home and have to leave again – I am afraid it would be ten times as hard leaving a second time. I often feel that I would like to stay here until the show is over and then go home and stay home. Then again, Heaven alone knows how long this war is going to last and we are all longing to see all you people again, and soon. I have had a long argument with myself and I don't seem to have reached any conclusion except

---

36 Personal correspondence, Joan Gutridge to Derrick Norton, 24 July 1941
37 South African UDF servicemen referred to the Western Desert as 'up north.'

that I wish this '__' war would end soon. Anyway we must keep our chins up and keep on fighting until we have wiped every Gerry[38] off the face of the earth – yes, those are my bloodthirsty sentiments.[39]

The battles in the Libyan Desert seemed to give Derrick the impression that they were making progress against the German forces. On 3 June 1942, he optimistically, if somewhat misguided, gave his views on their German and Italian adversaries.

> I suppose you know by now that there is an enormous flap going on here, I heard about it on my way back and hurried up to hear – foolish of me! However, we are all very confident that we have Gerry absolutely taped and we are going to give them one of the soundest whackings he has had yet. The Ito's are as usual absolutely laughable, poor devils…[40]

A few days later, on 11 June 1942, it seemed that Derrick had accepted that home leave was not an option, but he had hoped for some leave in Cairo, which was a very busy city during the war. The city held many different options for entertainment, including tea rooms, gardens, film theatres and an opera house.

For those who needed it, Cairo was also home to a number of Allied military hospitals, including hospitals staffed and run by South African, British, American, Australian and New Zealand forces.

> The war here is now over a fortnight old and we are all wondering how much longer it can last at this pace. I don't think much more than another fortnight and then maybe we will get our well-earned rest which we so narrowly missed a little while ago then I may see all my Cairo girlfriends again, let me see there must be at least 20 of them all charming and talented young South African girls. The stories you hear of these girls only going out with officers is all boloney – they are doing very well, more particularly the nurses for all of whom I have a very soft spot. The others are not always so well behaved.[41]

Derrick's assessment of the military situation in the Libyan Desert was ill-informed, but if he did have in-depth knowledge of the situation, he would have kept it to himself as the ever-present censors were still doing their work. On the other hand, Derrick's misjudgement of the situation was not unique and commanders, British and South African, were also caught unprepared. The centre of attention was the harbour town of Tobruk; whoever controlled this town would be able to bring in supplies for troops.

Although it is not known if Derrick knew anything about General Klopper's experience as commander of the Tobruk Garrison, or of his inexperience in military

---

38 "Jerry", German, the use of "Gerry" is a not uncommon term in use by South Africans.
39 Personal correspondence, Derrick Norton to Joan Gutridge, October 1941.
40 Personal correspondence, Derrick Norton to Joan Gutridge, 3 June 1942.
41 Personal correspondence, Derrick Norton to Joan Gutridge, 11 June 1942.

strategy, it can be assumed that Derrick may have heard about Rommel, a master of military strategy. Seven months earlier the German commander had dealt a heavy blow to the UDF forces at the Battle of Sidi Rezegh. Since that victory, Rommel had been running amok in the desert, and had been nicknamed 'The Desert Fox'. While UDF forces were attempting to improve the defences around Tobruk – and thereby remaining static, Rommel's *Afrika Korps* were embarking on risky mobile manoeuvres.[42]

The day after Derrick wrote his letter, his unit was sent towards Tobruk to relieve the Cameron Highlanders.[43] Ten days later, on 21 June 1942, Rommel overran the forces at Tobruk, gaining control of the town and taking almost 30,000 Allied prisoners.[44] Derrick was among them. It is unclear how Joan heard about Derrick's capture, but as was the case with the 'white flag' incident, Derrick never related the details of his capture in any of his letters.

During his captivity he received the news of Joan's engagement to a friend of his, but Derrick remained a loyal letter writer throughout his captivity, although prisoners were limited in the number of letters they were allowed to write.

By the time the war ended, Derrick found himself in *Stalag VIIA*, a prison camp near Moosburg, about 320 kilometres east of Weinsberg. It is possible the Derrick was forced, like thousands of other prisoners, to evacuate the camp and join the so-called hell march, the Germans' last attempt at avoiding the approaching Allies. Once he had been liberated and arrived in England, he resumed his correspondence with Joan.

Derrick eventually returned to Pietermaritzburg on 26 June 1945. Seeing Derrick again must have had a profound effect on Joan. Her engagement ended and she got married to Derrick on 8 December 1945, less than six months after his return from the war.

---

42 David B. Katz, *South Africans versus Rommel, the Untold Story of the Desert War in World War II* (Johannesburg: Delta Books, 2018), pp.178 & 192.

43 A. F. Hattersley, *Carbineer, The History of the Royal Natal Carbineers,* (Natal: Gale & Polden, 1950), p.105.

44 Andrew Stewart, 'The "Atomic" Despatch: Field Marshal Auchinleck, the Fall of the Tobruk Garrison and Post-War Anglo-South African Relations', *Scientia Militaria: South African Journal of Military Studies,* 36:1 (2008), p.80

3

Sydney Stuart and the 11th Field Ambulance

Sydney Stuart was born in the Orange Free State in 1919. Like many others, his chosen career after school was mining, and he joined the Simmer and Jack Gold Mines Limited in Germiston, on the Witwatersrand. Unlike many South Africans of British descent, Sydney did not volunteer his services to the UDF when the war began. As a junior official on the mine, he enjoyed benefits that others did not have, among which was a fairly good salary and advanced first aid training.

Waiting until after his 21st birthday, Sydney volunteered his medical knowledge to the 7th Field Ambulance Unit. However, it was not long before he found himself with the 11th Field Ambulance, attached to the 5th South Africa Infantry Brigade in the 1st Division.

So, Sydney was on his way to war. After training, he embarked from Durban to Mombasa in Kenya. Many servicemen who fought in East Africa and in the Western Desert, dismissed the campaign in East Africa as insignificant in terms of battle experience. The battles in Libya were on a much larger scale and demanded more from them in terms of combat. It becomes evident from Sydney's memoirs that the men saw Kenya almost as a holiday destination. He describes his war experience there as a list of places visited by his field ambulance:

> From Mombasa we were dispatched in short order to GilGil where the bulk of the South African forces were encamped at that time. There were the usual drill marches and general physical exercises to prepare us for the forthcoming battles. After a further couple of months our particular unit, which was the 11th South African Field Ambulance, was dispatched to a place called Londiani, further north in Kenya.[1]

Quickly realising that the natural threats were greater than the dangers of battle, the men focussed their attention on Mother Nature. It was the noises at night, those they could not see, that caused their nerves to rattle. Standing guard alone at night was the perfect time for imaginations to run riot, and Sydney was not spared. While still at Londiani, he described one such night:

---

1   André Erwee, and Louis J. Eksteen (eds), *The Second World War Experiences of Sydney Stuart: A South African soldier of the 2nd World War (1939 – 1945) who served in the 11th Field Ambulance of the SA Medical Corps* (Newcastle: Fort Amiel Museum, 2017), pp.31-32.

> Not long after sunset, whilst on guard duty the roaring of lions could be very clearly heard in the close vicinity, and there was evidence of a multitude of buck and other wild animals… It was an extremely dark night. After I had reached the end of my beat and turned to come back again, clattering through these multitude of stones [in the dry river bank] and reaching one of the bushes on the right side of the so-called path that I was on, which was my beat, there was a sudden scurry and flurry, and I saw a vague shadow leaping across the pathway, that I was moving along, and with a further clatter of stones, disappeared in the bush. At this stage I was fully prepared for anything that could happen, having put a bullet up the breech and carrying my rifle at the port. However, the sudden shock of this animal of whatever it was jumping across my path caused me to fall back and involuntarily fire a shot into the air.[2]

When the others arrived to see what the commotion was about, Sydney said it was a lion that jumped across his path. Taking into account that a lion's roar can be heard as far as eight kilometres away, the mistake, if it was one, was easily made. Of course, it would be unthinkable for him to fall back and fire a shot if a scrub hare had jumped out in front of him.

Leaving this wilderness behind them, Sydney and the rest of the 11th Field Ambulance men reached Abyssinia. It was here that battle casualties became a more common occurrence; one of which was a UDF pilot whose Hawker Hartebees fighter aircraft was shot down during the attack on Hobok. Obviously hit by Italian anti-aircraft fire, the Hartebees descended so slowly that it settled in a tree. Sydney described the pilot 'a little worse for wear', but otherwise alright.[3]

The mountainous terrain of Abyssinia presented the field ambulances with challenges, especially with the evacuation of patients to casualty clearing stations. Sergeant Major J. L Hartzenberg remembered that it often took days to get the casualties from the front lines to the casualty clearing stations. The terrain was very difficult to navigate and when the rains came, it soaked the ground for weeks on end. Blood transfusions were performed from person to person and the unfortunate volunteers who donated their blood were rewarded with a small bottle of Guinness Stout, and if they were lucky, they got the afternoon off as well.[4]

It was also here that Sydney's experience in the mines probably came in very useful. Because there were so many obstacles in the rough ground, it was found that, 'the canvas stretcher as used in the mines can be invaluable. This canvas stretcher is tiring on the carrying personnel if used over long distances but a patient can be readily moved in it over rough ground and hillsides.'[5]

The next casualty came when Fort Mega was overrun by the South Africans. The Italians had laid pipe landmines as defences, and the unfortunate Major Alfred

---

2   Erwee and Eksteen, *The Second World War Experiences of Sydney Stuart*, pp.33–34.
3   Erwee and Eksteen, *The Second World War Experiences of Sydney Stuart*, pp.37–38.
4   DOD CF Scheepers Box 17: Die Suid-Afrikaanse Geneeskundige Diens [The South African Medical Service], JL Hartzenberg. 15 April 1995.
5   DOD CF Scheepers Box 9: Subject: Warfare in Mountainous Country.

Ward Clare stepped on one. One of his legs was blown off below the knee and the other was shattered. Sydney's field ambulance now became 'mobile surgical team.' The efforts to save Major Clare involved amputating both his legs, but, as Sydney believed, the major was so overcome with shock that he died a few hours later. The other wounded were evacuated to Moyale, and then the 11th Field Ambulance was on its way again. This time to Egypt.

Although Sydney and the rest of his field ambulance members had no experience of desert warfare, the authorities knew that the conditions in Libya demanded considerably more from the men and their vehicles. A range of adaptions were needed for field ambulances that moved from the African bush climate and geography of East Africa to the dry desert conditions of North Africa.

The increase of battle activity between belligerents was also anticipated and so it was recommended that while field ambulances had to remain mobile, they would also have to develop a greater capacity for treatment of a high number of patients. The quick transfer of patients to a casualty clearing station was priority, and for this reason, field ambulances would each receive 14 ambulance cars. It was hoped that this would also help with the long distances that would have to be covered in the desert.

In terms of what was expected of the men of each ambulance, it was made clear that at least one officer in each ambulance unit had to be able to perform emergency surgery. This was especially important as the distances between the battlefields and the surgical units were often great.[6]

Soon pressed into service at Mersa Matruh, Sydney and his fellow medics set up an underground hospital. The wards were below ground level, almost like an enormous foxhole, and protected against air raids with sandbags. The hospital was flanked by a searchlight battery on the one side and a battery of anti-aircraft guns on the other.

To deal with the increased number of casualties, six nurses were sent to Mersa Matruh. According to Hartzenberg, this hospital was the target of many Stuka dive bombers, day and night, especially in the first weeks of its existence.[7] The lions of East Africa faded into obscurity as the realities of war became obvious.

Sydney remembered the burn cases that arrived at Mersa Matruh all the way from Tobruk, more than 370 kilometres distant. It was 1941, and Tobruk was occupied by Commonwealth forces, surrounded by Rommel's *Afrika Korps*. Because the Allied forces held Tobruk, the casualties could be evacuated from the harbour. When the number or casualties were high, minesweepers were used, taking men to the hospital at Mersa Matruh.

However, Sydney also had a chance to see the action at Tobruk from the harbour's side: '[At] certain times we congregated in force with ambulances, troop carriers, et cetera at the harbour to collect and evacuate these wounded to the casualty clearing station…'[8]

---

6   DOD CF Scheepers Box 9: GHQ., MEF ME/MEDITERRANEAN/3122: 'The Formation of Field Ambulances in Desert Warfare.'
7   DOD CF Scheepers Box 17: Die Suid-Afrikaanse Geneeskundige Diens, JL Hartzenberg. 15 April 1995.
8   Erwee and Eksteen, *The Second World War Experiences of Sydney Stuart,* p.43.

In November they were on their way again, moving closer to Sidi Rezegh. According to Captain Caldwell, also with the 11th Field Ambulance, they heard artillery fire coming from Sidi Rezegh on 20 November. Moving further on, the came across evidence of a 'terrific tank battle having taken place, indicated by numerous criss [sic] crossing of tracks and derelict vehicles.'[9] By the time the sun set, they were being machine gunned by low-flying aircraft.

Sydney recalled the same experience in his memoir and identified the aircraft as Stuka dive bombers, a favourite ground attack plane of the Luftwaffe.[10] The next day, 21 November, the attacks from the air continued, but Caldwell reported that this time the Stukas were driven off by Allied fighters. Throughout that day and the next, they treated many wounded men, especially from the Transvaal Scottish who were in the midst of the battle.[11]

He remembered the same day as one of confusion, and his writing of this episode of the war reflects the so-called fog of war:

> At the end of the second day's battle, things became rather chaotic and our Division came to a virtual standstill. The [4th] Indian Division had actually reached the coastline according to reports. As a consequence of the [German] Panzer attacks the New Zealand Division was unable to join up in the line of battle and therefore directed their attack through Sidi Rezegh towards the south of Tobruk. Of course the ordinary soldier in the field has very little idea of what is happening over the whole of the battle front, but it would seem that the South African forces took the brunt of the attacks from the panzers, and there were a considerable amount of casualties and prisoners taken. It was probably around this time that General Armstrong gave the order 'every man for himself.'[12]

The next day, the German forces were among them, and had it not been for the Red Cross on the vehicles, they would have been taken prisoner, or shot, if they put up resistance. Caldwell's account of the day is more detailed, and described in his report how an officer of the Transvaal Scottish spotted light armoured vehicles in the distance. When Caldwell took a closer look through his binoculars, he realised that they were withdrawing while being pursued by German tanks. The 11th Field Ambulance soon found itself withdrawing when the Germans began firing in their direction.

It is here that Sydney's account and Caldwell's report begin to deviate from one another. Sydney remembered how the *Afrika Korps*' tanks moved through their lines close up, while this is not part of Caldwell's report. However, an account in Sydney's memoir stands out as an event that could not be easily forgotten, although the event

---

9   DOD CF Scheepers Box 9: Diary of events from 18th Nov 41 to 30th Nov 41 By Capt P.M. Caldwell, 11th FD AMB.
10 Erwee and Eksteen, *The Second World War Experiences of Sydney Stuart*, p.45.
11 DOD CF Scheepers Box 9: Diary of events from 18th Nov 41 to 30th Nov 41 By Capt P. M. Caldwell, 11th FD AMB.
12 Erwee and Eksteen, *The Second World War Experiences of Sydney Stuart*, pp.45–46.

was not experienced by Sydney himself, he did witness part of it. Apparently, as the Germans moved through their unit, one of the drivers of the Cape Corps reacted angrily when

> … one of the German tank commanders had opened the turret of his tank and was looking around in a sort of imperious manner at the multi [racial] collection of troops standing around. Although I didn't actually hear the dialogue, it is reported that one of the Cape Coloured drivers, seeing this snatched his rifle and without further ado shouted *"Kyk daai donnerse Duitser!"* [look at that damn German!], and shot him through the throat. He [the German], of course, tumbled over the turret and in that position passed where I was standing, and I actually saw that he was dead.[13]

The men of the Cape Corps served as non–combatants and did not carry arms, as was the case with the rest of the non-European army services of the UDF.[14] The man in question would therefore not have had a rifle to grab and shoot with. While Sydney may have seen a dead German hanging from a tank turret, he may have come to his death by other means, leaving the first half of the story in the realm of myth.

After this encounter, Sydney and the medical personnel continued to treat the wounded, with one man from an armoured car whose arm was completely shattered by a hit to his elbow.

Of the 5th Infantry Brigade to which Sydney's field ambulance was attached, no equipment or vehicles remained after the battle. The reequipping of the 11th Field Ambulance would only take place once the New Zealanders and the British field ambulances had been resupplied with their field requirements. All the ambulances in the service of the UDF at that time were deemed to be 'aged and in poor mechanical condition.' Those that were not completely destroyed during the battle, had also seen service in East Africa, putting them well past their 'use by date.' All the field ambulances were also staffed with new, often inexperienced, personnel.[15]

Sydney was reported missing in action on 'approx. 20/11/41' and was confirmed as a prisoner of war on 2 February 1942.[16] He was one of 3,000 UDF men captured during the battle which almost wiped out the entire 5th South African Infantry Brigade.[17]

His first hours of captivity were very unusual. The Germans ordered the prisoners to load the wounded on the vehicles that were still in working condition. They were then told to drive southwards in convoy. Alongside the line of trucks were German motorcycle troops. Sydney drove one of the trucks, and on the back of that truck was a Scottish major who tried to convince him to drive slowly. In this way they

---

13 Erwee and Eksteen, *The Second World War Experiences of Sydney Stuart*, pp.46–47.
14 Van der Waag, *A Military History of Modern South Africa*, p.175.
15 DOD CF Scheepers Box 9: 'Present state of Medical Services: 1SA Div. 21 January 1942.'
16 DOD PF RS, Sydney Stuart, 29338.
17 Christopher Sommerville, *Our War How the British Commonwealth Fought the Second World War* (London: Orion, 1998), p.94.

would fall behind the rest of the vehicles and make their escape. This left Sydney in a difficult position:

> Seated next to me in the front of the truck, there was a German soldier with some sort of automatic rifle or sub-machine-gun who soon saw through my ruse of pulling the choke out and stalling the truck and [the German] quietly told me in perfect English to stop playing silly buggers … and despite the fact that the Scottish Major beat his fists on the top of the cab in an effort to try and get me to slow down, I thought discretion was the better part of valour.[18]

His attention was soon diverted when a unit of New Zealanders began firing at the convoy. The German quickly abandoned their captives and took off in a westerly direction, leaving the South Africans in the line of fire. Feeling desperately brave, Sydney grabbed the Red Cross Flag and waved it from the roof of the truck, but, 'at this moment there was a burst of machine-gun fire, which only just cleared the top of the truck and without further argument I dived off the side, and took shelter behind the wheel.'[19]

Sydney speculated that the Germans 'delivered' them to the New Zealand troops because they did not want to have the burden of wounded POWs. Of course there is no way to verify Sydney's view, although it is more likely that the Germans did not expect to come across Allied forces while on their way to a temporary prisoner-of-war camp. Taking into account that their prisoners were attached to a field ambulance, the Germans could have left them were they found them.

Unfortunately, the luck of the 11th Field Ambulance ran out a few days later. The German forces surrounded them, along with the New Zealand unit, and all were taken captive. This time they were marched to Benghazi on the coast of Libya, from where they were transported to Italy some months later.

Of those captured at Sidi Rezegh, Sydney included, the Medical Directorate considered several honours and awards for the medical corps. Four members of the 11th Field Ambulance received medals.

Major Melzer, commander of the 11th Field Ambulance, was recommended for a Military Cross. He 'showed extreme bravery and courage and a tenacity to duty that was truly admirable for he carried on giving medical aid to the wounded … despite cross tank fire, anti-tank, machine-gun and artillery fire…'[20]

Private McGillivray's Military Medal was for remaining at the operating theatre following an attack which caused a fire.[21] McGillivray extinguished the fire before making it ready to use within 20 minutes.

---

18   Erwee and Eksteen, *The Second World War Experiences of Sydney Stuart,* p.48.
19   Erwee and Eksteen, *The Second World War Experiences of Sydney Stuart,* p.49.
20   DOD Medical (hereafter MED), Box 12. ADMS 142/1 Awards. May 1942.
21   The Military Cross (MC) and the Military Medal (MM) were considered of the same quality and had the same criteria for their award. However, only commissioned officers were eligible for the MC, other ranks received the MM – incidentally the two looked distinctly different. This distasteful and prejudiced system was abandoned in 1993, since when all ranks of the British Army are eligible for the MC.

Lance Corporal Purchase also received a Military Medal because he continued to treat the wounded while under artillery and machine-gun fire; 'One of the wounded was killed by a machine-gun bullet while Lance Corporal Purchase was actually attending to him, however, undaunted he moved on to the next [patient] and carried on his work.'[22]

Lastly, Private Roberts received a Military Medal as he continued driving his ambulance to pick up wounded on the battlefield at Sidi Rezegh. He conducted many of these rescue missions despite his ambulance being 'badly shot up. By his action he brought many wounded quickly to medical aid. Finally his ambulance received a direct hit and was destroyed.'[23]

---

22 DOD MED Box 12. ADMS 142/1 Awards. May 1942.
23 DOD MED Box 12. ADMS 142/1 Awards. May 1942.

4

The Birch Brothers, *Die Middellandse Regiment*

Young men from the Great Karoo filled up the ranks of *Die Middellandse Regiment* (DMR). Established in 1934, the regiment was to expand the UDF from 12 regiments to 24. The chances were good that those who volunteered for war service with the DMR at the start of the war would have known each other. The regiment was made up of men of the same families, friends, and acquaintances. From the Dordrecht district, three brothers from the Birch family offered their services when Smuts called for volunteers. They were Sydney (Syd), John Vyvyan (Vyv) and Walter.

Syd was the oldest of the three brothers, and when the war started he was the father of three children and husband to Margaret, known as Peggy. Vyv and his wife Kay had just become parents to a baby girl. Walter, the youngest, was unmarried. A fourth brother, Edward (Ted) was unable to enlist for medical reasons. Emma, Hilda and Anne were sisters to the four brothers. Their parents, Ernest and Mildred Birch were the owners of Vogel Vlei, a farm that would become a well-known name in the horse-breeding world.

The DMR was mobilised in September 1940 and the men were sent to Premier Mine near Pretoria on 22 September for training. Soon afterwards, they were posted to various internment camps to guard those who were against Smuts's pro-war stance and who had been interned as a result. With the War Measures Act of 1940, the Smuts government was able to intern enemy aliens and South Africans whom they suspected of subversive activities.[1]

If the DMR men regarded guard duties tedious, things soon changed when the regiment was incorporated into the 2nd South Africa Division in March 1941. The Birch brothers were placed in B Company of the DMR.

Now the reality of what they had let themselves in for must have become clearer as they were sent to Pietermaritzburg for intensive training on Vickers machine guns. The culmination of their training came when they assembled with thousands of others on a parade ground early in June 1941, when Smuts gave a stirring speech to inspire them as they set off to war.

By this time, the victories of the 1st South Africa Division in East Africa would have been common knowledge, and the relative ease with which the enemy was

---

[1] A. M. Fokkens, 'Afrikaner unrest within South Africa during the Second World War and the measures taken to supress it' in *Journal for Contemporary History* 37:2 (2012), p.128.

overcome in East Africa may have left many of the new recruits confident that they would carry out their duty and return to the Union as defenders of freedom.

On 10 June, the three brothers left Durban on the *Mauretania* with the rest of the DMR, but not before they sent a cheerful telegram to their parents, informing them that they had departed for Egypt. They arrived at Suez on 22 June. Syd was one of 39 officers in the DMR and Vyv and Walter were part of the 551 rank and file.[2]

With their departure, new experiences assaulted the brothers in quick succession as their horizons were broadened from the farming life in the Karoo. The sea voyage offered a glimpse into their immediate future and hinted at some discomfort. Four days after leaving Durban harbour, Vyv wrote his first letter to his parents, complaining of feeling 'slightly giddy', but remaining optimistic for the most part:

Sydney Birch. (Photo: Chris Roux)

> My dear Mom and Dad,
> Well we left Durban last Tuesday as you probably know and have been going full speed ahead since then, covering I suppose about 500 or 600 miles in 24 hours.
>   It was only the first night that I felt slightly giddy [sea sick] but since then I haven't felt a thing; mind you I must say that this ship hardly rolls or rocks at all and also the sea has not been at all rough...[3]

The arid landscape and climate of North Africa was challenging to most men, and as the DMR arrived in June, their first few months in the desert were hot with no hint of rain. Yet, the letters that reached Vogel Vlei told cheerful tales of new adventures, with minor references to adverse conditions. At the end of July 1941, Walter wrote, 'we have managed to borrow a gramophone which makes the air (?) rather interesting. One can hardly say we are having a tough time in fact the dust and flies are a nuisance. Managed to catch a swim at some coast it was grand and easily the best...'[4]

---

2   G. E. Visser, 'Die Middellandse Regiment', *Scientia Militaria* 8:4 (1978), p.14.
3   Personal correspondence, Vyv Birch to parents, 15 June 1941.
4   Personal correspondence, Walter Birch to parents, 29 July 1941.

The rest of Walter's letter reads like that of a tourist describing the scenery and oddities of a newly explored destination.[5]

While Walter wrote about his sightseeing, Syd wrote from Cairo, busy with a course that would keep him away from the rest of his regiment until the middle of August. Not greatly enamoured with Cairo, Syd concentrated on aspects close to his heart, writing about soil fertility, irrigation and crops in the area around the Nile. Like all his letters, and those of his brothers, much space was allocated to asking about the state of the farm and the horses at Vogel Vlei. At this point, the three brothers remained preoccupied with what was familiar to them, their parents, horses, wives and the farm.

Having joined the same regiment, their brotherly bond gave them a sense of security. Even the relatively short time that Syd spent away from his brothers while on his course in Cairo made him aware of their absence, writing that 'Vyv & Walter are very fit & full of beans. I shall be pleased when I get back to them again.'[6]

By August, the DMR had not yet seen any action, but they were being prepared for desert warfare. Their days consisted of driving lessons in the desert sand and navigating with compasses in the featureless landscape. Towards the end of the month, the DMR found themselves near El Alamein with the task of digging defences.[7]

Avoiding the military censor's cut, Vyv's letters during this time did not reveal any of their activities related to war matters. His skilled compositions carefully obscured the less pleasant aspects of desert life. Descriptions of flies, dust, water rations and unpalatable army food were hidden among tales of enjoying South Africa's Castle Beer and swimming. Things were so good that Vyv apparently gained weight:

> Last night we had South African Castle Beer for the first time served to us and it was really great drinking something from our own country for a change. As I sit here on my stretcher writing this letter I can feel the cool sea breeze blowing on my back and it is beautifully cool. I have just to raise my head and my eyes meet the blue waters of the Mediterranean and now I can understand why they always refer to these waters as being blue. For most of the day the water is a clear sky blue in colour and hardly a ripple on it. Fortunately, we are allowed to bathe fairly often and the water is very warm but one get [sic] no surfing. This bathing is of course our only means of washing as water is naturally limited & controlled. Some chaps are giving to try their hand at fishing and I sincerely hope they have a spot of luck as then we might have fried fish for a meal. Hell but it would be a pleasant surprise to have a such a meal. Sometimes when I think of those beautifully fried chops and eggs we used to have at home my mouth just waters from greedy lust. It is mighty strange but this desert appears to agree with most of us and we still continue to put on weight daily. I am collecting a few rolls in my body these days.

---

5   Personal correspondence, Walter Birch to parents, 29 July 1941.
6   Personal correspondence, Syd Birch to parents, 29 July 1941.
7   Visser, 'Die Middellandse Regiment', p.14.

Fancy no more flies & dust to worry about and one can have a bit of peace and always feel clean.[8]

Shortly after he wrote this letter, Vyv was sent to attend a section commander's course at the Weapon Training School. He passed this with distinction, with his certificate including remarks that it was, '[an] excellent result due to hard work', 'thoroughly well deserved' and 'a good platoon sergeant.'[9] His future in the UDF was on track.

In a similar way, Walter sidestepped military reality and wrote about farming issues and horse racing results, with occasional references to swimming in the Mediterranean and football matches, which kept the men busy while they were off duty.[10] Understandably, digging defences did not make for riveting news, but throughout the war, the brothers' letters were characterised by their deep interest in events at Vogel Vlei.

August 1941 seemed almost idyllic, yet changes were afoot. Rommel had been besieging thousands of Australian forces in Tobruk since April. With control of Tobruk, Rommel was in a good position to invade Egypt, which at that time was swarming with British and Commonwealth troops with varying levels of experience in desert warfare. With General Sir Claude Auchinleck in command of the 8th Army, all hope was placed on Operation Crusader to relieve Tobruk and secure Egypt.[11] When the 2nd South Africa Division was placed under the command of 8th Army in October, they became part of that strategy.

At first, their daily duties were tedious and dull. Most of the time they guarded the railway between Mersa Matruh and Bagush.[12] It would not be until December that the DMR first encountered enemy forces, and the letters written during the preceding months showed that the brothers, along with their fellow servicemen, were being prepared for momentous matters. In October, Vyv wrote how:

> …things are going on very well here these days and boredom is a thing of the past as there is always something on the go to pass the time away in fact there is very little time to rest & collect one's thoughts or scattered clothes.
>
> Last week we spent messing around in the desert practising this that and the other thing and it was great fun except that one runs short of sleep because it makes no difference whether it is night or day things carry on just the same. The week passed by like a flash of lightning and I still can't realise that that [sic] it has passed being out in the desert is very much like being out at sea. Direction sence [sic] of bearing means nothing as wherever you look the country is the same and all that one is thankful for is that there is a north, south, east & west so as to help navigate in the correct direction.

---

8   Personal correspondence, Vyv Birch to parents, 17 August 1941.
9   DOD PF RS, John Vivian Birch, DMR.
10 Personal correspondence, Walter Birch to parents, 24 August 1941.
11 David B. Katz, *South Africans versus Rommel the untold story of the Desert War in World War II* (Johannesburg: Delta Books, 2018), 96 – 97, p.106.
12 Visser, 'Die Middellandse Regiment', p.14.

It is useless trying to remember what a spot looks like as the next one you stop at is most likely very similar.[13]

The brothers thought that the training sessions were keeping them exceptionally busy, but when the battles began, they would look back fondly at this time of relatively easy living. For now, they still had time for hygiene and Vyv wrote how he took the time to boil his socks on a small primus stove, 'as I find it much easier to boil them than to attempt to wash them.'[14]

While Vyv laundered his uniform, Syd was recovering from an appendectomy. The operation in a military hospital in Cairo postponed his reunion with his brothers following the completion of his course there. It would seem that the medical personnel were very careful with his health, and that they prudently controlled his recovery, despite him declaring that, 'I feel fit enough to be up & walking around all day.'[15] Following his discharge from hospital, he spent some time in an officers' convalescent home, then he went to the South African base camp before returning to his unit in the desert.

For Walter it was different, and as late as 16 November he wrote, 'In fact with no work and easy hours one can say I have been to the coast for a holiday. The difficult thing is always trying to find some news to write about … Once a week we get some really nice tomatoes which are very cheap up here…'[16]

Two weeks later, the DMR moved to Sidi Omar,[17] an inland town on the Libyan border that was specified as a concentration area for the Crusader offensive. When Walter wrote his letter on the 16th, he must have been unaware that the offensive was put in motion the day before. Embarrassingly for the UDF commanders, the South Africans were not seen to be ready for combat, at least in Auchinleck's opinion, and he put off the offensive for three days. In an effort to save face, Lieutenant General G. E. Brink agreed to commit the inexperienced UDF units to the offensive, improvising the units training as they travelled towards the combat zone.[18]

With Operation Crusader in full swing, the plan was to divert Rommel's attention from the siege at Tobruk, allowing for a breakout there. On 19 November, for instance, the 7th Armoured Brigade took control of the airfield of Sidi Rezegh in Libya. They were soon joined by the 5th South Africa Brigade under Brigadier Armstrong, while Pienaar and the 1st South Africa Infantry Brigade moved towards Bir El Gubi.

For a time, it seemed as if the strategy was effective. The German forces were spread out, but unfortunately, the commanders underestimated Rommel, and a fierce battle took place at Sidi Rezegh from 21 to 23 November.[19] It was here that the

---

13 Personal correspondence, Vyv Birch to parents, 9 October 1941.
14 Personal correspondence, Vyv Birch to parents, 9 October 1941.
15 Personal correspondence, Syd Birch to parents, 5 October 1941.
16 Personal correspondence, Walter Birch to parents, 16 November 1941.
17 Today known as Sidi `Umar.
18 Gustav Bentz, 'From El Wak to Sidi Rezegh: The Union Defence Force's First Experience of Battle in East and North Africa, 1940 – 1941', *Scientia Militaria* 40:3 (2012), p.190.
19 Andrew Stewart, *The Early Battles of Eight Army Crusader to the Alamein Line, 1941 – 42* (Mechanicsburg: Stackpole Books, 2002), pp.20–21.

war correspondent, Uys Krige was taken captive, along with Sydney Stuart and the rest of the 11th Field Ambulance with which he served.

As the battle was raging at Sidi Rezegh, the three Birch brothers were guarding the Fuka aerodrome. They missed all the action, yet news of the battles reached them. For some in the DMR it must have been frustrating to have been left out of the battle, on the other hand, when news of the destruction of the 5th Brigade reached them, they may have been quietly relieved that they were not involved in that battle.

For Vyv these developments were thrilling. Three days after the Battle of Sidi Rezegh, he wrote enthusiastically about the events:

> Since last writing a great deal has happened according to the wireless up here and judging from it they appear to be working very well. It is not much good my commenting on the news because by the time you get this lots may have happened and also you get it as soon as we do. Our wireless is working overtime these days.
>
> Since last writing I have had a rather varied experience and there is very little that I can write about except that we have been extremely busy and have been moving from place to place in rapid succession. I have already lost count of the different places. At one place I had a very interesting time indeed and come into contact with some RAF pilots and I bagged a flight off one in a Blenheim bomber and spent about ¾ of an hour in the air and you can imagine the kick I got out of it and also when he dived at a rocky outcrop out at sea and gave them a good burst with his machine guns. The sensation was simply marvellous and I had a wonderful view of the desert and sea also the coastline and I must say I learnt a devil of a lot from the experience which will come in very handy sometime later.[20]

Despite the increase in activity and excitement, it was also at this time that Vyv began to feel the effects of being away from home for so long, and not even the thrill of a flight in a Blenheim bomber aircraft could ward off his growing wistfulness. He concluded his letter by making it very clear that he would have preferred being at home:

> Before we realise it we will be on the way home again and this trip we be [sic] as a bad dream… To think of home and you people these days is like having a marvellous dream about something you very much want but it is always just out of reach.
>
> Well that is about all I have to say for the time being and I will write again when I can, I guess from now onwards out letters to you people will be very irregular, but I hope not too much.[21]

In his first letter home after the battle at Sidi Rezegh, Walter did not write about the battle, but mentioned, 'These damn flies are somewhat awful haven't much time to

---

20   Personal correspondence, Vyv Birch to parents, 26 November 1941.
21   Personal correspondence, Vyv Birch to parents, 26 November 1941.

write now but am crammed with news which will have to come later as every thing [sic] just seems in a rush while strange and funny things happen which gives one a good laugh.'[22]

Perhaps the three brothers did not include news of the battle because they were not involved in it, yet it could also be that they were trying to spare their parents from worrying about them. When writing to their parents, wives or girlfriends, many servicemen were scarce on details and skimmed over significant war experiences. The aim was to reassure those on the home front, and as such, the men hardly ever made known details of danger, bad living conditions, poor morale or inadequate leadership. On the other hand, military censors did not allow any information in letters that could place their armies at risk.[23]

Early in December, Syd was again with officers, 'as a number of officers & men from each company are being kept in reserve.' For Syd, things were becoming busier, and he confided that, 'we have been on the move nearly the whole time & we have covered a good bit of the desert.' Just like Vyv, Syd was looking forward to returning home:

> It is only a few weeks to Xmas. I must wish all of you everything of the best, I wish I could be there to share Xmas with you but we will make up for it next Xmas when all of us will be together again.
>
> We are just as keen on listening to the wireless news now a days [sic] as you are, to hear what is happening in other parts & by all accounts everything is going well. I hope we can mop up the Jerries up here soon & then it will all be over in North Africa & won't we have fun when all is peace and quiet again.[24]

He repeated the same wish in a letter to his wife, ending with, 'won't we give it a bang when we are all together again.'[25]

With the rest of the DMR on its way to Sidi Omar, Walter wrote a quick note to his parents on 6 December. Moving closer to Sidi Omar also meant moving closer to the enemy and to combat. For once, he did not write of boredom, but stated, 'have not much time to write but am crammed with news which will have to come later as everything seems in a rush while strange and funny things happen which gives one a good laugh.'[26]

Had the censors been absent, Walter may have written to his parents about the German Army's retreat to Halfaya and Bardia, which was the result of at least two weeks' fighting. The DMR came under fire from the *Afrika Korps,* pinning them

---

22   Personal correspondence, Walter Birch to parents, 6 December 1941.
23   Memoirs, written after the war, were free from the censors' restrictions, and often provide more detailed accounts of battle. On the other hand, one has to take into account the effect of failing memories and the influence of hindsight. In the case of the DMR, the memoirs of S. G. Wolhuter, published as *The Melancholy State* (details below), and those of Jack Mortlock (unpublished) give some insight into the experiences of the men during the war, including the Battle of Bardia and later the fall of Tobruk.
24   Personal correspondence, Syd Birch to parents, 4 December 1941.
25   Personal correspondence, Syd Birch to T. H. Wood, 5 December 1941.
26   Personal correspondence, Walter Birch to parents, 6 December 1941.

Officers of *Die Middellandse Regiment*, Sydney is front right. (Photo: Chris Roux)

down in slit trenches, on occasion one DMR man found himself in a trench strewn with letters left behind by a German soldier.[27] Walter's wish for a hot bath and his references to dust and flies were the only indication he gave of his annoyance with life in the desert, and he made no mention of the battle that in time would be remembered as a mere prelude.

Concerns about Christmas, flies and dust would soon seem irrelevant to the brothers, yet their letters remained optimistic, perhaps not wanting their parents to worry about them. In mid-December, Syd wrote, 'The Jerries are having a bad time up here & I don't think it will be long now before we clean them up, although they still have a few strong points.'[28]

When Syd wrote this letter, the disastrous outcome at the Battle of Sidi Rezegh was old news to him, but he was clearly putting on a brave face to reassure everyone at home. The Germans' 'bad time' may have been the retreat to Halfaya and Bardia, but to write so optimistically at this stage was premature.

The tone in Vyv's letter, on the other hand, was more realistic and he hinted at something significant that was about to take place. He warned his parents that, 'letters will be very irregular, so don't expect them weekly.'[29] At the same time, referring to the earlier combat, he also tried to reassure his parents, saying, 'an occasional

---

27 S. G. Wolhuter, *The Melancholy State: The Story of a South African Prisoner-of-War* (Cape Town: Howard Timmins, nd), p.10.
28 Personal correspondence, Syd Birch to T. H. Wood, 14 December 1941.
29 Personal correspondence, Vyv Birch to parents, 3 December 1941.

Jerry shell that came our way, but as we know how to dissolve into the ground they weren't too bad.'[30]

On Christmas Eve, the 2nd South Africa Division received an order to launch an assault on Bardia, a town which had been occupied by the British in January 1941, but was then lost again to Rommel's forces. By the end of 1941, the Australians broke out of Tobruk and the long siege came to an end. Rommel retreated westwards, away from the Egyptian border. Situated on the coast, Bardia was the closest Libyan town to the Egyptian border, and when the Germans and Italians retreated, a number of unfortunate members of their forces were left behind. It was then that the 2nd Division, including the DMR, were instructed to take the town.[31]

When the DMR reached Bardia, the regiment was at first stationed on the outskirts of the town. Their main task, initially, was to go out on patrols to gather information, or to capture enemy soldiers, and get information by interrogating them. These night-time excursions were not to everyone's liking, to say the least and one man in the DMR described them as 'pussy-foot' patrols that were better suited to infantry, not for a member of a machine-gun regiment.[32]

When the time came at last to start the attack on Bardia, the regiment had to move closer to their target during the night. Halfway there, Jack Mortlock and others from the DMR's A Company removed the windscreens from all the trucks as the light of the moon caused the glass to reflect, announcing their approach for anyone interested enough to cast a glance in their direction. Apparently, though, the Germans were expecting an attack to come from the opposite direction.[33]

The South Africans' first task upon arrival at their designated position was to dig defensive ditches, then they waited. Just before dawn, an enormous barrage opened up, with Matilda tanks advancing towards the enemy. Despite heavy returning fire from the Germans, the infantry followed in the tank tracks, with covering fire provided by the DMR's machine guns. A desert mirage and a dust storm made rangefinders almost useless, but the men continued to fire in the general direction until they were withdrawn to the rear for a quick meal and a restless night.[34]

Dawn on the second day of the battle revealed that the new positions were badly selected, and that the guns had been set up to face the wrong direction. To make things worse, the enemy was much closer than they had expected. Working quickly to put things right, the rest of the day passed without much action. The second night was spent in abandoned enemy dugouts, but sleep eluded the men when the DMR B Company, the Birch brothers' company, moved past them on their way to start the next phase of the attack.[35]

The third morning saw the South Africans entering the town, where they came across grim remnants of battle. As the men came to grips with their first battle, a

---

30   Personal correspondence, Vyv Birch to parents, 3 December 1941.
31   Katz, *South Africans versus Rommel*, pp.92, 156–157.
32   Jack Mortlock, *The Endless Years: Reminiscences of the Second World War* (Unpublished memoirs, 1956).
33   Mortlock, *The Endless Years*, p.10.
34   Mortlock, *The Endless Years*, p.10.
35   Mortlock, *The Endless Years*, p.11.

German bomber flew overhead and bombed the town, killing a number of stretcher bearers and wounding others. As the bomber flew off in the direction of Crete, the Battle of Bardia finally came to an end.[36]

A day later, Walter expressed his feelings without saying much about the battle itself:

> While all is going well I still think the less said about the past few weeks' benefits all of us. While we were in training at the various camps at home chafing & playing the fool. It's strange now how one really realises that it's all good work. Anyway it's still very cold…[37]

The Battle of Bardia was followed by victories at Sollum on 12 January and at Halfaya Pass on 17 January. On 24 January, Vyv found time to write and summed up the recent fighting:

> When last writing we were still in the thick of the Hellfire [Halfaya Pass] business and we were just getting ready for a final crack at them when [the German forces] surrendered, for which we were all very thankful because they were in strong fortifications there and it saved us a great deal of unnecessary trouble … I may have grumbled before about this and that but once I get onto the farm again you won't hear a word from me, it will be too marvellous for words to sweat and strain there after all this up here.[38]

The DMR now returned to the coast near Sollum for a break, a brandy and a long sleep.[39] Further west, Tobruk remained strategically important and in the months ahead the Allies and Axis would again meet there. In other parts of the world, the various battlefronts remained fluid, giving the brothers cause for optimism, and giving them reason to continue to fill their letters with reassurances. Vyv's letter early in February 1942 revealed that the DMR men were relaxed and that he was becoming accustomed to the dust covering every meal, changing his physical constitution:

> We're still at the same spot on the coast having a very easy time and I wonder how much longer it will last. Walter left on Sunday for seven days leave in Cairo, and I should imagine is having a marvellous time with hot baths and no dusty food, anyway my tummy should be brick-lined by now and I guess it could stand anything.[40]

Two weeks later things changed dramatically for the Allies with the fall of Singapore. In the weeks before the defeat, telegrams flew between London and the Allied

---

36 Mortlock, *The Endless Years,* p.12.
37 Personal correspondence, Walter Birch to parents, 5 January 1942.
38 Personal correspondence, Vyv Birch to parents, 24 January 1942. As a result of the intense fighting, Halfaya Pass became known as 'Hellfire Pass.'
39 Wolhuter, *The Melancholy State*, pp.14–15.
40 Personal correspondence, Vyv Birch to parents, 4 February 1942.

headquarters in Singapore, debating strategies of defending the city, or abandoning it to the enemy forces. Very few seemed to consider the practicalities of achieving a defence, or the consequences for those who would inevitably be left behind in the city if a retreat were ordered. Between 7 and 15 February the Japanese forces first besieged the city, then defeated the Allies inside.[41] The news of the enormous setback and of the thousands of POWs soon reached the 8th Army in the desert. Vyv, however, wrote optimistically yet with an underlying tone of reality:

> So the Japs [Japanese forces] have taken Singapore, but no matter how much damage they do now they will pay for it in the long run and I don't think the time is very far off when we will start on the long uphill journey of clearing this mess up. The Russians are still doing extremely well and I sincerely hope there will be no stopping them during the coming spring. Well we shall see what we shall see and I don't think we will have overmuch to worry about.[42]

Singapore was a long way from the desert, but the events there were a foretelling for those who were preparing to confront the *Afrika Korps* later that same year. By the end of January, however, Syd's thoughts were far from war and he must have longed for home as he wrote: 'It was wonderful news hearing that I had a brand-new daughter & that everything went off well I only wish that I could be there to see all of you.'[43]

This was to be Syd's last letter for some time.

For most others in the DMR things were quiet and laundry, card games and beer drinking were the main activities:

> Nothing has been happening here since last writing and things are very quiet indeed. We spend most of the day amusing ourselves with card games or having a wash when there is sufficient water accumulated. Yesterday I spent most of the day washing my clothes which I am pleased to say mean I need not worry about washing clothes for another six weeks as a shirt lasts about a month before being changed.
>
> At the moment [I] have been extremely fortunate in that I have just been able to buy four bottles of Castle Beer a luxury I have only had once before since being in Egypt.[44]

When the rest period came to an end, the DMR was split temporarily, with B Company, including the three brothers, going to Gazala to dig defensive trenches. It was most probably from here that Vyv wrote:

---

41 Martin Gilbert, *Road to Victory Winston S Churchill 1941 – 1945* (London: Heinemann, 1986), pp.45–55.
42 Personal correspondence, Vyv Birch to parents, 16 February 1942.
43 Personal correspondence, Syd Birch to parents, 31 January 1942.
44 Personal correspondence, Vyv Birch to parents, 23 February 1942.

Vyvyan Birch (right). (Photo: Chris Roux)

> Being back in the desert is not quite so boring as it was before because we now have some digging to do and that keeps us busy for about eight hours a day and also we get plenty of exercise from the digging with the result that one can't but help to get perfectly fit again … things are quiet and I wonder for how much longer, still it makes not much difference because the days have got to be passed somehow or another … somehow I expect great things to happen in Europe this summer and I think it will be Hitler's last summer, then he will start to crumble … I don't think there is much to worry about as far as this part of the world is concerned, as I think Rommel will find it very difficult to build up his forces again.[45]

Three weeks later, Vyv wrote again, this time from a different position:

> Since last writing we moved our position and as you heard over the wireless we are now in the forward areas but there is less doing here than there was from where we came from except that one hears and sees a bit of bombing and artillery fire etc. which we didn't have there. All we do here is sleep eat and play cards and when we get something to read we read … one thing we have been fortunate in, was that the ground was soft here and digging ourselves in was easy not like the last place where it was so stony one couldn't get two inches down without blasting…[46]

---

45 Personal correspondence, Vyv Birch to parents, 15 March 1942.
46 Personal correspondence, Vyv Birch to parents, 29 March 1942.

It seems that the rank and file believed that retreat signified imminent defeat or at the very least, weakness. Early in May, Walter wrote that 'Rommel will be running back hard again he [is] getting quite good at that well this will be his last time.'[47]

With their earlier success at Bardia, Sollum and Halfaya, the men must have become very confident in their ability to defeat the Germans, but Rommel was also optimistic, and on 12 May wrote to his wife, expressing the hope that the war would be over before the end of the year.[48] There are very few letters from the three brothers during May, most probably because they were kept busy with more pressing matters.

The disagreements among the Allied forces' leaders created a situation that could only lead to disaster. It was especially Auchinleck and the Commander of the 8th Army, Lieutenant General N. M. Ritchie, who did not see eye to eye. To avoid another siege at Tobruk, Auchinleck wanted to create a large space between Rommel's forces and the 8th Army.

Because Tobruk was a harbour town, it remained important for both sides. Essential supplies were offloaded there along with reinforcements and extra materiel. Whoever held Tobruk, also had a lifeline.[49]

Auchinleck, however, had different ideas. As early as February 1942 he made it clear that Tobruk would not be held at the expense of risking another Allied loss. Auchinleck wanted divisions to be as mobile as possible; Ritchie, on the other hand, believed that by creating static defensive lines between Gazala, Alem Hamza, and Bir Hakeim, they would be able to withstand Rommel's attack. The defensive boxes were placed in such a way as to repel the enemy who, it was thought, would come from the west.[50] They were wrong.

The town of Gazala lies 60 kilometres west of Tobruk, and between the two Libyan towns, the defensive lines were supposed to keep the Germans away from Tobruk. It was also where numerous battles raged between 26 May and 21 June.

Ignorant of their precarious position and the battles that awaited them, Walter wrote philosophically on 10 June about being away from home for one year, saying, 'it is a year less in this land of the living.'[51]

On 9 June, Vyv wrote about time either dragging or flying, depending on his mood. As was his habit, he reassured his parents, this time saying, 'we are all keeping fit well & cheerful and are not worrying over much as things are going well generally speaking.'[52] These were the last letters from Vyv and Walter for some time.[53]

All three Birch brothers were in for a rude shock. Their letters gave no indication of the dangerous reality that surrounded them, yet they must have known that

---

47 Personal correspondence, Walter Birch to parents, 5 May 1942.
48 Gilbert, *Second World War*, pp.324–325.
49 Neil Orpen, *War in the Desert, South African Forces World War II Volume III* (Cape Town: Purnell, 1971), pp.169–182.
50 Orpen, *War in the Desert,* pp.169–182.
51 Personal correspondence, Walter Birch to parents, 10 June 1942.
52 Personal correspondence, Vyv Birch to parents, 9 June 1942.
53 Between January and August 1942 there were no letters from Syd, however, these letters were most probably lost, as his brothers would have mentioned his absence, or the reason for his silence in their letters.

something big was about to happen; they had been working to strengthen their defences and were laying minefields.[54]

Vyv was not the first, or the last, to underestimate Rommel. The brothers were clearly labouring under the same misapprehensions that bedevilled the decisions of the 8th Army Command. Rommel had in fact launched his assault on 26 May, yet the brothers and their commanders remained secure in their belief that they were safe behind their defences. With Rommel advancing, Ritchie and Auchinleck agreed at last, they would not retreat but would see out the battle. Their decision was approved by Churchill, who viewed retreat as a fatal error.[55]

On 13 June, B Company joined the rest of the DMR at Point 208.[56] Along with other brigades, the DMR was to make sure the defensive lines would hold the German forces at a safe distance from Tobruk. The fight was already well underway, and Rommel's forces were closing in on the isolated defences which were scattered along the Gazala Line.[57]

One by one the 8th Army defences were surrounded by German units, closing off lines of retreat. Despite things worsening, the 8th Army command, and the rank and file, was under the impression that Rommel's days were numbered. It was only on 14 June that the Guards Brigade was withdrawn from the Knightsbridge area, south–west of Tobruk.[58] It was also on 14 June that Walter, Syd and Vyv were captured by enemy forces, in what became known as the Battle for the Via Balbia, the coastal road between Gazala and Tobruk.[59]

Next in Rommel's sight was Tobruk, the gateway to the Mediterranean and the supplies that would be delivered to there. With the 8th Army dismissing some of Rommel's advances at this time as 'diversionary', the *Afrika Korps* was actually taking advantage of defences created by the British. In this way, they were able to attack the static defensive boxes as well as the mobile forces of the 8th Army.

Ritchie was still convinced that his approach would prevent another siege at Tobruk because those who were stationed there would be able to break out while the Germans were kept at a safe distance. Ritchie put his hopes on the defensive lines in the south and south–east, and Klopper was also satisfied that his forces were relatively safe at Tobruk. In his understanding, there would be time enough to withdraw by the time the German forces turned their attack towards the southern sections of the Tobruk area.[60]

Rommel, however, was not inclined to frontal attacks and he had his forces circle around the defensive lines, and with the Tobruk Garrison under Klopper looking towards the west, Rommel surprised them from the east.[61] While all this was going on, there was still no agreement between the British commanders as to whether or not

---

54   Orpen, *War in the Desert,* p.260.
55   Orpen, *War in the Desert,* p.265.
56   Visser, 'Die Middellandse Regiment', p.15.
57   Orpen, *War in the Desert,* pp.267–269.
58   Orpen, *War in the Desert,* pp.267–269.
59   DOD PF RS John Vivian Birch, DMR. DOD PF RS, Walter Ernest Birch, DMR. DOD PF RS Sydney Birch, DMR. Orpen, *War in the Desert,* p.272.
60   Orpen, *Wat in the Desert,* pp.194–196.
61   John Pimlott (ed.), *Rommel in his own words* (Barnsley: Greenhill Books, 1994), p.89.

Tobruk should be held at all costs, or abandoned to Rommel. They were still arguing about the practicalities, the risks and the realities of defending or abandoning Tobruk while most of the 2nd South Africa Division stared captivity in the face.

After the war it became clear that Ritchie had arrogantly assumed that he could predict Rommel's strategy. When the *Afrika Korps* descended on Tobruk on the morning of 20 June, they did so from the south–east, not from the west, where Ritchie and Klopper had been expecting him. By nightfall, the situation compelled Klopper to ask permission from 8th Army commanders to retreat from Tobruk. The answer he received remains a point of contention to this day, nevertheless, it is doubtful if a successful breakout would have been possible as by then the surrounding areas were held by German and Italian forces.[62] The next morning, believing he had no other option, Klopper surrendered, and thousands of 8th Army soldiers became POWs.

In the weeks that followed, the brothers, along with almost 30,000 other POWs, endured hunger, thirst and living conditions that robbed the most hopeful of men of their fortitude. The temporary prison camps in Libya were hastily erected, and consisted of nothing more than barbed wire enclosed spaces. With the Italians, who were themselves ill equipped, in command of these POWs, the state of affairs deteriorated rapidly and men began to lose weight. The emaciated bodies offered no resistance to illness, and the unsanitary living conditions caused break outs of dysentery, typhus and typhoid.

Confusion also characterised the first weeks of captivity. Regiments were scattered and men were left to their own devices as they searched for familiar faces.[63]

Needless to say, letter writing was not a priority among the captives during the first days in the so-called hell camps of North Africa. When news of the defeat at Tobruk reached South Africa, thousands of families were left waiting anxiously for news about their sons and husbands. At first the messages from the military authorities stated vaguely that the man was 'missing in action', and in some cases it was months or years before confirmation of a man's status could be established, for some it was 'confirmed POW', for others it was 'killed in action.'

Months after the fall of Tobruk and the end of the Gazala battles, when the POWs were transferred to Italy and settled in permanent camps, the Red Cross was able to help with food parcels and information. The Red Cross inspectors also visited camps to make sure that the Italians were adhering to the regulations of the Geneva Convention, including living conditions and access to news to and from home.

Even with the efforts of the Red Cross, the reality was that food and letters often took months to reach their destinations, extending physical and emotional hardships for the captives and their families.[64]

The first letters to arrive at Vogel Vlei came from prison camps in Italy. On 18 August, Syd wrote from Camp 21, 'I am very well. The Red Cross are doing great

---

62   Katz, *South Africans versus Rommel*, pp.178–208.
63   Karen Horn, *In Enemy Hands South Africa's POWs in WWII* (Cape Town: Jonathan Ball Publishers, 2015), pp.61–65.
64   Joan Beaumont, 'Protecting Prisoners of War 1939 – 95' in Kent Fedorowich & Bob Moore, *Prisoners of War and their Captors in World War Two* (Oxford: Berg Publishers, 1996), p.279.

work…'65 Next, news came from Camp 60, where Walter found himself imprisoned. Early in November Walter's short note asked about letters from home and for parcels to be sent as often as possible.66

Three weeks later, Vyv wrote that he found himself in the Caserta military hospital in Naples. The Red Cross was able to supply food to this hospital, there was also enough food, although not plentiful.67 When Vyv was admitted, he must have been very ill, but he optimistically wrote, 'I am writing this in hospital in Naples suffering from diarrhea [sic], making slow progress but very thin and weak keeping cheerful though & will be here some time recuperating. Hope you are all well at home and hope to see you soon, who knows?'68

It seems Vyv had hopes of medical repatriation.

The postcards on which prisoners were allowed to write did not leave much space for news, but the endless hours in prison camps did not generate much to write about anyway. The unreliable mail service to prison camps, and the frequent relocation of POWs, made communication very difficult.

The three Birch brothers were all in separate camps. In an effort to find information about his brothers, Walter wrote to the Red Cross. It was October, and Walter had been placed in a permanent camp where the conditions were much better compared to the first days of captivity in the make–shift camps in the desert. On 8 November Walter heard from the Red Cross and immediately wrote to his parents to tell them about Vyv's dysentery, saying in the same letter that he also suffered from the same illness.69 Four days later Walter was out of hospital and asking his parents to send parcels with warm clothing, cigarettes and reading matter.70

Syd was also in the dark about his brothers, and his first letter home he wrote about the cold weather.71 It was only in February 1943 that he started receiving letters from home.

In the Caserta hospital near Naples, Vyv was still struggling against the illness that affected thousands of POWs. The hospital itself was one of the few that offered sound medical treatment, as one POW wrote that he received 'excellent treatment' there.72 In Vyv's correspondence a similar opinion was expressed when he wrote in January 1943 that the, 'treatment in new ward excellent & have confidence in new doctor and orderlies… Red Cross parcels were excellent.'73

A friend and fellow prisoner, Arthur Short, wrote the letter on behalf of Vyv, who was too weak to sit up in bed. Arthur included his own note in the letter, saying that

---

65 Personal correspondence, Syd Birch to parents, 18 August 1942.
66 Personal correspondence, Walter Birch to parents, 5 November 1942.
67 DOD Correspondence (hereafter CE) 4/15. Union of South Africa Censorship. Correspondence suspected to require special attention.
68 Personal correspondence, Vyv Birch to parents, 25 November 1942.
69 Personal correspondence, Walter Birch to parents, 8 November 1942.
70 Personal correspondence, Walter Birch to parents, 26 November 1942.
71 Personal correspondence, Syd Birch to parents, December 1942. NB There is no actual date on this letter but Syd says, 'It's getting near x-mas and the snow could start in earnest soon…'
72 DOD CE, 4/15, Union of South Africa Censorship, Correspondence suspected to require special attention.
73 Personal correspondence, Vyv Birch to parents, 10 January 1943.

Vyv, 'is very weak but putting up a good fight. I keep him company & attend to his wants. He is bright and cheerful.'[74]

From December British doctors and orderlies were allowed to work at the hospitals to assist the Italian medical staff. Before the British doctors arrived, patients suffered from bedsores and endured unhygienic conditions, as the Italians did not, or could not, adequately attend to all the patients.[75]

It was January 1943, almost seven months since he was captured and Vyv was still waiting to receive his first letter from home. Remaining optimistic, he wrote again and the tone of his letter seemed hopeful, although Arthur Short was still doing the writing for him:

> I am still in hospital & am very thin but pegging [sic] away slowly. I am still very weak & Arthur Short feeds me as I am not able to help myself just yet I must say that my appetite is improving as I manage to eat almost all of my diet (?) foods that are brought along. If I can keep this up I should soon be able to regain a little strength.[76]
>
> Yesterday there was great excitement in the hospital as the first South African who came over on the same boat as I did receive three letters from his wife. They were addressed to the Red Cross & they were dated September of last year. I am looking forward to receiving my mail at some later date & to hear all the good news of home & farming after these months of captivity…[77]

Vyv died two days later, still waiting for a letter.

The news of Vyv's death travelled slowly. On 1 February, Walter wrote that he had 'joined the rest of the Dordrecht boys who are also well. It's just Vyv & Dad Hartley missing now they must be somewhere.'[78] The next day he wrote again: '…have not got in touch with either Vyv or Syd.' He was also still waiting for his warm clothes to arrive from home, but he did get his first letter on 16 February.[79]

When Walter at last received the news of Vyv's death, it was March, and he immediately wrote to his parents:

> I simply don't know what to say as have received the sad news of Vyv's death through Red Cross. Believe me Mom that he had the best of fighting spirits in him I will remember him on 15 June 1942 also October 2 – 1942 when I said goodbye to him. I recovered from disintry [sic] but not by the fight Vyv

---

74 Personal correspondence, Vyv Birch to parents, 10 January 1943.
75 R. E. Owen, (ed.) *Official History of New Zealand in the Second World War 1939–45*, http://nzetc.victoria.ac.nz/tm/scholarly/tei-WH2PMed-pt2-c4.html, accessed on 19 November 2020.
76 Personal correspondence, Vyv Birch to parents, 17 January 1943.
77 Personal correspondence, Vyv Birch to parents, 17 January 1943.
78 Personal correspondence, Walter Birch to parents, 1 February 1943.
79 Personal correspondence, Walter Birch to parents, 2 February and 16 February 1943.

put up & will not forget it. Cheer up all at home … As I can see you when we return then be able to say what a man he is…[80]

Presumably, Walter was going to tell his parents about the battles they fought in and how Vyv acquitted him of his task.

A month later, Syd wrote:

Bill Birch got a letter from his wife saying that you had been notified that Vyv had passed away. I just can't believe it, as I thought he was quite well. What a tragic thing to happen. You people must try not to take it too hardly (?). Remember that in this great struggle some had to be taken & it was God's will that he had to be one of those. Vyv was the best of pals & was always such a staunch ally. I just cannot imagine life at home without his cheerful personality.[81]

After this, Syd tried to keep his parents' spirits up and he wrote about good news. As in the beginning of his service in the UDF, he wrote about the horses at Vogel Vlei, that he hoped they were not worrying too much about him and that he was 'getting on well.'[82]

Vyv was only 26 when he died on 23 January 1943. The official cause of death was amoebic dysentery. He is buried in the Caserta war cemetery in Italy along with 43 other South African servicemen, most of whom were POWs when they died. In total, 768 Commonwealth soldiers are buried in this cemetery, many of whom fought in the Italian campaign from 1943 onwards.[83]

Soon after Italy capitulated and changed sides in 1943, Syd and Walter found themselves in German occupied territory. Late in 1944, Syd was repatriated to go home. Although he wrote in August 1944 that his parents, 'need not worry about my health as there is nothing to complain about', his condition must have been serious as the belligerents repatriated relatively few POWs during the war.[84]

When the war came to an end in 1945, Walter also returned home, and the two Birch brothers once again focussed on horses, achieving considerable success in the racing world.

---

80   Personal correspondence, Walter Birch to parents, March 1943. (NB there is no precise date on this letter but internal evidence puts it before 26 March).
81   Personal correspondence, Syd Birch to parents, 16 May 1943.
82   Personal correspondence, Syd Birch to parents, 7 August & 16 October 1943.
83   South African War Graves Project, Caserta War Cemetery, http://www.southafricawargraves.org/search/view-paginated.php?page=1&cemetery=480, accessed 17 Nov 2020.
84   Personal correspondence, Syd Birch to parents, 12 August 1944.

5

Captain De Villiers Graaff

De Villiers Graaff found his father lying on the floor in the middle of the night. It was April 1931 and Sir David Graaff was dying.[1] Years later, De Villiers described the trauma of this event when he wrote his memoirs. Throughout his life, his father had effortlessly balanced humanitarianism, business and politics. Among his friends and acquaintances, he counted prime ministers and leaders, locally and internationally. His opinions were valued and his contribution to society substantial.

At the age of 17, the young De Villiers had a lot to live up to, and although his father's death was a huge loss, he would grow to fill his father's shoes in no small measure. The Great Depression had by then left its mark on the country's economy and the family business was suffering the consequences. De Villiers and his brother David were forced to make changes and these he described as 'responsibilities … which would have been difficult to cope with for one much older and more mature.'[2]

Seven years later De Villiers wrote the advocate's admission exam, and the following year he married Ena Voigt. It was the same year that the Second World War started, and when the country's participation was put to a vote in Parliament, De Villiers witnessed it from the inner circles.

He had also become close with the soon to be Prime Minister, J. C Smuts, whom he viewed as a man of remarkable foresight. His admiration for Smuts is clear and De Villiers' position was never in doubt – he would volunteer to fight.[3] His completed his application for enlistment on 17 June 1940, but he was only called to duty on 6 May 1941.[4] In the meantime, De Villiers embarked on months of training and military courses.

Initially a member of the Durbanville Commando and then of the 6th Mounted Regiment, De Villiers was sent to Roberts Heights. David Graaff, De Villiers' younger brother, soon joined him in Pretoria, and De Villiers remembered the day when he wrote to his mother in July 1940:

---

1   De Villiers Graaff, *Div Looks Back: The Memoirs of Sir De Villiers Graaff* (Cape Town: Human & Rousseau, 1993), p.36.
2   Graaff, *Div Looks Back,* p.37.
3   Graaff, *Div Looks Back,* pp.59–63.
4   DOD PF RS, De Villiers Graaff E4/110116, WS/Lieut Unit DMR.

> My Darling old ma,
> Dave arrived this morning & the regiment has been in fits ever since. Capt. Reeve of the Remount Squadron served under Dad in the old Cape Garrison Artillery & said he was only too pleased to help in any way. He applied for Dave's transfer in person & sent him round here to report at once. Fortunately, the colonel was here & saw him in person. The old colonel then drafted him straight through to my section so we sleep in the same hut, drill next to each other all day…
>
> Saturday was, I think, one of the most miserable days I have ever spent & I have seldom felt so like howling. Saying goodbye to you all & having to try & be cheerful all tough was just too much. I do hope all will go well – I think of you all so much…[5]

When De Villiers left home, his son was five weeks old and he appealed to his mother to:

> Keep an eye on Ena & little David old Darling – I worry about them so much & you are the only one who really can help them. Best love to you & Jannie – the only thing for any of us to do now is to try & keep a stiff upper lip…
> ps. Dave says he will write as soon as he gets a chance – or runs short of food![6]

As was the case with so many other volunteers, the tension between duty to country and love of family was a sore point. For Dave, life in the army was far more adventurous and carefree, and food was indeed on his mind soon after the regiment arrived in Piet Retief a few days later:

> De Villiers seems to be full of beans. Whenever he isn't doing anything, he writes letters to Ena. So he is really living quite a model life. I'm afraid I can't tell you any spicy things as all our letters are censored. So I'll have to remember all the good stories until the end of the war!
>
> Food. Please send me dried fruit, rusks, biscuits, nuts, raisins, etc. Don't worry about cheese, I am glad to say I at last seem to have lost my desire for cheese. Our food here consists entirely of meat and bread, so I'm really longing for some dried fruit … I can't say I'm feeling terribly fit. I don't get enough exercise, and I can't get rid of my cold…[7]

If it wasn't for Dave's good humour, his health would have discouraged him.

---

5   De Villiers Graaff personal correspondence, July 1940.
6   De Villiers Graaff personal correspondence, July 1940.
7   David Graaff personal correspondence, July 1940.

Unlike Dave, De Villiers wanted to get on with things, and he complained to his mother, 'our only real grouse is the interminable delays almost all of which seem to be due to incompetence somewhere or other…'[8]

From their letters, it seems as if the two brothers did not do much else except standing guard, but things got moving when they were sent back to Roberts Heights for an NCO training course. By September De Villiers' days were full as he acted as Sergeant-Major and his 'day starts at about 5 a.m. and I can be called upon at any time to all hours of the night. Also I seem to be responsible for seeing that everyone else performs his duties satisfactorily – never a pleasant task.'[9]

Dave also completed the course, but as he contracted measles at that time, it is not clear if he attended the course with his brother or at a later date.

In Cape Town, De Villiers' mother collected money for the war effort, and the colonel was, 'anxious for it to be paid into our Regimental Fund [which] is controlled by a committee on which the men are well represented and used for all sorts of good works like helping needy fellows, buying sports equipment & the various odds & ends the army can't or won't supply like kitchen utensils etc…'[10]

Another thinly veiled stab at the army's incompetence did not detract from his deep commitment to the Union's participation in the war, and in the same letter he wrote excitedly that Ena was going to Pretoria to see him. De Villiers was also hoping to see his mother and wrote that he believed that they 'really shall go north one day though, of course, no one knows when. Perhaps you might consider paying us a visit before long too? We should love it.'[11]

De Villiers' eagerness to see his wife and mother was matched by his impatience to go to war, however, he would have to wait. When he wrote his letter in September 1940, it would be four more months before any UDF servicemen engaged in combat – in December 1940 against the Italian forces at El Wak.

It was unclear if De Villiers' regiment would 'go north' to help bring the East African campaign to an end, or if they would go straight to Egypt, as they did eventually, to become part of the British 8th Army that fought against Rommel in the Western Desert Campaign.[12]

With the end of the year approaching, De Villiers' thoughts of war were interrupted by politics at home. Hertzog and Havenga formed a new alliance, and De Villiers wondered 'What are the repercussions of the reorganisation (?) of Hertzog & Havenga going to be? I have a feeling "*dat die poppe nou sal dans.*"'[13]

Hertzog, the Prime Minister at the outbreak of war, resigned when Parliament voted against his neutrality stance. Hertzog then joined D. F. Malan's re-established National Party (NP), but he became more discontented as the more radical nationalists within the party weakened his position. In his letter, De Villiers was most

---

8   De Villiers Graaff personal correspondence, July 1940.
9   De Villiers Graaff personal correspondence, September 1940.
10 De Villiers Graaff personal correspondence, September 1940.
11 De Villiers Graaff personal correspondence, September 1940.
12 Gustav Bentz, 'From El Wak to Sidi Rezegh: The Union Defence Force's First Experience of Battle in East and North Africa, 1940 – 1941' *Scientia Militaria* 40:3 (2012), p.179.
13 The dolls will dance, an Afrikaans saying that implies trouble is brewing. De Villiers Graaff personal correspondence, 11 November 1940.

probably referring to founding of the *Afrikaner Party,* a union of Hertzog's parliamentary followers under N. C. Havenga, a nationalist who supported Hertzog's views on a neutrality stance in the war.[14]

January 1941 did not start on a happy note for De Villiers. He was sent away on yet another course, as was Dave. The consequences were that they were also removed from their regiment, De Villiers going to DMR and Dave to the 7th Reconnaissance Regiment, although they were both at Roberts Heights for the course;[15]

> It was a terrible wrench leaving the regiment & I can't tell you how really miserable I felt. Somehow, I had put everything I had into that show & was really beginning to see some daylight at long last. When we were ordered off on the course I realised that we had small chance of returning but only really had the point driven home when I got Major van Zyl's letter. I am afraid it made me very disinterested in this course for a while but I suppose everything will come right in the end.
>
> Dave, oddly enough, didn't seem to mind leaving the regiment at all & have settled down here quite happily despite all his grumbling. He is quite stupidly impatient to get into action & is always talking or trying to get himself taken off the course & sent north at once. Of course it is quite impractible [sic] because although we may be trained mounted men we know nothing of other branches of the army & could not carry a commission successfully elsewhere.
>
> This course is very disappointing in many ways ... we hear an awful lot of nonsense about etiquette & the behaviour of officers...
>
> Please don't worry about Dave. He will find himself all right before long. Just at present he has the idea that he can get everything he wants by pulling strings which worries me a lot but doubtless he will revise his views in time. Otherwise he is doing very well and is already very popular with everyone. He spends all his spare time in the swimming bath & playing cricket.[16]

With all of this going on, De Villiers also knew that there would be no sense in Ena visiting him in Pretoria, although he 'longe[ed] for her and little David more than I can tell you...' However, Ena did visit him, and when she returned home, De Villiers wrote that he felt more 'lost' every time they said goodbye. His brother's health was also a concern, but an incident resulting in an officer's court-martial took up much of his letter:

> The various enquiries into the riot up here & the Court Martial of that officer have led to a lot of bad feeling in these parts & in Johannesburg

---

14 H. Giliomee, *The Afrikaners Biography of a People* (Cape Town, Tafelberg, 2003), p.441.
15 Graaff, *Div Looks Back*, pp.68–69.
16 De Villiers Graaff personal correspondence, 18 January 1941.

particularly people are very angry. Beyers' evidence today seemed to me quite disgusting as he spent all his time blaming his junior officers & then refused to be cross-examined in public.[17]

Riots were common as anti-war groups attempted to oppose the Union's participation in the war. It was especially the OB that organised protests which often led to violent street fights between opposing groups.

The specific riot that De Villiers referred to in his letter is not clear, but it may have been a consequence of the War Measures Act that was passed in 1940. This Act gave the government the power to act indiscriminately to ensure the safety of the public, among which was the internment of those deemed to pose a threat.[18]

Government measures such as these set the pro-war and anti-war factions against each other and the use of the red tab on those soldiers' uniforms who had taken the oath to fight intensified the situation as each man's viewpoint was literally on his sleeve. Members of the *Stormjaers* and the *Terreurgroep*, for instance, tried to keep UDF soldiers busy so that the Union could not spare them for the service on the battlefields against Axis forces.[19]

In 1941, more steps were taken to control subversive elements, and all public servants were prohibited from joining an organisation such as the OB. Later in the same year, the measure was extended to state employees. Smuts's attempts to rid the country of the so-called 'fifth element' was only partially successful as the government measures merely served to inspire anti-war groups to continue with their work. Nevertheless, the English press reported on any and all government successes to eliminate anti-war activities.

In December 1941, a newspaper article described how an attempted coup d'état was prevented when the OB tried to take control of military stores, wireless stations and other key positions in Durban. This harbour was of great importance for the UDF, not only because most troop ships left for East Africa and the Middle East from this point, but also because it formed part of a merchant shipping route. It was in December 1941 when the route around Africa became busier and a target for German U-boats when the Americans entered the war.[20]

With Italian and German submarines threatening the security of the maritime routes, control of the harbours was equally crucial, and had the OB succeeded in their takeover, a door would have been opened to Axis forces into the Union.

---

17   It is not clear if De Villiers Graaff is referring to Adjutant General Beyers, or another officer. De Villiers Graaff personal correspondence, 18 January 1941.
18   A. M. Fokkens, 2006. *The Role and Application of the Union Defence Force in the Suppression of Internal Unrest, 1912 – 1945*. Thesis presented in partial fulfilment of the requirements for the degree of Master of Military Science (Military History), Faculty of Military Science, Stellenbosch University, p.105.
19   Anna La Grange, 'The Smuts Government's justification of the emergency regulations and the impact thereof on the Ossewa-Brandwag, 1939 to 1945', *Scientia Militaria*, 48:2 (2020), p.44.
20   Evert Kleynhans, '"Good Hunting": German Submarine Offensives and South African Countermeasures off the South African Coast during the Second World War, 1942–1945', *Scientia Militaria* 44:1 (2016), pp.169–170.

The newspaper article, based on a speech by the Minister of the Interior, Mr H. G. Lawrence, contained information that must have been a cause of great concern for those who were pro-war and supporters of Smuts. The reporter asserted that, 'Most of the subordinate officers [who participated in the attempted coup d'état] were in Government employment and were placed in positions where they could carry out sabotage on a large scale. It was beyond doubt that they were the eyes and ears of the Nazi spying organisation in Durban.'[21]

No doubt information on such acts was collected by military authorities and filed securely. A report on the response to anti-war activities, 'Stamping out the Saboteur', stated that acts of sabotage increased during the early part of 1942. Apparently, 'the outrages included bombing of buildings, dynamiting of telegraph and telephone poles, and cutting telegraph wires, as well as attempts to blow up theatres and troop-carrying trains.' Among other incidents, the report mentioned the arrest of Robey Leibbrandt and six others on 24 December 1941. Ironically, it was the OB who informed the authorities of Leibbrandt's whereabouts and his plan to assassinate Smuts.[22]

The authorities also engaged in 'an extensive drive ... at the houses of certain [police] constables and a number of men were detained.'[23] The report speculated on Leibbrandt's contacts in the police and expressed the hope that with his arrest, the authorities would 'get to the bottom of all subversive activities, more especially as far as bomb outrages were concerned.'[24] In the same month it was reported that £200,000 had been spent on internment camps.[25]

De Villiers' attention, however, was taken up by his course and the speculation on which regiment he would eventually join when going 'up north':

> These days there is no more question of either wanting or not wanting to go north – we shall all land up there and jolly soon too. It is just a matter of which unit. Of course I should have liked to have gone up with the 2nd Division but there is no chance of our training being completed in time. The big snag at the moment is Dave who chops and changes from one day to another & really worries me a great deal ... I should love to be with him but sometimes I wonder whether he wouldn't be better on his own where he can make his own friends. What do you think?[26]

Personal differences quickly became of little consequence when the two brothers eventually left the home front, albeit on separate ships. De Villiers was posted to the DMR in May 1941; the following month he boarded SS *Mauritania* and arrived at

---

21 Unisa: United Party Papers: Sir De Villiers Graaff Collection. File 118: Sabotage; 118.1 General Acts, press cuttings, 1941 – 1943, 1964.
22 F. L. Monama, 'The Second World War and South African society, 1939 – 1945' in Potgieter, T. and I. Liebenberg (eds) *Reflections on War Preparedness and Consequences* (Stellenbosch, Sun Press, 2012), p.51.
23 DOD PP PR61. Stamping out the Saboteur (up to end of March 1942).
24 DOD PP PR61. Stamping out the Saboteur (up to end of March 1942).
25 DOD PP PR61. Stamping out the Saboteur (up to end of March 1942).
26 De Villiers Graaff personal correspondence, 11 April 1941.

Suez 10 days later.²⁷ On the same ship were Sydney, Walter and Vyvyan Birch. It is very likely that Sydney and De Villiers knew each other as they were both officers in the DMR.

While at sea, De Villiers, like many other servicemen, complained about the heat as they crossed the equator. For him it was worse, as he was, 'Put in charge of the men's messing arrangements & have to spend about 9 hours a day in the kitchens. I feel now that the 'hereafter' will hold no terror for me as the fourth furnace on the left can't be any worse than this.'²⁸

Ena went to Durban to see De Villiers off on his travels, and he, 'was just too miserable for words…'²⁹ It would be the last time they saw each other for five years. De Villiers and David would also not see much of each other during the rest of the war. In his first letter from Egypt De Villiers described David's condition:

> I saw David a few days ago after he arrived & have seen him twice since then. I am afraid that he has not been improving as rapidly as we had hoped and is looking terribly thin. I had a long chat to the doctor in his unit and together we wangled him a spell of leave. He is now staying with private people near Alexandria and we are full of hope.³⁰

During the sea journey, David developed boils on his body, and when he arrived in Egypt, he was treated with the wrong medication, resulting in his condition worsening considerably. He spent some time recuperating but was eventually found unfit for service. Severely underweight, David was sent home on recuperative leave.³¹

In a letter to his *Skataardetjie*,³² De Villiers's news was more pleasant, saying that he had been meeting some friends in Egypt: 'Last night Corp Grock called me to meet an old friend & whom should I find but Tubby van der Horst – well concealed behind an enormous floppy moustache. I could not help smiling when I saw him in view especially of his Dad's connection with *Die Burger*!! Still we all know that a funny world this is!'³³

Die Burger newspaper supported the nationalist stance against participation in the war. Along with other Afrikaans newspapers, most notably the *Transvaler*, the Afrikaans press attempted to influence the home front and gain support for prominent anti-war and anti-Smuts persons such as J. B. M. Hertzog, Dr H. F. Verwoerd, J. G. Strijdom and Dr D. F. Malan, all of whom would later play leading roles in the post-war apartheid government.³⁴

With David on his way back to the Union, De Villiers had time to see the sights of Egypt. In August, the regiment moved to a new camp, and the main activity at the

---

27   DOD PF RS, De Villiers Graaff.
28   De Villiers Graaff personal correspondence, June 1941.
29   De Villiers Graaff personal correspondence, June 1941.
30   De Villiers Graaff personal correspondence, 2 July 1941.
31   Graaff, *Div Looks Back*, pp.71–72.
32   'Darling treasure.'
33   De Villiers Graaff personal correspondence, 3 July 1941.
34   J. Mervis, *The Fourth Estate: A Newspaper Story* (Johannesburg: Jonathan Ball Publishers, 1989), pp.225–227.

time was 'marking time', which did not do much to quell the impatience of the men. De Villiers wrote that their camp was:

> Right on the sea in quite pleasant surroundings. There is no dust, usually a cool breeze & we have a lot of bathing. Needless to say that suits me very well & I continue to flourish – although I am very bored at times.[35]

The camp from which De Villiers wrote was near El Alamein and received a few important visitors such as General I. P. de Villiers, Commander of the 2nd Division, and later the General Officer Commanding, Frank Theron. When they met, Theron promised De Villiers that he would ask for David to join them again as soon as he was healthy.

At the time, De Villiers was busy with a course for 'motor contact officers' and felt slightly awestruck by the 'famous characters' who also attended, for him, 'the resultant tone of the show is too, too high.'[36]

Responding to news from the home front took up much of De Villiers' writing. He gave his opinion on his younger brother's pigeon training scheme and commented on the floods that had been ravaging the Cape. Union politics also featured from time to time and in September he remarked:

> The fun between Malan & van Rensburg has caused us no little amusement in these parts & I was delighted with your story that Emmie du Toit was also "*in die gesous.*"[37] Perhaps when she is in the OFS [Orange Free State] her mother will talk a little sense to her!!![38]

D. F. Malan, the leader of the NP and Hans van Rensburg, the leader of the OB, did not get along and towards the end of 1941 a series of letters between members of these two organisations emphasised the conflict. Malan was willing to work with the OB to prevent a split among nationalist Afrikaners, but the OB regarded Malan as a 'villain' and suggestions were made that OB members resign from the NP. The cause of the dispute was a government intelligence investigation into links between Adolf Hitler's Nazi Party and the OB. Rumours emerged that Nazi agents would penetrate the Union, and the government reacted by focussing their attention on the OB.[39]

In January 1942, investigations led to the arrest of 314 policemen and 59 railway policemen who were seen as subversive elements. Those arrested were members of the *Stormjaers* section of the OB. Soon after, the Minister of Justice, Colin Steyn, announced that bomb saboteurs would receive the death penalty.[40] Despite the serious developments on the home front, De Villiers sense of humour did not abandon him, and he ended his letter about a friend's admiration for his moustache:

---

35 De Villiers Graaff personal correspondence, 20 August 1941.
36 De Villiers Graaff personal correspondence, 26 September 1941.
37 'in the thick of things'.
38 De Villiers Graaff personal correspondence, 17 October 1941.
39 La Grange, 'The Smuts Government's justification of the emergency regulations, p.54.
40 DOD PP, PR61. 'Stamping out the Saboteur' (up to end of March 1942).

> He was most intrigued with my moustache & simply couldn't take his eyes off it. Incidentally I have had some marvellous photographs taken of it & have asked Ena to show them to you. I am sure you will be thrilled with it.[41]

In his next letter, De Villiers complained that, 'War news seems something of a riddle at the moment as no one seems able to make out just how the Russians are doing. However, we continue to hope for the best.'[42]

Despite his lack of news, the war was moving closer and his regiment's turn at combat was nearing, keeping him 'Snowed up with work & so busy that I haven't known which way to turn. Even Ena's birthday, a Sunday, was spoilt by our having to spend the whole night wandering round the desert – tomorrow morning we are off again.'[43]

He continued a few days later…

> …as you will know by now the Big Push began up here on Nov 18th & although I have not been involved as yet I am still sitting safely in the rear life has been so full of 'alarms' & excursions that letter writing has been practically impossible … for obvious reasons I can't give you news of our activities in the past few weeks and can only say that I am amazingly fit & well & have really been most comfortable. We have, of course, been moved about a great deal & I seem to have had more than my share of lightening moves at all hours of the night & day … Tomorrow is my birthday so I shall be thinking of you all a great deal … For a time, I am afraid letters will be very scrappy so please don't worry if you hear from me only at irregular intervals. That will not necessarily signify that I am in the battle because I am still only a reserve.[44]

A week later he tried reassured his mother again…

> I am at present sitting in reserve some old Italian fortification miles from the fighting & other of all danger. My only troubles are boredom, cold, lack of water and the eternal dust storms. I have never in my life seen anything which quite equals them. However, we are very comfortable despite the impossibility of washing and have no complaints … we seem to get further from [Cairo] each day.[45]

While he was not fighting at the time, it is doubtful if his mother found this news comforting. As always, De Villiers expressed his interest in the news, and war news was understandably a priority:

---

41 De Villiers Graaff personal correspondence, 17 October 1941.
42 De Villiers Graaff personal correspondence, 26 October 1941.
43 De Villiers Graaff personal correspondence, 3 November 1941.
44 De Villiers Graaff personal correspondence, 16 November, continued on 7 December 1941.
45 De Villiers Graaff personal correspondence, 14 December 1941.

De Villiers Graaff (left) in Egypt, 1941. (Photo: Sir De Villiers Graaff)

The entry of Japan into the war has been something of a mixed blessing to Hitler because USA seems to have woken up with a bump at last & the Germans well know what that means. The rumour is that Hitler promised the Japs all sorts of assistance & I can't help feeling that he intends to gamble on a drive through Spain. In that case our loyal & ancient allies, the Portuguese, will be involved & I can't help feeling that soldiers from the Union will take up their abode at the Polana Hotel, Lourenco Marques before long. Tell Dave that may prove a great deal more entertaining than the dusty (?) of Cairo he might consider the matter seriously before making too determined an effort to return here.[46]

Since the outbreak of the war, Winston Churchill had been unsuccessfully trying to convince President Franklin D. Roosevelt to enter the war, but it was only when the Japanese attacked Pearl Harbour on 7 December and badly damaged the American Fleet there, that Roosevelt committed his country to war.[47]

Landing on African soil on 8 November 1942, the American forces had the potential to make a significant dent in the Axis forces in North Africa, especially as their Grant tanks were superior to those of the German forces.[48] Nothing came of the

---

46 De Villiers Graaff personal correspondence, 14 December 1941.
47 M. Gilbert, *Churchill and America* (New York: Free Press, 2005), p.242.
48 Katz, *South Africans versus Rommel*, p.172.

rumours that De Villiers mentioned in this letter, and Portugal did not participate in the war, although their sympathies leaned more towards the Allies than the Axis.[49]

As the possibility of combat became a reality for him, De Villiers intensified his attempts to reassure his mother. A few days after Christmas, he again stated that he remained, 'out of the danger zone' and was kept busy with administrative duties. His attempts at humour also persisted and he ascribed his good health to his theory that the:

> …mixture of sand with our food which results from the continual dust should be recommended as a new diet. Xmas here promised to be rather a grim affair as we are very much on our own but I managed to arrange a shooting competition and a party which helped to cheer the chaps up quite a bit. Getting gay on just a tiny tin of American beer is no easy matter but somehow, we managed it and the show went off most successfully. Needless to say, though, most of the time I am afraid the overwhelming majority of us had our thoughts very far away from this particular part of the world … Have you had any news from or about Jimmy Attwell since the Sidi Rezegh affair? I know he was attached to the 5th Brigade for a time but since he was connected with supplies should not have been involved.[50]

It is not known what Jimmy Attwell's fate was, but from the ranks of the 5th Brigade, 224 were killed, 379 wounded and 3,000 captured.[51] Yet again, De Villiers' mother was most probably not very comforted by his words.

The new year saw the end of De Villiers' – and the 2nd Division's – time in reserve. The first weeks of 1942 were marked by successes as the German forces were pushed back to El Agheila, leaving only stragglers behind.

While the rank and file of the DMR fought in the Battle of Bardia, at Sollum and Halfaya in mid-January, De Villiers was not personally involved in combat, but he had obviously heard good news, writing, 'our chaps really have done wonders [in the fighting] I was to have been in the assault on Halfaya and was actually receiving my orders when they surrendered. I suppose I must regard myself as lucky. Anyway I don't mind confessing that I was very relieved.'[52]

The experience of luck and relief were not comparative, as one of De Villiers' acquaintances had a very different experience:

> Ian Simpson had two strokes of luck. He was blown up in an armoured car but only got a scratch & then was taken prisoner at Sollum but released 48 hours later at Halfaya quite unhurt. Now he has got seven days Cairo leave to recuperate so I have not seen him to talk to.

---

49 Joaquim Da Costa Leite, 'Neutrality by Agreement: Portugal and the British Alliance in World War II' *American University of International Law Review* 14:1 (1998), pp.188 & 192.
50 De Villiers Graaff personal correspondence, 27 December 1941.
51 C. Somerville, *Our War How the British Commonwealth Fought the Second World War* (London: Weidenfeld & Nicolson, 1998), p.94.
52 De Villiers Graaff personal correspondence, 28 January 1942.

> We are at present in a very pleasant camp right on the sea with green grass and palm trees quite plentifully scattered over the landscape. After months of desert dust, we can hardly believe our eyes or credit our luck. The thrill of getting wet all over at the same time in the sea is just marvellous. …
>
> Just at present I am up to the ears in a number of cases in which our natives have been involved. The whole series arises from their having got at some brandy somehow. Needless to say they partook unwisely and too well…
>
> Our adjutant is again away for a few days so I am once more acting in his stead… fortunately, however, I have been able to move into his quarters and am now most comfortably situated in a beautiful captured Italian tent right on the sea…
>
> We hear that Rommel is advancing again but no one seems the least bit worried about that. The only person who appears to be really excited about it is Hitler who had announced that it is to be a great offensive…[53]

When De Villiers wrote this letter, on 28 January, Rommel had already made his move seven days before, and he was about to recapture Benghazi, about 580 kilometres from where De Villiers found himself at the time. Rommel was on his way to Tobruk, and with the 8th Army retreating to the Gazala Line, a defensive line between Tobruk and the Egyptian border, the harbour town was within Rommel's reach.

General H. B. Klopper took command of the 2nd Division, within which De Villiers served, and remained in Tobruk. The offensive, most probably the one which De Villiers referred to in his letter, would only start in May.[54]

The break in combat allowed De Villiers a break in Cairo, although: '…despite 6 months in the desert the place holds no real attraction for me. However, I dare say I shall go before long – even if only for the break.'[55]

His leave did remind him again of the luxuries which had been forgotten in the desert:

> …can't you just imagine how we revelled [sic] in proper mattresses, sheets, hot baths and gallons of iced beer. Four of us went together and we even had champagne in a nightclub just to show there was no ill feeling. We found a glorious sporting club on an island in the Nile to which we went each morning for squash. We then had hot baths, cold showers and rounded off the visit with iced beer under the palm trees. It was quite like a bit of the glamorous, glorious Egypt so often described in romantic fiction. The only trouble about the party was that we are all four married and we missed our wives so much in those surroundings that we became quite miserable. However, there was always beer.[56]

While the general tone of the letter is very positive, the war and the nearing reality of combat played on this mind. His brother David had regained his strength to such

---

53   De Villiers Graaff personal correspondence, 28 January 1942.
54   Katz, *South Africans versus Rommel*, pp.160–161.
55   De Villiers Graaff personal correspondence, 3 March 1942.
56   De Villiers Graaff personal correspondence, 8 April 1942.

an extent that he was planning to return to North Africa, but De Villiers felt that, 'it would have been so very nice to feel that at least one of us was in the Union in these times.'[57] De Villiers had also been feeling cut off from the world as they were struggling to hear news. The radio that he bought in Cairo, however, did not bring good news and he reflected:

> The news has not been too bright of late. This evening we heard of the Japanese victory in the Philippines ... I wonder what the next move will be – an attack on Australia or a move Westward??[58]

De Villiers may have referred to the Battle of Bataan in the Philippines. The Japanese cemented their victory over the Allied forces on the day after De Villiers wrote this letter when the American forces surrendered on 9 April, with 35,000 taken prisoner.[59] Worried about the progress of the war brought his mind back home, and he expressed his hope of leave to the Union:

> The tragedy is that it will be such a time before there is even a chance of leave for me. We now hear – only "rumour" – that after another 6 months married men in exceptional circumstances may be considered [for leave], but not before, and if things don't improve even that won't materialise. However, one feels that America must make herself felt very soon.[60]

De Villiers must have realised by now not to pay attention to rumours. Yet, when it came to his son, his homesickness got the better of him, 'I do feel that this miserable war has robbed me of some of the most blessed moments of [my son's] life. Is he really so grand ma? – or do you chaps just tell me that to make me happy?'[61]

By late April the Japanese successes were still on De Villiers' mind and although he tried to avoid the subject by boasting about his mother's invite to have dinner with Jan Smuts, he returned to the subject, writing that '*Oom Jannie*[62] may well be worried about India. Things seems to have gone very wrong there and I have to doubt the Indians will welcome the Japs...'[63]

He was worried about the influence that these victories might have had on the 'coloured and native peoples' of South Africa, writing, '...the Union really is going to have a wealth of further problems now.'[64] For De Villiers, these concerns lay in the future and for the present he expressed his relief that Smuts advised his mother to stay at the inland family farms of Zonnekus, as the government apparently feared an Axis invasion from the sea.[65]

---

57 De Villiers Graaff personal correspondence, 8 April 1942.
58 De Villiers Graaff personal correspondence, 8 April 1942.
59 Gilbert, *Road to Victory*, pp.46, 86–87.
60 De Villiers Graaff personal correspondence, 8 April 1942.
61 De Villiers Graaff personal correspondence, 8 April 1942.
62 Uncle Jannie (Jan Smuts).
63 De Villiers Graaff personal correspondence, 21 April 1942.
64 De Villiers Graaff personal correspondence, 21 April 1942.
65 De Villiers Graaff personal correspondence, 21 April 1942.

The next letter from his mother contained news about the war elsewhere, and De Villiers replied that he was, 'thrilled to hear the news of the taking over of Madagascar [and] the action against the Japanese fleet off Australia.'[66]

While these victories were real, there was still much to do to ensure a decisive victory over the Axis forces in North Africa, especially as Rommel was planning an assault which De Villiers and his comrades-in-arms were not prepared for and did not expect. If De Villiers had any information about the Axis movements in the desert at the time, he would not have shared them in his letters, so he continued in a witty manner:

> I am very sad that you and Ena are so apprehensive of my moustache. In fact, it gives me great dignity and is very frightening to all evildoers. The other day we were to have had an inspection by certain brass hats who failed to turn up. When I had ultimately dismissed the parade one of my sergeants told his chaps he was so relieved that the brass hats had not come as he was so afraid they would lose me. 'You see,' he said, 'with a moustache like that he simply can't fail to impress.' In Cairo, too, Plum Lewis was really shaken by it and Charlotte Bishop just couldn't stop looking at it. As a matter of fact, if only you had me at home now you could tackle any nationalist constituency with impunity – a mother with a son with a moustache like mine would just romp home.
>
> Incidentally, joking apart. I am thrilled that you have been asked to stand for Parliament again. But don't you let them jockey you into fighting a forlorn hope for them. Wait until something that is a certainty turns up and then give them all beans.[67]

Three days after De Villiers wrote this letter, the three Birch brothers were captured by German forces. On 15 June 1942, six days before the fall of Tobruk, De Villiers was promoted to captain, but he only became aware of this after the war.[68] De Villiers never had the chance to 'give them all beans.'[69]

De Villiers found himself near Tobruk where he and his comrades spent most of their time removing booby traps and mines set by the Germans before their most recent evacuation from the area. It was dangerous work, but luck favoured him when a device did not detonate fully when he stepped on the tripwire. De Villiers was hit by shrapnel, but when a fellow soldier ran towards him to help, De Villiers threatened to shoot the man unless he stopped in his tracks – there were trip wires all around.

When it became evident that Tobruk would not hold out against Rommel, De Villiers' plan was to escape immediately. However, he was reminded that he was responsible for his men and that when he had made sure they were safe, he could escape. By that time, it was too late, and De Villiers became part of what he called

---

66   De Villiers Graaff personal correspondence, 11 May 1942.
67   De Villiers Graaff personal correspondence, 11 May 1942.
68   DOD PF RS, De Villiers Graaff AG (1)736/55/48.
69   De Villiers Graaff personal correspondence, 11 May 1942.

De Villiers Graaff dancing with Princess Elizabeth on her 21st birthday in Cape Town, 1947.
(Photo: Sir De Villiers Graaff)

'the most tragic gathering' of prisoners.[70] Escape remained on his mind, and when he received an MBE (Member of the Order of the British Empire) after the war, the citation stated that he:

> …was camp adjutant – did excellent work for the whole camp – his efforts were untiring. Acted as camp IO [Information Officer] and assisted in many escapes. He attempted an escape in Germany but was unsuccessful.[71]

While an MBE must have been a welcome acknowledgement of his efforts and sacrifices during the war, De Villiers' own words made clear his priorities when he wrote his memoirs some years later, 'My practice grew, things on the farm improved and David [his son] and I slowly began to understand each other.'[72]

---

70 Graaff, *Div Looks Back*, p.83.
71 DOD PF RS, De Villiers Graaff: Union of South Africa. DAG (P) 801/1/2889. Honours and Awards Sub-Section, 25 February 1947.
72 Graaff, *Div Looks Back*, p.117.

6

Fred Anthony Ernstzen of the Cape Corps

Recruitment for the Cape Corps began in July 1940. During the First World War, the Cape Corps provided labour for the forces in East Africa. They served as drivers, mechanics, servants and in any other capacity, but officially not in combat. In 1916, a contingent set off to France and served there until July 1919, well after the fighting came to an end in 1918. It was only the Cape Coloured Infantry Corps that served as combatants, leading to an early integration of servicemen of different races in the UDF.[1] By the time the Second World War began, the Cape Corps once again faced racial restrictions and the prospect of serving as non–combatants only.

In Cape Town, Fred Anthony Ernstzen bided his time. He waited until the war was well past its 'phoney' stage and volunteered his services on 9 January 1941. By this time, Hitler's forces had invaded Norway and Denmark. Attacks on Belgium, The Netherlands and Luxembourg had resulted in these countries surrendering to Germany. By mid-1940, the northern half of France was under German control and Italy had joined the war on Germany's side.[2]

In the meantime, the Soviet Union had been grabbing its share of European countries, and by October 1940, the only hope for the Allies came from the Battle of Britain, in which the RAF defeated the Luftwaffe. At the same time though, Greece's struggle began when Italy invaded the country. In Africa, the Italians caused further chaos with a short-lived invasion of Egypt.[3] With all of this going on, perhaps Fred was hopeful that he could make a fighting contribution? He was wrong.

Fred became a member of the 17th Mechanical Transport Company, Cape Castle. A week later he was moved to Barberton for a period of training before he left the Union in September 1941 on the SS *Dunera*. His unit went straight to the Middle East, and when they disembarked at Suez on 2 November, they joined the 1st

---

1 Anri Delport, 'South African Troops in Europe and the Middle East (Union of South Africa)', 1914-1918 International Encyclopedia of the First World War, (2017), https://encyclopedia.1914-1918-online.net/article/south-african-troops-in-europe-and-the-middle-east-union-of-south-africa/#toc_cape_corps_labour_battalion_cclb, accessed 22 August 2024.
2 Anon, 'World War II Dates and Timeline', United States Holocaust Memorial Museum, https://encyclopedia.ushmm.org/content/en/article/world-war-ii-key-dates, accessed 22 August 2024.
3 Anon, 'World War II Dates and Timeline', United States Holocaust Memorial Museum, <https://encyclopedia.ushmm.org/content/en/article/world-war-ii-key-dates>, accessed 22 August 2024.

Division Transport Company. A mere 21 days later, he was reported missing – and this is when his war began.

It was during the Battle of Sidi Rezegh that Fred was captured. Like others who served in the Cape Corps, the Native Military Corps and the Indian Corps, Fred did not carry arms. As with most other unarmed drivers, mechanics, batmen, cooks, stretcher bearers, he was taken into captivity without the option of at least an attempt at defending his position. In practice, and unofficially, however, and when the situation demanded it, the support workers were roped in to help the fight.[4]

It is not known if Fred ever held a gun in his hands during the devastating battle before he was captured, but there is no doubt that men such as Fred, with inadequate and short training periods, which focussed on non–combative duties, were ill-prepared for combat.[5] In addition, because Fred arrived from the Union and did not gain any experience in the East African campaign, the battle at Sidi Rezegh must have been a wholly distressing experience for him.

In the chaos of the battle at Sidi Rezegh, Fred's transport unit was hit by a German tank shell which killed his friend. However, Fred was resilient and the burden that the war laid on him made him self-reliant and inventive. With the trauma of the battle and the shock of capture still palpable, Fred may have caught a glimpse of Rommel as he inspected the POWs the day after the battle.

Bernard Schwikkard, a member of the 3rd Transvaal Scottish Regiment, was also watching as Rommel addressed the large group of POWs. He remembered how the German commander explained that the captives were to be handed over to Italian control and that, according to Rommel, 'these [Italians] are not soldiers they are rebels, so I am sorry to do this to you.'[6]

One may argue that Bernard's memory had become less accurate in the years after the war, but the crux of his statement is verified by a declaration which was made before the war came to an end. A POW who had been repatriated claimed that he heard Rommel say to the prisoners that they, 'had a long way to go, and [had] to be prepared for privation.'[7]

Rommel's words were no empty threat and Fred soon felt the full impact of hunger and deprivation in the desert camps that came to be known as the hell camps of North Africa.

Most of the belligerent countries were signatories to the Geneva Convention, which set out how prisoners of war were to be treated. The measures were aimed at maintaining a sense of humanity between the captor and captive, so for example, one of the points stipulated:

---

4 J. S. Mohlamme, 'Soldiers without reward Africans in South Africa's Wars', *Military History Journal* 10/1 1995), samilitaryhistory.org/vol101jm.thml, accessed 7 April 2021.
5 N. Cowling, (ed.) 'Historical Survey of the Non-European Army Services Outside of the Union of South Africa Part 1', *Scientia Militaria, South African Journal of Military Studies* 24:1 (1994), pp.29–31.
6 Bernard Schwikkard, interview with Karen Horn, Johannesburg, 17 March 2010.
7 DOD Narrative Report (hereafter Narep), ME/3. *Account of the adventures of the fellows taken at Sidi Rezegh. Statement by repatriated POW, 'Mr W.'*

> Prisoners of war are in the power of the hostile Government, but not of the individuals or formation which captured them. They shall at all times be humanely treated and protected, particularly against acts of violence, from insults and from public curiosity. Measures of reprisal against them are forbidden.

In addition, it sought to uphold military custom and equality, stipulating:

> Differences of treatment between prisoners are permissible only if such differences are based on the military rank, the state of physical or mental health, the professional abilities, or the sex of those who benefit from them.[8]

In Libya, at Tobruk harbour, the black captives were made to unload war materiel from ships. Corporal Job Maseko's decision to sabotage a German freighter was made on his estimation that they were being ill-treated by their captors.[9] They were also accommodated in Tobruk and were not allowed to enter shelters when the Allies bombed the town. They were living on starvation rations of one biscuit per day and, '…beaten and kicked by both Germans and Italians.'[10]

Soldiers of colour would have realised that they were being treated differently than their European counterparts, and no doubt they would have taken the initiative to improve their circumstances as best they could. Although Section II, Article 9 of the Convention states, 'Belligerents shall as far as possible avoid bringing together in the same camp prisoners of different races or nationalities', it does not make any mention of men of different races receiving equal treatment, it was implied, but not necessarily applied.[11]

The Geneva Convention was revised in 1949, and the issue of equality was one of the points that changed considerably with new wording: 'All prisoners of war shall be treated alike by the Detaining Power, without any adverse distinction based on race, nationality, religious belief or political opinions, or any other distinction founded on similar criteria.'[12]

The 1929 Convention had good intentions, but to put the theory into practice, the captors would have had to assert an appropriate attitude, and on a battlefield soldiers were preoccupied with survival, not with upholding humane measures, especially if

---

8   International Committee of the Red Cross, *Convention Relative to the Treatment of Prisoners of War. Geneva, 27 July 1929*, 305-IHL-GC-1929-2-EN PDF, https://ihl-databases.icrc.org/en/, accessed 22 Aug. 2024. European prisoners of war were not treated much better and in most cases the circumstances of the war dictated access to food and accommodation. In other instances, camp commanders with a sense of sadism employed unlawful methods of discipline.
9   DOD AG (Prisoners of War) (hereafter POW). Box 128. Western Desert Campaign, Statement by No. 4448 L/Cpl Job Maseko alleging to have sunk a boat in Tobruk harbour.
10 DOD AG (POW). Box 130. Western Desert Campaign, Axis cruelty to native prisoners (Tobruk). Statement given on 11 September 1942.
11 International Committee of the Red Cross, *Convention Relative to the Treatment of Prisoners of War. Geneva, 27 July 1929*, 305-IHL-GC-1929-2-EN PDF, https://ihl-databases.icrc.org/en/, accessed 22 Aug. 2024.
12 International Committee of the Red Cross, *Convention Relative to the Treatment of Prisoners of War. Geneva, 12 August 1949*, www.un.org/en/genocideprevention/documents/atrocity-cirmes/Doc.32_GC-III-EN.pdf Accessed 7 April 2021, accessed 7 April 2024.

their opponents were seen as violent and barbaric, as fascist propaganda had been portraying people of colour for some time.[13]

Very soon after becoming captives, Fred and his fellow captives were forced-marched towards Benghazi, a distance of about 550 kilometres. This became known as 'the thirst march,' and here again it is possible to gain information on the experience of Cape Corps men from the oral testimony and memoirs of other UDF servicemen who marched alongside Fred. As the POWs became desperate for water, their Italian captors used their desperation to maintain control over them and to manipulate them to continue walking. With the promise of water at the end of each kilometre, the men were made to complete their journey in three days.

When a truck with a water tank stopped, scuffles to reach the water further delayed opportunities to drink. The Italians captors tried to impose order, which inevitably put the Cape Corps and African soldiers at the back of the line. European POWs got to the water first and more often than not, the water would run out before everyone got a chance to drink.[14]

After some time in the Benghazi POW cages – barbed wire enclosures where food and water were scarce – dysentery became commonplace. Following an unknown time in Benghazi, Fred and others were eventually transported to Italy.

Many ex–POWs testified that they expected better conditions in Italy. In permanent camps, so they hoped, they would be better fed and would be able to settle into a routine. Disastrously for Fred, however, he was one of about 2,000 men who boarded the *San Sebastian*.[15]

The cargo ship was used to transport captives across the Mediterranean to Italy. The trip would take about 36 hours to complete if all went well. The captain stayed close to the Greek coastline, hoping to avoid any attacks from Allied ships. This was important – the *San Sebastian* did not have any markings showing that it was carrying POWs.[16]

The captives were held in three holds below deck. Official descriptions include ladders which the men could use to climb out of the 12-metre-deep hold to use the toilets above. The 'toilets' were wooden structures that hung over the side of the ship, giving the men no privacy.

Each hold had one ladder, and with more than 600 men in each of them, some captives became claustrophobic and panicky.[17] When the men boarded the *San Sebastian*, a few still had their rations with them, but considering that many more still suffered from dysentery and that the cargo holds had no inlets for fresh air, appetites were most probably not huge.[18]

---

13 R. Scheck, '"They Are Just Savages": German Massacres of Black Soldiers from the French Army in 1940', *The Journal of Modern History*, 77:2 (2005), p.326.
14 P. Ogilvie, and N. Robinson. *In the bag* (Johannesburg: Macmillan, 1975), pp.22–23.
15 Also known as the *Jason* and the *Bastiano Veneri*.
16 M. Leigh, *Captives Courageous South African Prisoners of War World War II* (Johannesburg: Ashanti Publishing, 1992), p.40.
17 K. Wright, 'Sebastiano Venier – Mediterranean 1942: Tribute to an Enemy', Naval Historical Society of Australia, https://navyhistory.au/sebastiano-venier-mediterranean-1942-tribute-to-an-enemy/, accessed 8 April 2021.
18 Karen Horn, '"A sudden sickening sensation": South African prisoner-of-war experience on board the San Sebastian, December 1941', *Historia* 63:1 (2018), p.119.

On 12 December 1941, Lieutenant Commander Pizey spotted the *San Sebastian* from his submarine, HMS *Porpoise*. A torpedo was launched, and it hit its target between the first and second hold, instantly killing about 300 men.[19] Others were severely injured and scrambled over each other to get out of their enclosures. Fred did not give his account of the events that followed the attack, but some sense of the disaster comes from other first-hand accounts.[20]

As soon as the torpedo hit the San Sebastian, pandemonium erupted among the prisoners who were literally and figuratively in the dark. According to some, the Italian crew, including the captain, saved themselves by boarding lifeboats, while many POWs who were thrown into the water were being sucked under by the ship's propellers.[21] The details of the events are sketchy, and different witnesses recall different details. With the Italian crew absconding, a German engineer then took control of the ship in an effort to maintain order.[22]

Other sources testify that a German captain who, 'from the moment of disaster had kept to his post, and [he] did his best to inspire the crew to remain on board.'[23] In yet another version, Whittaker's wartime narrative report stated that a South African, Sergeant Tillard of the 1st South African Irish Regiment, took control once the captain and his officers had gone.[24]

Whatever the actual situation, all of the POWs recalled the confusion, and many testified seeing their Italian guards 'running all over the place, shouting and cursing…' Many POWs took this chaos as an opportunity to wreak their revenge, and a number of guards were thrown overboard by prisoners, 'without any qualms at all.'[25] The captives clearly felt justified in their actions because they had endured extreme conditions in the 'hell camps of North Africa,' 'the thirst marches' and then the days of darkness in the ship's hold with no sanitary arrangements and little or no food and water.

The POWs were not the only opportunists and it seemed that some Italian guards demanded an exchange of goods for services. One POW had to bribe an Italian

---

19 Wright, 'Sebastiano Venier', Naval Historical Society of Australia, https://navyhistory.au/sebastiano-venier-mediterranean-1942-tribute-to-an-enemy/, accessed 8 April 2021.
20 These include the accounts of Newman Robinson, Cyril Crompton, Herbert Rhodes (Aussie) Hammond, and Vivian Rees-Bevan. Ogilvie and Robinson, 1975; Crompton and Johnson, 2010; Chambers, 1967. Narrative reports of the sinking are also available in the DOD archives; DOD Union War Histories (hereafter UWH) Narep ME/3. *Mr Whittaker Sidi Rezegh and captivity afterwards (Greece and Italy) related to Mrs G. R. de Wit by Mr Whittaker*. Lastly, an interview with Bernard Schwikkard in 2010 provided more insight into the torpedo attack. Bernard Schwikkard, Johannesburg, 17 March 2010.
21 Schwikkard, 1999, 26; DOD UWH Narep ME/3. *Mr Whittaker Sidi Rezegh and captivity afterwards (Greece and Italy) related to Mrs G. R. de Wit by Mr Whittaker*.
22 A. Gilbert, *POW Allied Prisoners in Europe 1939–1945* (London: John Murray, 2006), p.49; W. W. Mason, *Prisoners of War Official History Prisoners of War New Zealand in the Second World War 1939–45* (Wellington: Oxford University Press, 1954), p.111.
23 J. Chambers, J. *For you the war is over. The story of H.R. (Aussie) Hammond* (Cape Town: HAUM, 1967), pp.16–18.
24 DOD UWH Narep ME 3. *Mr Whittaker Sidi Rezegh and captivity afterwards (Greece and Italy) related to Mrs G. R. de Wit by Mr Whittaker*.
25 Crwys-Williams, *A Country at War*, p.198.

guard with his prize riding gloves before the man would tell him where he had hidden the lifebelts.[26]

The ship was struck near the coast of Greece and ran aground on the rocky coastline. In an effort to escape the sinking ship, a number of POWs constructed a precarious rope bridge by which many were helped to reach the shore. Others, realising that the ship would not sink immediately, had a feast as they helped themselves to the contents of the food store, a case in point was Aussie Hammond, who took time to deliver cognac to the medical orderlies, and then 'dashed back to join the feast in the galley.'[27] Newman Robinson, on the other hand, went on a 'marauding expedition [for] blankets, coats and curtains for cover, and towels and pillowslips for bandages, and got to work splinting broken limbs.'[28]

While the discrepancies in the sources mirror confusion on the ship, Fred apparently was not part of the chaos, at least not for long. Somehow, he found his way onto a raft. He hung on for dear life, but it was 24 hours before he was picked out of the water.[29]

Fred was obviously one of the men, who, according to Newman Robinson, jumped overboard hoping that the Italian destroyers would come to their rescue. Unfortunately for them, the Italians had other priorities as they dropped depth charges in an effort to sink the British submarine, leaving the POWs fighting for their lives in the turbulent waters. [30]

Once on dry land, the injured POWs were taken to a hospital at Caserta, while the rest were taken to temporary camps. It was in one of these camps that Schwikkard's recollections included one of the,

> …coloureds from Cape Town who had a blanket, so we smooched up to him, and said look, come on man, let us share, and he was very kind, he agreed, but provided that he had the middle, and so four of us had a blanket…[31]

Fred soon found himself, along with Bernard Schwikkard, in a prison camp that became known as Dysentery Acre. As the name indicates, the hygienic conditions were appalling, resulting in the rampant spread of disease. In addition, the lack of food and water left the weakened prisoners unable to recover from illness or to rebuild their health. When they were moved to warehouses near Patras harbour, a severe lice plague forced them all to spend their days, 'like monkeys catching fleas.'[32]

A 45-gallon drum served as a toilet in each warehouse that housed approximately 300 men. The sheds were so crowded that they had to take turns to fetch

---

26 DOD UWH Narep ME 3. *Mr Whittaker Sidi Rezegh and captivity afterwards (Greece and Italy) related to Mrs G. R. de Wit by Mr Whittaker.*
27 Chambers, *For you the war is over*, p.19.
28 Ogilvie and Robinson, *In the bag*, p.33.
29 Zane Boltman (grandson of F. A. Ernstzen), personal correspondence, 11 November 2016.
30 Ogilvie and Robinson, *In the bag*, p.31.
31 Bernard Schwikkard, Johannesburg, 17 March 2010.
32 Schwikkard, 1999, pp.28–29.

their food when it arrived, as the floor space was too small for all of them to occupy simultaneously.[33]

Although Fred's official record of service gives no indication of his experiences in Italy, the official list of Imperial POWs in Italy show that Fred first arrived at Camp 85 near Tuturano.[34] In this camp, like all the other Allied POWs, Fred would have been deloused, had his hair shaved, received additional clothing and had his first hot shower in months.[35] Following this, POWs were then sent to permanent camps, and although it is unclear where Fred spent these early months of captivity, he most probably would have adopted a more fixed daily routine once he arrived in the new camp.

For many POWs, settling down in a permanent camp that, for men with no rank, were work camps provided a sense of normality, despite the continuous shortage of food and intermittent news from home. Reports by the Red Cross inspectors who visited the camps on a regular basis provide some information from which inferences may be made about Fred's experiences in Italy.

The Red Cross reports describe camp conditions under headings such as 'general conditions', 'interior arrangements', 'camp capacity', 'toilet facilities', 'food and cooking facilities', 'medical attention and sickness among POWs', 'clothing, laundry, money and pay,' 'canteen,' 'religious activity,' 'recreation and exercise,' 'mail,' 'welfare work' and 'complaints'. In addition, reports were also completed on satellite work or hospital camps. In most camps, the POWs selected camp leaders, also known as the 'man of confidence', and the inspectors relied on these men for information. The main aim was to ensure that the detaining powers adhered to the Geneva Convention.

In June 1943, a South African Red Cross representative in London questioned Monsieur Zollinger, the Head of Prisoner of War Parcels Department of the International Red Cross. The information derived from the interview was sent to South Africa and provided insights into the living conditions and the camp arrangements of South African POWs in Italy. Regarding Camp 82, near Laterina, and Camp 85 near Tuturano, the following was sent:

> I asked a good deal about the conditions etc. of the Native and Coloured Prisoners of War. In Camps 82 and 85 there are a number of white prisoners as well. I find that the natives are housed in separate sleeping huts, but that the white prisoners probably have to share cooking arrangements. [Zollinger] says we never need fear that they are not being well treated. Confidentially: However many South African Prisoners may complain that they have not got this or that, for propaganda reasons they, both white and native, are treated better than any of the other Prisoners.[36]

---

33   Schwikkard, 1999, p.29.
34   DOD AG (POW) Italy Imperial Prisoners of War Alphabetical List. Section 5. South Africa. Union Defence Forces.
35   Leigh, *Captives Courageous*, p.60.
36   DOD AG (POW) 1527, vol. 1. *An airgraph received from the London Committee of the South African Red Cross Society*. 9 June 1943.

In stark contrast with the accounts of ill-treatment that the POWs received shortly after capture on the battlefield, this report gives an indication of the more relaxed attitude of the non–combatant Italian camp commanders, all of whom were conscripts. On the other hand, the South African Red Cross man may have been deceived by Monsieur Zollinger, who may or may not have been biased in his opinion of the UDF prisoners.

Most rank-and-file camps in Italy were allocated to agricultural work. Working on farms held many advantages, not only did the POWs have access to more food, but they also enjoyed more freedom of movement. Another benefit was that many POWs established tentative friendships with local farmers, a welcome reprieve from the boredom and frustrations of the large POW camps where food was slow to arrive, accommodation cramped and recreational activities often non–existent, especially during the first few months in Italy.[37]

Because the Geneva Convention stipulated that different races be accommodated in separate camps, it is unlikely that Fred, or any Cape Corps men would have been sent to the same work camps as white servicemen. A number of coloured and black POWs were sent to Camp 122 in Cinecittà near Rome, where an elaborate complex of film studios was built in 1937. The POWs were used as actors in films that were produced for propaganda. The virtues of Mussolini and Fascism were of course celebrated in these films, while the so-called actors received double food rations for their work. Cinecittà had first been established as a film studio complex with the aim of producing fascist propaganda films for Mussolini's regime.[38]

According to Red Cross reports, Camp 122 held British POWs and South African 'coloured' POWs, albeit in two separate sections. The two respective camp leaders were Private Henry Suetsane and Sergeant Paling.[39] Another report, compiled on 2 October 1942, showed the camp held 407 'Coloured South African troops' with one Tunisian and one French Cameroonian POW. The tone of the report is remarkably positive and described the POWs as 'quiet, peaceful and docile' and their morale as 'very satisfactory.'[40]

Other inspectors also found positive aspects on their visits to the camp. One of them stated that the conditions in the camp were in accordance with the stipulations of the Convention, and that discipline was 'good [and] there have been no punishments (with the exception of a few hours of arrest for brawling) there have been no attempts at escape.'[41]

As the war began to take its toll on Italy, so the POWs in Italian camps started to feel the consequences. By March 1943 inspection reports show that conditions

---

37 William (Bill) Hindshaw, *An Account of my Experience as a Prisoner-of-War and Escapee in the Italian Alps During the Second World War* (unpublished memoirs, nd), p.24.
38 N. Steimatsky, 'The Cinecitta Refugee Camp (1944–1950)', *October Magazine* (2009), pp.28–31.
39 DOD AG (POW) 1527/122. *Prisoners of war camp no. 122 visited by Dr de Salis on the 11th of April 1943.*
40 DOD AG (POW) 1527/122. *Prisoners of war camp no. 122 visited 2nd October 1942 by Cap L. Trippi.*
41 DOD AG (POW) 1527/122. *Prisoners of war camp no. 122 visited 14th October 1942 by Dr de Salis.*

in Camp 122 had deteriorated, especially with regard to a shortage of clothing for POWs. Mention was also made of the complaints of Speelman Makita, a South African POW, regarding private parcels that he did not receive. The last page of the report stated that a long conversation with four coloured South African NCOs was conducted, and that 'various misunderstandings were cleared up and Speelman's exaggerations reduced to their true proportions.'[42]

By the following month a follow-up report mentioned that the camp leader in the coloured section, 'had no complaints to make and he did not express any wishes.' However, there was still an, 'urgent need of clothing and shoes', indicating that nothing had been done in this regard since the previous report was compiled in March. In addition, the toilet facilities were 'obviously inadequate' – there were only six for the more than 400 captives.[43]

Camp 122 continued with film production until the coup d'état in July 1943, but once the German forces arrived shortly after the armistice, the studios were used as a transit camp for POWs who were being sent further north towards German occupied territories.[44]

On 25 July 1943, Benito Mussolini was at last deposed in a coup d'état and negotiations on an armistice began without delay. This process lasted until September when the terms were finally agreed upon.

In the meantime, the Italian guards were confronted with Allied propaganda in the form of pamphlets that were dropped on POW camps. The pamphlets stressed the deterioration of Italy and its relationship with Germany and made much of the overthrow of Mussolini. The effect on Italian morale became evident in the way they treated the prisoners still under their guard. Depending on the Italian guards' political ideology, they either became more benevolent or more antagonistic towards the POWs. In some cases, POWs were held back in camps, but at other camps, the Italians seemed pleased at the news of the armistice, and simply walked away. At one camp, a POW recalled how, 'every sentry bar one changed into civvies and destroyed his rifle.'[45]

Many captives naturally took this opportunity to make a dash for freedom, but it is not known how Fred reacted at this time. Many POWs in agricultural work camps established friendships with Italian farmers, and once they were at large, they could rely on the goodwill of the locals for food and shelter. While most successful escapees aimed to reach neutral Switzerland or sought to join an Allied unit, many others were not so fortunate, they were recaptured by German forces and transported to camps in German occupied territory.[46]

In other cases, POWs chose to remain in their camps, believing that Allied forces would reach them before the Germans could do so. Unfortunately for them, the

---

42   DOD AG (POW) 1527/122. *Prisoners of war camp no. 122 visited 6th March 1943 by Dr de Salis*.
43   DOD AG (POW) 1527/122. *Prisoners of war camp no. 122 visited 11th April 1943 by Dr de Salis*.
44   Steimatsky, 'The Cinecittà Refugee Camp', pp.30–31.
45   Hindshaw, *An Account of my Experience*, p.27.
46   Paul Schamberger, *Interlude in Switzerland: The Story of the South African Refugee-Soldiers in the Alps* (Johannesburg: Maus Publishing, 2001), p.6.

Germans forces arrived before the Allies, and the POWs soon found themselves in cattle trucks, also going northwards to German occupied territory.[47]

Some years after the war, Fred imparted some information about the events following the Italian capitulation, and it would seem that he did evade the German takeover of Italian camps and survived for some time on, 'the generosity of civilians, stolen foods, discarded potato skins, stale bread and even rats.'[48]

By December 1943, however, Fred was once again a prisoner, as his record of service indicates that he was 'interned [at] *Frontstalag 133* Beauvais.'[49] *Stalag 133*, near the town of Beauvais was a camp originally set up to accommodate British Colonial South African prisoners from the Native Military Corps. The men in this camp were in the unfortunate position that a nearby transit camp, or *Dulag*,[50] for RAF officers were dependant on their camp. This meant that, according to the Red Cross report:

> Failing British, Canadian or American parcels, in sufficient quantities, the Delegate despatches to the Dulag British parcels from the South African Red Cross drawn from trucks which had originally been intended for British Colonial South African natives at Stalag 133 at Chartres, Orleans, or Beauvais … on the 15th, in accordance with the request of the camp authorities, the camp leader of the British Colonial South African natives handed 606 food parcels to the Dulag (which is one parcel per two men); but he refused to give any cigarettes saying his stock was too low; but, as the Delegate has stated in his report on the South African camp, he found, on checking the returns, that the stocks of cigarettes and tobacco were higher than they should have been when compared with the number of food parcels in store…[51]

While the exact details of Fred's experience of this time remain unclear, it is known that German authorities adopted a policy of transferring black POWs to occupied France. This was in accordance with the fascist ideology that dictated that German territory be cleansed of non–Arian races.[52] As such, Fred was most probably recaptured in Italy and sent to France, while the recaptured white Allied POWs were transferred to camps in Germany and Poland.

Fred's service records also indicate that on 9 April 1944, he was, 'on strength with the CC [Cape Corps] Gen List [General list].'[53] However, he must have been captured again, and escaped again. This time, as an escapee, he came across the *maquis*, a French resistance group. It was 15 August 1944. Yet, his time with this

---

47 Horn, *In Enemy Hands*, pp.151–152.
48 Zane Boltman, personal correspondence, 11 November 2016.
49 DOD PF RS, C274832. Pte Ernstzen, F. A. Form DD.293 (W.R.6)
50 *Durchgangslager der Luftwaffe*, Transit Camp of the Allied Air Forces.
51 Red Cross Committee, *Frontstalag 133*, https://www.pegasusarchive.org/pow/FS133/cFS_133_RedCross18Jul44.htm, accessed 23 August 2024.
52 M. C. Thomas, 'The Vichy Government and French Colonial Prisoners of War, 1940-1944', *French Historical Studies*, 25:4 (2002), p.667.
53 DOD PF RS, C274832. Pte Ernstzen, F.A. Form DD.732.

fighting group could not have been a celebration of freedom; the *maquis* wanted men, 'to fight, live badly, in precarious fashion, with food hard to find. They will be absolutely cut off from their families for the duration; the enemy does not apply the rules of war to them…' By this time Fred was surely familiar with rules not being applied to him. The recruitment message also advised potential *maquis* members to bring along warm clothing and items such as, 'a torch, a compass, a weapon if possible.'[54] It is doubtful that Fred had any of these luxuries.

The resistance fighters were subversive groups who sabotaged the progress of German forces and assisted Allied networks to gain information. Many German soldiers who settled in France after the occupation in 1940 treated the black French population with the scorn they believed they deserved. Similarly, the racial outlook of the Vichy Government towards colonial POWs determined the inferior treatment of these prisoners. But there is also evidence to the contrary, which suggest that good relationships developed between the black POWs and their German guards.[55] This discrimination motivated many French citizens of African origin to join resistance groups, and however short-lived Fred's time with the *maquis* may have been, he most likely felt at ease in their presence, if not physically comfortable.[56]

The *maquis* operated as guerrilla fighters who, unlike other resistance groups, remained mostly in rural areas. Their successes can in part be attributed to the fact they were spontaneous in their attacks, acting on impulse. With no clear strategic planning on their part, the chances of them being betrayed was reduced.

It is unlikely that Fred made a significant contribution towards the actions of the *maquis*, as his time with them lasted only about two weeks, from 15 to 23 August 1944.[57] At more or less the same time, the *maquis* became part of a larger resistance organisation, the *Forces Françaises d l'Interieur,* the goal being the speedy and effective liberation of France.[58]

On 23 August 1944, Fred was captured for a third time.[59] Two days later, France was liberated by the Allied forces, and Fred was freed from his last POW camp on 2 September 1944. On the same day he was transferred to the United Kingdom.[60] A few days later, his parents at last received good news when the military authorities in Pretoria wrote:

---

54 P. Davies, *France and the Second World War Occupation Collaboration and Resistance.* (London: Routledge, 2001), p.62.
55 Thomas, 'The Vichy Government', p.661; R. Scheck, *French Colonial Soldiers in German Captivity during World War II* (New York: Cambridge University Press, 2014), pp.97–98.
56 L. Broch, 'Colonial subjects and citizens in the French internal resistance, 1940–1944', *French Politics, Culture and Society* 37/1 (2019), https://go-gale-com.ez, accessed 7 April 2021.
57 DOD PF RS, Private F. A. Ernstzen 274832, *Application for Campaign Medals* (1939–1945 and onwards).
58 Davies, *France and the Second World War*, pp.61–63.
59 DOD PF RS, Private F. A. Ernstzen 274832, *Application for Campaign Medals* (1939–1945 and onwards).
60 DOD PF RS, Private F. A. Ernstzen 274832, C274832. Pte Ernstzen, F. A. Form DD.293 (W.R.6).

> Dear Mrs Williams
> It affords me great pleasure to confirm my telegram informing you that your son, Private Fred Anthony Ernstzen who was a prisoner of war has been released by the Allied Forces in Northern France and arrived in the United Kingdom on the 2nd September.
>
> I am unable at present to furnish any further information but you may rest assured that immediately any news comes to hand concerning him you will at once be advised.[61]

By this time, Fred's physical condition was showing the stresses and strains of his war experience. By mid-1944, Germany was struggling against the odds, facing Allied forces from the east and the west. The more the tide of the war turned against Germany, the less they were able, or willing, to adhere to the Geneva Convention, and in many camps across German occupied territory POWs felt the impact of the worsening conditions. With Europe in tatters, the delivery of Red Cross food parcels became almost impossible. Hunger among POWs and their captors caused tempers to flare and frustrations to surge.

The Germans realised the inevitable outcome of the conflict and wanted to secure their safety and freedom from persecution after the war. The POWs, on the other hand did not care a jot. By this time, they had been losing weight just as they did in the strenuous months after capture. As in the beginning, disease and severe privations characterised the end of their captivity.[62] Upon his arrival in Britain, Fred's health had deteriorated to such an extent that he was 'spoon-fed water and food to combat malnutrition.'[63]

Unlike French colonial prisoners, Fred's identity, at least in terms of his nationality, must also have been confirmed by the Allied authorities because he was repatriated to Britain and from there to the Union. In contrast, POWs of West African origin, many of whom were held in France, were repatriated directly to their country of origin. Yet again, this did not go smoothly. Violent protests against bad treatment characterised the last days of the POWs held at a camp near Dakar.[64] It seems that for POWs of colour, even liberation brought about struggles for freedom.

Late in October 1944, Fred arrived in the Union where his recuperation continued in Durban, Cape Town and Robben Island. By February 1945 he was well enough to be transferred to the Apostle Battery in Cape Town and in November the same year he was discharged. Fred was awarded the 1939–1945 Star, The Africa Star, the 1939–1945 War Medal and the Africa Service Medal.[65]

---

61   Officer in charge of War Records, 7 September 1944.
62   Horn, *In Enemy Hands*, pp.64, 221.
63   Zane Boltman, personal correspondence, 11 November 2016.
64   Thomas, 'The Vichy Government', p.690.
65   DOD PF RS, Private F. A. Ernstzen 274832, *Application for Campaign Medals* (1939–1945 and onwards).

7

Chris Roux and the Transvaal Horse Artillery

At 35, Chris Roux was an old man, at least according to his fellow soldiers who joined him in the UDF. Born in 1904, no one would have held it against him if he had decided to stay at home. After all, by then he had already established a successful farm near Hopetown, had a wife, May, and two young children, Piet (7) and Elizabeth (9).

Yet, he also had dreams of becoming a fighter pilot with the South African Air Force, so, with that in mind, Chris took the oath to serve on 26 October 1940. The SAAF had other ideas though, and he was deemed too old to fly. Without ceremony, he was handed over to the South African Artillery (SAA). Soon after, he found himself at Potchefstroom and Zonderwater, near Pretoria, for training, leaving his wife to manage the farm, and his children in a Bloemfontein boarding school.[1]

Even at the young age of seven, Piet, or as he referred to himself, Peter, realised the importance of keeping his dad informed of the goings on at the farm.[2] Writing on 25 October, when Chris was still on his way to Potchefstroom, Peter wanted to give him the latest news,

> Dear Dady [sic]. They at catching out the Persians.
> The farm is in a good condition. Tommy was here last night and we were catching *torre*.[3] We were riding a calf too and the calf threw me off so I have a black eye.
> The calves are fat.
> Luve [sic] from
> Peter
> xxxxxxxxxxxxxxxxxxxxxxxxxxx[4]

---

1. This chapter is based on Chris Roux's UDF Record of Service and his letters to his family, sadly, in 2010 a fire destroyed many of the letters but those that survived nevertheless provide some insight into the war from a father's perspective.
2. Although Peter never signed his letters to his dad using the diminutive form of his name, Chris insisted on addressing his letters to 'Pietie'.
3. Beetles.
4. 27 kisses. Peter Roux to Chris Roux, 25 October 1940.

Chris, his wife May, son Peter and daughter Elizabeth. (Photo: Chris Roux)

From October 1940 to September 1941, Chris remained in the Union, travelling between the Zonderwater and Potchefstroom training camps. In November 1940 Chris received another letter from Peter:

> 19.11.40
> Dear Daddy
> To morrow [sic] I am going to write in ink. Ben gave a bonky his nam is xxxxx vossie. I in spand him to by.
> A wasp stung me on sunbay so my eye is swoln up. Wel I hov to clos up cors it is deb tim.
> Love from
> Peter
> Tears[5]

When Chris was posted to Zonderwater from Potchefstroom, he was not impressed with the living arrangements, and he complained to May that they were living in tents without mattresses. Also the ground was very hard and they found it very difficult to pitch their tents, in the end resorting to, 'knocking a hole with a mallet

---

5 Peter Roux to Chris Roux, 19 November 1940. The letter is copied as originally written by Peter.

into the hard ground. *Magtig dis hard*[6] oh hell what a life. We lived in luxury in Potch, and we are going to miss it...' Another source of discontent was that they were four miles from the nearest train station and would therefore not take any weekend leave.

In Libya things were moving at pace and those men still in training, Chris included, must have felt as if they were going to miss out on the action. When Chris joined the UDF, the Transvaal Horse Artillery had already been deployed to East Africa. Chris would join the THA the following year, by which time they had been converted to the 3rd Field Regiment of the SAA.

However, it must have been Operation Compass that captured the imaginations of the men still stuck in the Union. It was during this offensive that UDF men experienced large-scale battles against a more determined enemy than they had encountered in East Africa. The three Birch brothers and De Villiers Graaff all had a taste of combat at Bardia, Sollum and Halfaya Pass.[7]

Chris Roux in uniform. (Photo: Chris Roux)

A letter to May in March 1941, shortly after the fall of Benghazi and Rommel's appointment as *Generalleutnant* of the *Afrika Korps,* shows Chris's frustration:

> We are still being bull–shitted in the usual way. Had a very big show at gun drill the other day. It really means all four guns had to go into action at very short notice. And did we battle for position, D-sub again came first. Don't think there is much hope of us leaving shortly ... also beginning to believe we are for home–defence ... sorry to hear the farming gets you down at times cheer up May, it makes me feel so proud of you. Thinking of you all, constantly...[8]

At the time, Chris was with the 1st South Africa Heavy Battery (SAHA), but with the battles in North Africa demanding new combat strategies, Chris began to believe that he would leave the army soon because, in his opinion:

> This [SAHA] battery will now definitely be broken up, and what's more I think we will be back in Potch soon again where we will get smaller guns.

---

6   goodness its difficult.
7   Katz, *South Africans versus Rommel*, pp.178 & 192.
8   C. L. M. Roux personal correspondence, 17 March 1941.

Won't be long before the other two guns will be away/arty [?] also. Only the guns we wanted not the crews. It is painful to see our guns being prepared to move, it's heart-breaking to think some other fellows will mount them in future. Guess I'll say farewell to the army soon if we are going to be broken up and knocked about.[9]

Yet, it was not long before Chris realised that a soldier's life was not always a case of 'hurry up and wait.' Army life could be unpredictable, causing a man to find himself in unexpected places and filled with surprises, sometimes good, often bad. Sometime during 1941, while he was still in training and before he left the Union for active service, Chris wrote to his two children about one such surprise. Unfortunately, his letter leaves more questions than answers:

Daddy has only a little time to write this to you two. Daddy has been detailed with nineteen others for a special duty. I am not allowed to mention whereto. I hope its [sic] going to be a nice trip. I will write to you from time to time. We have to leave so suddenly not even time to run down [to Bloemfontein] and see you … goodbye be good and listen to what is told you. Always remember your Daddy.[10]

A few days later, he followed up with more news:

We are four days away from camp now still travelling with trees flying by all day long. So far we have seen no game at all. Last night while on guard at a station a lion kicked up a terrible row quite near by [sic]. Sorry he didn't come so that I could see him. We passed over the Victoria Falls very early this morning but we didn't get a very good view as it was still very dark … in another hour's time Daddy has to go on guard again … the air is hot and dry here *"en ons sweet dat dit so bars"*[11] Just at present we are all terribly dirty. It's only a case of washing our faces … We are in command of two strange officers but they are very nice, and we like them. Pietie we must come hunting here one day when you are man enough for such hard work…[12]

In later years, Chris told his family that they were sent on a 'secret mission' to Northern Rhodesia. Their task was to deliver ammunition to East African troops. At night, the men took turns to guard the train.[13] His record of service simply states

---

9   C. L. M. Roux personal correspondence, 19 March 1941.
10 C. L. M. Roux personal correspondence, nd.
11 We sweat a lot (literal translation: we sweat so much that we burst).
12 C. L. M. Roux personal correspondence, 21 September.
13 As told to Chris Roux, grandson of C. L. M. Roux. E-mail correspondence, Chris Roux to author, 6 November 2024.

that he was temporarily excused from military service for one month. When he returned from this trip into Africa, he was given 10 days' leave without pay.[14]

Northern Rhodesia committed two battalions to the war. The country was a British colony that shared borders with German East and German West Africa, as well as with British Nyasaland. It is safe to say that the British East African colonies were the least important issue for Britain at that time of the war.

The events in Europe, including the Blitz in most large British cities, held their attention. What is more, the Italians, who had declared war the previous year, had shown that they were not overly keen on provoking battles with British and Commonwealth forces. As such, East Africa suffered from a lack of military staff and materiel. With the railway running through Livingstone, over the Victoria Falls bridge and continuing into Northern Rhodesia, Chris's 'secret mission' was most likely being tasked with delivering ammunition to the border with German East Africa from the Union. Bringing in ammunition and supplies from Britain would not have been feasible at the time.[15]

It seems that this trip to East Africa was Chris's only excitement during his training phase. On 3 November he was back, and was transferred to the 6th Field Regiment SAA. Contrary to his predictions, his service would continue regardless of the demise of the Horse Artillery. It was just as well, because the UDF needed more men; Operation Crusader was about to begin in North Africa, and the disastrous battle at Sidi Rezegh in November would see almost the entire 5th South African Infantry Brigade fall victim to German forces. This was also the battle where Uys Krige and Fred Ernstzen were captured.[16]

Nine days later, Chris's fate was sealed as he boarded a train and set off to Durban to embark on the *Llandaff Castle* towards Cairo. As always, his children were on his mind, and he reminded them:

> You two must write often Daddy will always be on the lookout for post. Do not miss any days at school as I would so like to see two clever little children soon. Will send you a few little things from Up North, if you behave very well. You must be good and listen to mummy very nicely ... Do not forget you two monkeys write and write often. With a loving kiss for each from yours ever loving Soldier Daddy.[17]

On Christmas day, his first while on active service, Chris wrote again:

> Dearest Elizabeth and Pietie,
> Thank you so much for your letters of good wishes. Daddy received your letters this morning, Xmas day. Goodness knows how you timed it so well to get your letters here on the day. I appreciate your letter very much, and it so nice of you to give your love to my fellow soldiers, they also appreciate

---

14   DOD PF RS, C. L. M. Roux, Record of Service.
15   Stewart, *The First Victory*, pp.32–33, 42, 250.
16   Katz, *South Africans versus Rommel*, pp.178 & 192.
17   C. L. M. Roux personal correspondence, 29 November 1941.

Chris Roux and two friends in a tent in a dugout. (Photo: Chris Roux)

your kind thoughts ... we toasted your health so far away ... Yesterday we received a box of cigarettes as a Xmas present. A small tin with General Mrs Smuts' face on it. We are moving higher up today sometime ... you two must write often, because every time I see a plane I just imagine it carries post from you to me. You should love to hear all sorts of news from me, but our letters are censored, and therefore cannot tell you of all our movements. Let's hope this old war will end soon, so I can see you again soon...[18]

This was also the day the Chris was transferred to the 3rd Field Regiment Transvaal Horse Artillery and the convoy began to move towards Gazala.

> Dearest Elizabeth and Pietie,
> Daddy hasn't had post for a week, I suppose there is some delay somewhere as I know you two will write regularly ... Two afternoons ago we were taken by troop carrier to see a travelling concert show, and I quite enjoyed it ... saw one girl acting the dead image of Aunty Dorothy ... lips painted red and eyebrows blackened with face heavily powered ... We were all taken to the sea for a compulsory swim and was the water cold. Have never experienced anything like it before. Couldn't stay longer than a few minutes and my teeth were chattering. This afternoon one battery played rugby against the other and what a scramble. Daddy is suffering from a cold but also

---

18   C. L. M. Roux personal correspondence, 25 December 1941.

The convoy on the move. (Photo: Chris Roux)

joined in after half time. No good anymore, too old, lost all my pep … Is the farm still being looked after or is it managing itself, I always think of how you are enjoying yourselves [on the farm] Don't let things go to [sic] badly or otherwise Daddy will have a lot to say when he returns one day…'[19]

Chris was trying to maintain a positive tone in his letters to Peter and Elizabeth, but in truth there were all kinds of frustrations the men had to deal with. These he let May know about in his letters. When the post did not get through in time, or was lost, Chris wrote how he found it, 'annoying to think all my time wasted. It's difficult to find time writing during the day and at night its blackout … May I'm truly worried about the farming…'[20]

May was alone on the farm, and while she may have dealt with the pressure of managing the different aspects of the business, Chris's concern for the farm grew the longer he was away from home.

A few days later, however, he was able to write encouragingly to the children who had just returned from a holiday at Kleinmond on the Cape Coast. Although his letter is devoid of any news of significance, Chris described his daily routine and the living conditions in the desert:

> … and now you two are at school again, fresh and full of energy to enjoy your work. Daddy can picture you dressing, having your breakfast and run for the school … Daddy does almost the same sort of thing here in the mornings. Have a quick shave and wash, slip on my boots, and some days I just manage to be in time for roll-call at 7:15 fastening buttons etc., as far as I go … being in the dug–out one doesn't hear the whistle, and its pitch dark

---

19 C. L. M. Roux personal correspondence, 14 January 1942.
20 C. L. M. Roux personal correspondence, 25 January 1942.

Chris Roux (left) and a friend taking a break in the desert. (Photo: Chris Roux)

in here when we get up to shave. All is done by candle light. As I'm sitting here now my candle is burning very low and have no more. Our canteen couldn't get any, so we'll just have to go to bed with the fowls … You can imagine the dust in here when the wind blows. While doing the cleaning up, John brought his little petrol primus in and in no time we had tea. It was a real treat. We can always do this sort of thing provided we have the tea and Klim … The moon is bright and the Western Desert is well lit up. There's a lot of fun going on outside. A few boys have caught a stray donkey and want to "go places" with it, but Mr Donkey is wise and not having any. He goes round in circles and that's all … I have a feeling they will before long land in the dugout with me … it's time you two do some writing, both of you … Do send Daddy cigarettes ever so often because it takes ages to get here. The boat is very slow…[21]

It was now that Chris began to experience combat. His diary shows that Stukas were active in their vicinity and that they spent most of their time digging gun positions.[22] The rainy season was also upon them and on 5 March Chris wrote that all of them were 'slushing about in the mud, drenched.'[23]

Letters to May often included matters of business, but Chris also felt free to express his feelings towards those who did not volunteer for service. The 'key men' for instance, were deemed to fulfil important positions in the Union and were not expected to volunteer for service. Those who were wearing the red tabs indicating their willingness to fight did not view the 'key men' with sympathy, and were of the opinion that they were ditching their duty.

On 16 February, Chris asked May to send money as there was a likelihood that he would spend a few days' leave in Cairo. Had it not been for a certain Badenhorst, his

---

21 C. L. M. Roux personal correspondence, 31 January 1942.
22 Chris Roux, War Diary, 14 March 1942.
23 C. L. M. Roux personal correspondence, 5 March 1942.

bank manager, Chris would not have had to ask May for assistance, but Chris had had: '…a letter from Badenhorst with only a third of the arranged amount enclosed. What is the matter with him? I suppose all key-men are alike, should have guessed that.'[24]

Frequent movement and intermittent skirmishes with the enemy obstructed mail and no parcels got through while outgoing letters took a month or more to arrive at their destination. Waiting for news from the farm tested Chris's patience, and it seemed as if May's letters, when they finally arrived, failed to reassure him:

> …from all accounts in your letter I gather you are having a though [sic] time again, what with sheep lambing and the season not suitable … you are going to have endless trouble there if you don't appoint some sort of manager there. for the love of God do not appoint an OB[25] B– by any means. It's impossible for you to run the three farms without a manager your health will not allow the strain, and it already worries me no end, to think what will happen…[26]

The next day Chris continued with his letter, wishing May a happy birthday and expressing his hope that by the time her next birthday came along, '…this bloody struggle [is] at an end with peace once more restored.'[27]

The cause to which Chris felt a duty and had left his family and farm for, now began to take a back seat as things at home clearly were not going well. Chris' state of mind towards his superiors also grew negative, as he informed May that:

> …our Sgt [Sergeant] is so conscientious he keeps us on the go from sunrise to sunset without a break to do even writing. At this rate our love for him will part and much against our will have to do some loafing. Tony and I are compelled this evening to miss our supper or otherwise no letters will ever be written. Must write to the kiddies but when? The sun is setting fast and I must try to finish this…[28]

It was March 1942 and the 8th Army was putting in everything they had to keep Rommel from making progress towards Egypt. The line between Gazala, where Chris was during that time, and Bir Hakeim was heavily mined and UDF forces were placed to the west and the east of the line, putting them in the front line against the *Afrika Korps*.[29]

Further to the east of the line lay Tobruk, El Alamein and Egypt. If there was anything to learn from the past, it was that Rommel was determined to achieve his

---

24 C. L. M. Roux personal correspondence, 16 February 1942.
25 *Ossewabrandwag*.
26 C. L. M. Roux personal correspondence, 5 March 1942.
27 C. L. M. Roux personal correspondence, 5 March 1942.
28 C. L. M. Roux personal correspondence, 19 March 1942.
29 James Holland, *Together We Stand North Africa 1942–1943: Turning the Tide in the West* (London: Harper Collins, 2006), p.xii.

Roux with his 25pdr gun. (Photo: Chris Roux)

goals. A case in point was the Battle of Sidi Rezegh in November the previous year, which would still have been fresh in the minds of the 8th Army command.

Not able to write about the defensive line in his letters, Chris kept the details for his diary entries:

> Arrived Gazala 2nd March. Dug gun pits and slit trenches day after day … Busy digging gun positions had to call in engineers for blasting … our aircraft and German aircraft very active … Arrived at our new destination when once more we had to dig gunpits … We stayed till 18th [March] at our almost completed gun position when orders came through to the effect that we are now attached to the Hare Column which meant that we left that night for the front line … [20 March] To-day captured two German 75mm guns and 200 primers after a two-hour artillery duel. Laying [mines] was the order of the day … [26 March] left at 6 in the morning on a raiding party into enemy lines. The 50 Div. was pushing on our left in a box formation and we had to "wrecky" [sic] on the right flank … [27 March] Twenty four bombers with a very big escourt [sic] of fighter planes passed over to bomb enemy concentrations … [1 April] We had to cover the infantry for the day while they were digging in …[30]

Later on the same day, Chris wrote to May, concerned with her health and the management of the farm, he expressed his shock when he read her previous letter.

---

30   Chris Roux, War Diary, 2 March to 1 April 1942.

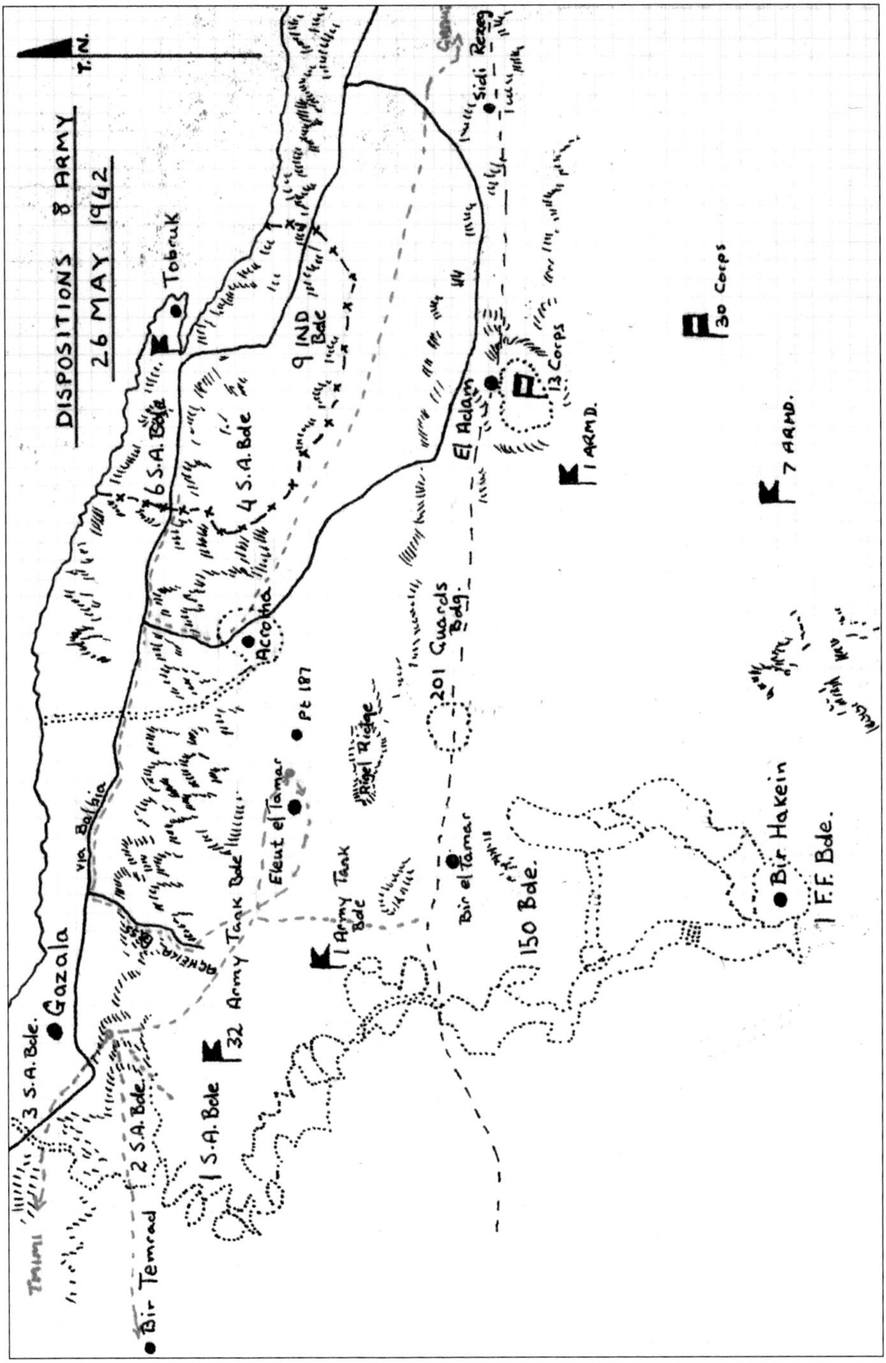

Chris' map of the Gazala Line. (Photo: Chris Roux)

He wanted to get back to her as soon as he could, and planned to put in his application the next day for permission to return to the Union. Unfortunately, he had the bureaucracy of the Defence Force to deal with. With the *Afrika Korps* and the 8th Army facing each other with an ever dwindling piece of no-man's land between them, it was unlikely that Chris would get his time off.

The rest of April turned out to be a hellish month. It is possible that it was not so much the censors who prevented Chris from sharing battle details in his letters, but more his concern for May's health. In his diary, however, Chris did not hold back, and he described how close he came to injury and death:

> 5 April 1942: 6 o'clock this morning was the beginning of a heavy artillery duel. It lasted all day and now at sunset is still going on. About fifty Jerry tanks approached our position, but were repulsed with losses. Any amount of enemy planes acting as spotters were seen above us. One enemy plane was brought [sic] down by ac-ac [anti-aircraft] fire. The pilot landed by parachute while the plane decended [sic] like a falling leaf and burst into flames on impact with the ground. We all gave a hearty cheer for the ac-ac. For once.
>
> 9 April 1942: Our 48hr patrol over we arrived back behind our main front line of defence tired, dirty, and hungry. Ammunition was checked … maintenance was ordered … nor far from us the RA gun pits and while two fellows were handling their ammunition (4.5) one shell exploded and killed the one, leaving the other seriously wounded. It was a terrible crash and the shell splinters whistled past us…
>
> 10 April 1942: [two] gunners [were] medically examined and may be rebaorded [sic], owing to deafness and being bomb happy at times … At 4.15 we had a pukka Stuka parade. Twelve planes dive bombed us. I was in the act of writing to Pietie and Elizabeth when I heard a scream of engines and they dived. I made a dive for my slit trench just in time. Bombs came hurtling down all round and at times it felt as if I had to hold on to the ground to keep down…
>
> 12 April 1942: Air activity was very active during the night. Planes could be heard machine gunning the roads … an artillery duel developed but after five hours firing enemy guns were silenced … the thought [sic] of a direct hit is very distressing…
>
> 15 April 1942: [Stuka dive bombers] dropped heavy bombs the other anti-personnel. Quite a few casualties. The earth vibrated with explosions and ground dust and what not poured over us from a bomb dropping eight yds away at the back of us and one 14 yds in front of us … we were damn near bomb happy the lot of us … Ambulances were on the spot and some ghastly sights were seen. Many wounded and bomb happy … as the planes pulled out of their dives the machine gunners in their rear cockpits opened up and the zip was most terrifying … we were damn near bomb happy the lot of us … a couple of whiskys would be most welcome…

On 19 April, Chris' Battery came under command of Lieutenant Colonel F. Theron.[31] By 25 April Chris at last had time to write home again, and although he had had no word on his application to return home, he remained optimistic despite a note of despondency over desert conditions creeping into his letters:

> Received Elizabeth's letter yesterday, poor little soul it seems an effort for her to write, but she seems full of her boarding school idea … Tony and I have just shaken all the dust out of our blankets … Tony has an awful job with his crop of hair. The dust gets into it, and with a little perspiration cakes his hair together … there are a few things I'm darn sick of now in the desert. Rolling blankets strapping them on to the vehicle, undo them again make up the bed, roll them again and so it goes on. As for camouflage net, creeping in under it, out again, with always something hooking somewhere. If I ever see a fisherman catching 'harders'[32] with a net, would walk away in disgust. Even a hairnet will worry me … we somehow carry on, adding a little humour to it all … Slit trenches we have no objection in digging because they give wonderful protection.[33]

The first few days of May were calmer, but it was not long before shells began bursting again. Chris narrowly escaped death:

> I heard two pop pops and simultaneously whistling of shells right over my head. I took one flying leap flat on to the ground. I was far too late as the shells had already burst 50 yds behind us.

He did this with a fractured foot which saw him go off to hospital where he lay about, 'doing sweet blow all.'[34]

Of the events between 26 May, when the Battle of Gazala began, and 20 June, when Rommel's forces overran Tobruk, only a summary of Chris' experiences is available, but the severity of combat is evident. For someone to emerge unscathed was a matter beyond their control, as is obvious from Chris' diary descriptions:

> On 26th May Jerry started his push and were kept busy day and night firing thousands of rounds each day … were continuously under shell fire from enemy long-range guns. Shells dropped perilously near our gun pits, some only ten yds away … Then news came through that Jerry had pierced our defences known as "The Cauldron" – Knightsbridge and the Free French at Bir Hacheim had to withdraw. We were sent out to help the 57th Brigade but the firing was hot and accurate and had to withdraw. [On 14 June] we pulled out and ran the gauntlet to Tobruk. All the time Jerry was following us. Very lights went up one after the other and had Jerry only known our position

---

31 Orpen, *The History of the Transvaal Horse Artillery*, p.109.
32 A type of fish.
33 C. L. M. Roux personal correspondence, 25 April 1942.
34 Chris Roux, War Diary, 4 May 1942.

we would all have been summering in Italy … Jerry opened up with arty [artillery] fire and in no time thousands of vehicles were careering all over dodging the shell bursts. Ghastly sights were seen when shells burst under vehicles. We were fired at by anti-tank, machine guns and tanks. How we managed to get through is still a miracle [20 June] News that Tobruk has fallen shocked us … at this position we are again in readiness to fight a rearguard action allowing troops to move out.[35]

As Rommel prepared to move his panzers on Tobruk, confrontations with the enemy became more demanding during June as the 7th and 8th Field Batteries patrolled the Gazala Line. Close encounters with Messerschmitt fire and small ambush parties kept them alert, but as ever, Chris did not give details in his letters.[36] He wrote to May early in June:

all that matters is I'm well and OK, no need to worry … Tony and I remarked how well we are taking it. Sleep is about all we want … May, I still intend writing to the kids but for the present they must wait … *Dit gaan maar barstens*!![37] Just at present I reckon you can rule out hearing anything definite from me, until such time when things are quiet again…[38]

Seven days later Chris and the rest of his battery was deployed at Bir Hakeim in a dangerous undertaking. Rommel wanted to rid the Gazala Line of all pockets of resistance, the most tenacious being the Free French. The first attack against the French came on 1 June from the Italians, but when Rommel realised that the Italians were not making any progress he sent in German troops. Seven days later, Rommel had other British units on the run, and turned his full attention to the French at Bir Hakeim.[39]

Chris' regiment had to provide rearguard cover allowing the French to withdraw safely. Being in this position obviously put them in the path of the oncoming German forces and Chris and his comrades made full use of their slit trenches. Bir Hakeim fell into Rommel's hands and the 8th Army was in retreat.

Another defeat awaited the 8th Army, and more specifically the UDF, when Rommel turned his attention to Tobruk. On the day that Tobruk fell, 21 June 1942, Chris' unit was away from the action, and he was able to write to his, 'Darling May, We are parked here in a desolate bit of desert, away from all that has taken place. You would be worried about me, but rest assured I am safe and well and so is Tony.'[40] On 25 June he continued, 'I am lying flat out under my truck in the shade after travelling more than two hundred miles over a [?] barren desert…'[41]

---

35 Chris Roux, War Diary, 26 May to 20 June 1942.
36 Orpen, *The History of the Transvaal Horse Artillery*, p.111.
37 Things are tough going!
38 C. L. M. Roux personal correspondence, 3 June 1942.
39 Katz, *South Africans versus Rommel*, pp.179–181.
40 C. L. M. Roux personal correspondence, 25 June 1942.
41 C. L. M. Roux personal correspondence, 25 June 1942.

The chaos of the battle extended into the aftermath and no one was sure who had been captured, killed or escaped as the remnants of the defeated army retreated towards El Alamein. Chris was reported missing on 20 June and it was 10 days before he was found and struck of the list of missing men.[42] It was indeed a time of confusion, as Chris was under the impression that a friend of his was also missing. Chris and this friend met each other by chance just after the friend posted a letter to Chris's family informing them that Chris was taken prisoner by the Germans.

Chris related this story in a letter early in July, and knowing how unreliable and slow the mail was, he wrote:

> I quite understand how worried the people in the Union are; everybody sort of waiting to hear where their near and dear ones are. Do let mother know from time to time that I'm OK. I'm writing as regularly as possible so that you'll know, *alles is nog reg*.[43] … *Tell Pietie he must stadig met die droë-wors, anders sal ek moet afreken met hom eendag.*[44] Tell him I appreciate his wanting to come and help Daddy fight, but his war effort looking after his mammy is enough, that's to say if he does. Often when I view all this, my wonderings go back to you all. It usually happens at night when I doss down next to my vehicle, smoking my last cigarette of the day … *Word nou stadig moeg vir die sort neukery.*[45] Do you know May I've heard absolutely nothing as yet [about my application to go home] and suppose with all this, nobody cares if you lose all and everything. I can say one thing and that is if any farmer with a concern joins up, well then he's a b-g fool, and so am I for that matter.[46]

The large number of men who were taken prisoner and the slow flow of reliable information caused rumours to flourish. The defeat at Tobruk meant that there were so few men left in the THA that the regiment was removed from the order of battle.[47] Chris must have suspected that news of the disaster would reach home first, and he must have been worried about May's state of mind. Hoping that his letters would reach her, he continued to write:

> You can rest assured that Tony and I are still on the go. It was a near thing, but we got through and out unscathed. There would be wild rumours knocking about but as I have mentioned before, don't take any notice of any until you receive genuine confirmation … I haven't written to the kids for a long time, but as soon as we come to a standstill will drop them each a card

---

42 DOD PF RS, C. L. M. Roux, Record of Service.
43 Everything is still okay.
44 He must not eat the *droëwors* [dried sausage] too quickly, or I shall have to deal with him one day.
45 Slowly getting tired of this type of messing about.
46 C. L. M. Roux personal correspondence, 8 July 1942.
47 Staff writer, 'A hundred and ten not out for the Transvaal Horse Artillery', https://www.defenceweb.co.za/land/land-land/a-hundred-and-10-not-out-for-the-transvaal-horse-artillery, accessed 6 November 2020.

… Tell Pietie one day I'll take him for a Springbok shoot again, *hy moet net 'n bietjie wag en nie so haastig wees nie*.⁴⁸ Will never forget the joy on his face the day he popped off his first buck. I suppose he worries you no end when Hendrik & co go to the veldt. Very pleased to hear Elizabeth is satisfied, had fears she wouldn't be. She with her tennis and hockey makes me feel an old man. Will soon be at the stage sitting with my *pyp in die bek*,⁴⁹ watching them at their games.⁵⁰

Sometime during this confusing time, May had undergone an operation, escalating the difficulties of the circumstances in which she found herself. It is not known when May received Chris' letters that he wrote in the days and weeks after the fall of Tobruk, but on 17 July, she received a telegram informing her that her husband had gone missing on 20 June and that he was most probably in enemy hands.

On the same day that May read the official telegram at home, Chris wrote to her from somewhere on the coast of the Mediterranean:

> Darling May
> We have just been relieved for a few hours after being very busy, so I am taking this opportunity … this morning we had a photo taken while in action by a press photographer, so if you see a crew at their job, and you spot a fellow with hands all bandaged you will know who it is … the bandages are only covering some nasty desert sores which will be healed up in a week's time … *alles gaan goed*,⁵¹ don't worry about the news, *alles sal regkom*…⁵²

A month after the fall of Tobruk, May received 'the good news telegram' from a friend that Chris and Tony were safe. Only snippets of her letter remain,⁵³ but it is clear that the information on Chris came in fits and starts and caused a lot of confusion and worry:

> After my telegram came, the same thing – missing … I walked up & down here [?] & the tears just ready to flow … Lou phoned to say DHQ where she interviewed the head of this department [?] that if I had a letter from you dated after the 20th [?] that there is some mistake – so on Sat[urday] evening again … to tell them this piece of good news [and they said] "don't be too optimistic May" [I] just want to go back to the subject of the telegram etc about you & what a relief it is now … am just anxious for a letter from

---

48   He must not be in such a hurry.
49   Pipe in my mouth.
50   C. L. M. Roux personal correspondence, 11 July 1942.
51   Everything is well.
52   Everything will be all right. C. L. M. Roux personal correspondence, 17 July 1942.
53   The letter was partially destroyed by fire.

you now & a confirmation of the good news from DHQ ... God bless you & keep you safe as He has...[54]

Almost as if to confirm the confusion, the UDF Headquarters in Pretoria wrote to May on 1 August to confirm that Chris had been taken prisoner on 20 June.[55] Three days later she received two telegrams, one from the South African Red Cross saying that they had been informed by the Department of Defence that Chris was reported as *not* missing and *not* POW.[56] The other telegram was from Pretoria, stating the same information.[57] By this time, however, May had received the good news through other channels.

On 31 July 1942 Chris boarded a ship in Cairo to return to the Union on leave. Soon after his arrival, he was granted temporary release from the UDF. He was supposed to report back on 11 March 1943, but on 12 October 1942 his release was converted to discharge, and he was finally free to go back to the farm.

Like many Second World War veterans, Chris hardly ever spoke of his war experiences, with one exception; his grandson remembers how he:

> spoke quite often about the attack from Bir Hakeim where his gun was involved in a rear-guard action for the Free French to withdraw. How they had to lie prone in [a] slit trench with machine-gun fire continually zipping over their heads. One of the guys, Visagie, as I recall, was due to go on home leave in a short time was fretting and concerned and kept peeping to see whether or not they would be captured. 'He took a bullet right here' I recall my grandfather saying putting his thumb between his eyes on his forehead. The attack was so swift that the *Afrika Korps* did not concern themselves with this lone gun and swept by. He told me they pretty much drove east in convoy with 'Jerry' until they could break away into the desert. He mentioned that it was four days before they could bury Visagie who was wrapped in a blanket behind the seat of the 'Garrie.'[58]

---

54 May Roux personal correspondence, 20 July 1942.
55 Officer in charge of war registers, Pretoria HQ to May Roux, 1 August 1942.
56 The South African Red Cross to May Roux, 4 August 1942.
57 UDF HQ to May Roux, 4 August 1942.
58 As told by Chris Roux, grandson of C. L. M. Roux.

8

Tom Mitchell and the Imperial Light Horse

Tom Mitchell[1] remembered May 1940 as a time of 'fire and fury.'[2] As his friends were mobilised, Tom was stuck at the University of Cape Town, writing, but failing most of his second year exams. He was desperate to volunteer for the UDF, but he had been rejected three times because his eyes did not make the grade.

Eventually, he memorised an eye chart and passed the medical exam. His intention was to join Dougie van Riet's transport unit, but as he exited the recruitment office, he met an officer of the Umvoti Mounted Rifles who would be 'going North very soon.' Three days later, Tom and the rest of the regiment were on their way to Pietermaritzburg for training. Tom had a nagging feeling when he said goodbye to his mother and sisters:

> I knew that we'd probably be fighting in Europe where conditions were likely to be far worse than in the desert … I said to myself that I was unlikely to see them again. The feeling didn't worry me, I just accepted it.

Early in 1941 he found himself driving a truck to East Africa. Along the way, which was tough going, Tom and his fellow volunteer drivers experienced what can only be called the ultimate adventure for a young man full of life. Lions in camp, scorpions the size of a man's foot and the odd Italian biplane strafing in their general vicinity failed in giving the men any sense of the seriousness of their work.

Tom was skilled at handling a rifle, he once shot a vulture from 600 yards, but this did not necessarily make him army material. When they eventually arrived in Egypt, they were greeted by a local man, who, in perfect Afrikaans, said, "*Goeie môre Meneer! Daar's kak in die land!*"[3] Obviously the man had come across South Africans before.

With very little to do in Cairo, boredom soon set in. Tom noticed how, 'morale went for a loop' amongst the men. Their frustration disappeared a few days later when his, 'introduction to the real bombing war came.'[4] They were unloading a ship

---

1 Tom Mitchell dictated his war memories during 1995 and 1996. In 2018 his son Charles made the memoirs available to the family as *Tom's War*, adding a preface and a chronology of the war to the memoirs.
2 C. Mitchell, *Tom's War*. Privately Published Memoir, p.9.
3 "Good morning, Sir, there is shit in this country!", Mitchell, *Tom's War*, p.59.
4 Mitchell, *Tom's War*, p.65.

when they became the target of an air raid and, '[Tom] realised that about two tons of steel per minute was being pumped into the sky [by anti-aircraft guns] straight above me, and within a short while bits would be raining down. Panic!'[5]

It was after this encounter that Tom and his mates grasped the value of teamwork: 'That night made us realise that as long as we didn't all panic at the same time, and some could reassure others, and we stayed together, we'd be okay.'[6]

Still, the war required more from young men than distributing bouts of panic amongst each other, and Tom remained stubborn. With fewer drivers needed, Tom felt unwanted, but his subsequent transfer requests were refused:

> I would've been quite happy to revert to private if I could get a place in one of the companies – any one – but no, the adjutant insisted that I should remain a lance-corporal, and acting corporal, until there was a place for me … eventually I became so fed up I went to see the adjutant, and in the ensuing argument, I ripped off my stripes and threw them on his desk, then marched out of his office.[7]

The adjutant's reaction was not recorded.

Tom still had a lot to do in the Western Desert, and by mid-1941, many battles between the British 8th Army and *Generalleutnant* Erwin Rommel's *Afrika Korps* lay ahead.

Rumours were rife of a potential 'push', but as the men got most of their news from the 'latronigrams', Tom did not trust the news. He volunteered again, this time for a 'special job with the signals.' It was the same night that the Battle of Bardia began, and Tom remembered how, 'Jerry was coming closer and eventually tried a bayonet charge. The boys shot straight and Jerry didn't try again.'[8]

He emerged unscathed, but the reality of war, and that he was in it, had begun to dawn on him.

During the battles around Gazala, it was the daily sitreps that made an impression on him:

> I remember one remark by a Tommy reading the latest sitrep that we'd again surrounded a group of Germans: 'Cor blimey! So we've surrounded them again, have we! Tomorrow we'll hear that they've fooked all our tanks again!' [Tom continued] The morale of the army sank lower and lower but confidence in a few of the leaders, among them "Strafer" Gott, remained high.[9]

Regardless of morale, luck seemed to remain on Tom's side, and he very narrowly missed being in Tobruk when it fell to Rommel's forces in June 1942. It was now that

---

5   Mitchell, *Tom's War*, p.68.
6   Mitchell, *Tom's War*, p.69.
7   Mitchell, *Tom's War*, p.71.
8   Mitchell, *Tom's War*, p.81.
9   Mitchell, *Tom's War*, pp.94–95.

Tom was able to evaluate the situation objectively, writing in his memoirs that the defeat at Tobruk:

> Brought home to the troops the fact that confidence and courage weren't enough, [it] resulted in a more determined professional attitude, especially among the junior regimental officers and troops who were at the cutting edge of the army. The necessary lessons were learnt quickly. For myself, I noticed a difference in attitude when I joined the ILH. I ceased to be a thing to be messed around and to do as I was told, and became part of a team.[10]

The defeat at Tobruk was followed by the retreat towards Egypt. This hasty retreat came to be known as the 'Gazala Gallop'. Tom remembered that their route took them into open desert, where:

> Some time during the night, we ran into one of the German laagers. There were tanks standing all around; I can remember the dark shapes in the faint light and a lot of random firing from the Germans, who seemed to fire at anything that moved. We just kept going … I put my foot down. I remember the tracer flying and bullets hitting the car; some of [the] kit was set alight and the steering wheel was hit … after about a mile or so, the engine gave up the ghost … there wasn't any time to do anything about it. We grabbed what kit we had, and jumped out one side, the colonel out the other. I never saw him again. I threw a match in the tank and climbed on the first truck that came past…[11]

Yet, his theory of fighting in teams during battle was still to be tested, and this came with the battles of Alamein towards the end of 1942. It was here that Tom and others joined the Imperial Light Horse Regiment under Captain MacIntosh, and at last they became 'frontline soldiers, and all our time and energy were directed to the prime job of beating the enemy.'[12]

To keep an eye on the approaching German forces, small patrols were sent out from Alamein, and Tom described these reconnaissance experiences as, 'intense nervous strain and mental concentration [and] we moved in an open box formation, with machine gunners on the flanks [a telephone wire] was connected to a gun battery so that if we got into trouble, we could call down artillery fire.'[13]

The aim of the patrols was to plot the German positions as well as to establish where the minefields were. On one occasion, the sound of snoring alerted them to an enemy position on their way back from a patrol.

Getting a new Bren Gun lifted Tom's spirits, but when a convoy of new 6pdr anti-tank guns appeared, the men became 'exhilarated at the big push' which they knew

---

10 Mitchell, *Tom's War*, pp.96–97.
11 Mitchell, *Tom's War*, pp.99–100.
12 Mitchell, *Tom's War*, p.105.
13 Mitchell, *Tom's War*, p.108.

was imminent. However, Tom's preparations for the battle reveal another side to his emotions on that night:

> As the Bren gunner, I was determined not to run out of ammunition, so I arranged my web equipment to carry my small pack six packets of 50 rounds of cartridges, as well as 10 full magazines and 2 hand-grenades – a total of nearly 600 rounds of ammunition … The total weight I planned to carry was close on 100 pounds … George Nel, our corporal, was worried that it was too heavy, so I did a couple of press ups to prove that I could carry it. Later I was told to carry a shovel as well, but that I refused![14]

When the sun set, they moved silently into no-man's land, so close to the Germans that they could hear one of them handing out mail. Tom and the rest of the men were in position, silently watching the full moon lighting up the desert around them.

At last the stillness was interrupted, '…the whole horizon lit up with continuous gun flashes, like intense lightning. Then we heard the shells passing overhead, then their explosions, and finally the roar of the guns, which blotted out all other sounds. The barrage, which was due to go on full-blast for five hours, had begun.'[15]

It was under this bombardment that Tom's unit started moving towards their objective, with the Germans firing 'backwards and forwards' over them. It was not long before Tom got hit, 'In my arse! Nugget looked me over and I felt him tear my trousers a bit, then he burst out laughing. A flat piece of shrapnel had cut through my trousers and lay against my bare flesh. It hadn't penetrated my skin but it was red hot.'[16]

Their laughter amid the chaos quickly died away when a Bren Gun Carrier close to them hit a mine and burst into flames. They all raced to help, throwing sand to douse the flames. Their efforts came to an abrupt stop when they realised that, along with the sand, they were also throwing a fair few mines that had been laid by the enemy.

Literally in the fog of war, Tom's unit approached their objective. A gun from their own lines was off target, causing smoke, dust and four letter words to fly through the air as the shells landed directly behind them instead of on enemy targets. In an exceptionally close call, a German machine-gun fired on them from a position to their rear. Taking cover, a section was sent out to:

> …hunt the gunner … I went back in the general direction the fire was coming from, and when the gun fired again I lay down and started firing on it in short bursts. I then thought it to be about 200 yards away. The Jerry gunner had spotted me and fired back. I remember the tracers coming straight towards me, then at the last minute lifting over my head. After a few bursts the hunting section shouted to me to cease fire and I heard them shouting and a grenade exploding. The smoke was dissipating and the

---

14   Mitchell, *Tom's War*, p.113.
15   Mitchell, *Tom's War*, p.114.
16   Mitchell, *Tom's War*, p.115.

moon was beginning to illuminate the scene. After a few minutes I stood up, but when I bent to pick up my Bren I saw that one foot on the bipod was resting on an S-mine, with the steel prongs shining in the moonlight. You may be sure I walked back to my section very carefully, placing my feet only in the footprints I'd made coming out.[17]

Near misses did not bring special treatment, and on 25 October, Sergeant 'Curly' Webb led a patrol towards the German positions. Upon reaching their objective, they found no Germans, only a minefield and above them a moon that lit up the desert around them. Tom asked Curly what they were supposed to do there, but no one seemed to know.

In the meantime, unknown to them, they were being watched by a German patrol. When the guns 'opened up' from both sides, Tom and the rest in the patrol decided to get out:

> There was a nasty 37mm anti-tank gun that was also shooting singly shots; each shot was a tracer and disappeared past me long before I could react, so I just ran with the others. I remember racing up to a treble concertina wire about four feet high, with two rolls on the bottom and one on top, and thinking, 'How will I ever get over this?' But the next thing I knew, it was behind me.[18]

Almost a kilometre further on, some of the men, Tom included, decided to look for cover. They found shell holes and stayed there until the guns went quiet. When they returned to their lines, they were informed that they had been recorded as missing and that a patrol was searching for them. Against all odds, there were no casualties. However, their luck was running out.

On their way to take over positions that the New Zealanders had captured, Tom's unit passed a convoy of 14 ammunition carrying trucks that had been bombed at some point. The truck at the head of the convoy suffered an almost direct hit, killing the driver at the wheel. The next driver got as far as opening the door, the next lay half out, and the next outside, the next some distance away. So it went, Tom counted 8 burned drivers. He did not mention if the trucks were German or British.

Once at their position, Tom and Nugget dug themselves into a foxhole just behind a minefield wire. A few steps into the minefield, they saw a dead New Zealander, and further away, a few more. Tom guessed that the bodies must have been there at least a week as they 'were beginning to smell.' Not given permission to enter the minefield to retrieve bodies, Tom and two others nevertheless took the risk when night fell:

> The others didn't want to touch him but I persuaded them each to lift a foot while I lifted the torso, and we carried him up to the grave [they dug earlier]. I opened his shirt and cut off one of his identity disks, and took his paybook. I saw his name was Leslie Burns. We lined the grave with

---

17 Mitchell, *Tom's War*, p.117.
18 Mitchell, *Tom's War*, p.119.

a blanket and carefully placed him on it ... I climbed into the grave and bent his arms across his chest. I must have expelled air from his lungs as [I crossed his arms] because he emitted a loud moan.[19]

No doubt exhausted, Tom was lucky to receive a slice of bread with Cape Gooseberry jam and a cup of hot coffee, but 'a salvo of shells landed. I dove flat, and the coffee and bread and jam landed in the dirt.'[20]

At last, on the morning of 5 November, they woke up to silence. Climbing out of their foxholes, many of them went to look for souvenirs. It was then that they were confronted by a group of Italians with a white flag. In broken English, the captives made it clear that they wanted to go to Zonderwater, a large prisoner of war camp near Pretoria where thousands of Italians were held since 1941.

As if the South Africans had not had enough of explosions, they put up a fireworks display that night. For them, a time of rest lay ahead at home, but in Tom's mind's eye, he could still see the sights that bore no description, '...like the 88mm gun that had been knocked out, probably in the opening barrage, and the bits of the crew were still laying around, covered with flies. A mutilated body that has been lying around in the hot sun for a couple of weeks is not a beautiful sight.'[21]

When his leave came to an end and it was time to return to war, this time to Italy, Tom once again had the nagging feeling that he would never see his mother again. Yet, he accepted this as by then he and many of his friends had developed a 'fatalistic attitude in action.'[22]

They did not go to Italy immediately, but spent 9 months in North Africa training and preparing for what was to come. They arrived in Italy in April 1944. He was now part of the 6th South African Armoured Division, and a member of an infantry battalion in an armoured brigade in C Company, under Major Oscar Strauss, who in turn, was under 'the brilliant' Lieutenant Colonel E. G. Papa Brits of the 6th South African Division.

They approached the Italian battlefields from the heel of Italy and made quick progress to the Cassino mountains south of Rome. There they were to relieve the Canadian troops who had been fighting in the front line for more than a month. The Abbey of Monte Cassino had already been destroyed, but the battle continued. On 11 May 1944, Tom experienced a barrage, 'which reverberated in the mountains for nearly eight hours [which] was far more impressive' than in the battle at Alamein.

When they moved past the town of Cassino, they saw, 'the wonderful defensive line the Germans had had. They'd been virtually blown out of it by our artillery...' Yet, the need for night patrols remained, bringing with it the danger of minefields and detection by the enemy:

> In Italy we were often much closer to the enemy than we'd been in the desert. Night patrols were quite different and very exhausting. In the Cassino line we sometimes crawled all night; we could occasionally hear

---

19 Mitchell, *Tom's War*, p.122.
20 Mitchell, *Tom's War*, p.122.
21 Mitchell, *Tom's War*, p.127.
22 Mitchell, *Tom's War*, p.131.

> Jerry and presumably he could hear us but we rarely saw each other. There were mines all over: jumping jacks [s-mines] or little Schu mines that would go off if you looked at them … we learnt to walk far apart from each other, fifteen to twenty yards at least, so that only one would get it. Our eyes had to be all round us, in the back of our heads, under our feet and up in the trees above. We lived on our nerves. So many men were needed to keep watch that we never got enough sleep … time meant nothing. Survival was everything. Men got leaner and leaner. They dropped out by ones and twos, killed or wounded.[23]

The German forces were retreating towards the North of Italy, but behind them they left booby traps and mines in every conceivable and inconceivable place. Initially they mined the paths, then they connected mines with tripwires in the crops alongside the paths. Cherry trees were also lined with wires, and when men pulled down branches to get to the ripe cherries, they were obliterated. Farmhouse kitchens became death traps, with the Germans setting their devices in such a way as to only go off when the room was full of people. As a result, Tom and his men searched, 'every bush, house or haystack, by either burning it down or firing into it.'[24]

Tom made it all the way to Rome, and his unit entered the city on the day after it had been taken by the Allied forces. He remembered flowers and kisses from liberated Italians, and feeling like a 'Roman Emperor at a triumph' until his second in command ordered him to take over at the 'wireless' so that he could take Tom's place on the scout car. On the same day, they began their journey towards Civita Castellana, 'where for us, the real war was about to begin.'[25]

Less than 10 miles away, Tom's war came to an end. Although the South African forces took the town of Chiusi from the Germans at the end of June, Tom was 'knocked out early.'[26] More than that he would not share, but he spent six weeks in the No. 2 British Hospital, with both legs in splints. Determined to return to the battle, he was told that the chances of him walking 'in a straight line' were minimal, and slowly he began to accept the fact that he would never again join his fellow combatants.

While forced into inactivity, Tom received intermittent news of his unit's progress over the course of his recovery. The news was never good. Most of his friends were killed in action in less than a month's time. Tom did not record the events that led to his wounds, and he never completed his memoirs. However, his reminiscences left a clue as to his subsequent silence on the topic of war:

> Active war is a messy business: your friends may be killed or wounded, and you pick up the pieces. Dead bodies aren't attractive, especially when

---

23 Mitchell, *Tom's War*, p.142–143.
24 Mitchell, *Tom's War*, p.143.
25 Mitchell, *Tom's War*, p.145.
26 Mitchell, *Tom's War*, p.149.

Allied forces entering Rome (Photo: Marianne Cilliers)

they've been lying in the sun for a week or more, so it's important not to become emotional...[27]

After Alamein, Tom tried to make sense of war. He wanted to know why men willingly entered battles when they knew they may die. When he dictated his memoirs in 1995 and 1996, he pondered on the motive and realised:

> ...men had been doing so since the dawn of history and presumably would continue doing so. I'd like to think that it's because their life is so good they want to protect it for their wives and families but if you read about the appalling conditions on Nelson's ships and the armies of bygone days, it becomes clear that there must be some other motive. I don't know what it is.[28]

---

27 Mitchell, *Tom's War*, p.131.
28 Mitchell, *Tom's War*, p.133.

9

Gerard Gafney and the Royal Natal Carbineers

Although he was the youngest of three brothers, Gerard Gafney did not hesitate to volunteer when the war began. His two older brothers, Stewart and Harden also joined the UDF, but it was Gerard who would serve in East Africa, Abyssinia, the Western Desert and in Italy.

In 1939 he had no idea what he had let himself in for, but by the time he arrived in Italy in April 1944, he already had the Military Medal pinned on his chest.

The medal confirmed to him what he already knew, he was tough enough to face the enemy head-on, and he had luck on his side. He also felt confident to draw a few conclusions about war, based on his experiences in Africa. He believed, for example, that the Abyssinian Campaign was a 'bow and arrow war,' that General Ritchie 'shouldn't have been a general, he should have been a corporal,' and that taking pot-shots at the Germans trying to supply their units at Halfaya Pass, was 'a wonderful game while it lasted!'[1]

Gerard Gafney in uniform. (Photo: Guy Gafney)

After the war, Gerard compared the Abyssinian Campaign with those of the Western Desert and Italy. For him, East Africa and Abyssinia was inconsequential and that, 'those who had taken part in Abyssinia only, it wasn't very complimentary to them.'[2] Perhaps for that reason, he skipped over these campaigns and began the dictation of his memoir from the time when he arrived in Egypt to prepare for the battles in the Western Desert.

---

1   Gafney, G. Oral reminiscences.
2   Gafney, G. Oral reminiscences.

Gerard with his two brothers, Stewart and Harden, and their mother. (Photo: Guy Gafney)

The Natal Mounted Rifles (NMR) was his first military home, but when the Western Desert campaign began he was transferred to the 6th South Africa Armoured Cars. When the Divisions were reorganised for the Italian campaign, Gerard requested to join the RNC. It was the camaraderie among the Carbineers that stayed with him long after the war, because, 'you always knew whatever jam you'd be in you could rely on these chaps to help you if they possibly could.'[3]

But before he became familiar with the Carbineers, he had a long and hard war waiting for him in the Western Desert. The 6th Armoured Car Regiment, to which Gerard was attached after the campaign in East Africa, arrived in Egypt in June 1941. There the 11th Hussars helped them with training.[4]

In one of their first encounters with Rommel's *Afrika Korps*, the armoured cars experienced confusion, something that did not bode well for future encounters with the formidable German forces.[5]

Yet Gerard was very happy to be one of the armoured car guys. Writing to his brother Harden a few months earlier from somewhere near Harar, Gerard's frustration at not getting into the regiment at first was evident, 'I was getting a transfer to an armoured car regiment, only some bastard sat on my application until the regiment embarked without me. Capt. Frikker … was going to work it for me. I would have kept 3 stripes too.'[6]

---

3   G. Gafney, Oral reminiscences.
4   Harry Klein, *Springboks in Armour: The South African Armoured Cars in World War II* (Cape Town: Purnell & Sons, 1965), pp.150–51.
5   Harry Klein, *Springboks in Armour*, p.217.
6   Gerard Gafney to Harden Gafney, 24 July 1941.

Searching for the enemy. Gerard can be seen atop the last vehicle.
(Photo: Guy Gafney)

A short while later, Gerard did join the Armoured Cars, and wrote to Harden again:

> As you can see I had to forfeit my stripes to get into this unit, but it is worth it in a way. None of those NMR fellows will be able to bullshit me about action, as I've already been in a couple of air raids while at one of those places you frequently hear mentioned in the news.[7]

Although Gerard seemed to remember only the 'fantastic experiences' in the desert, his first experience of battle against German forces was an eye-opener, as it had been for so many other UDF men whose combat experience was limited to the small scale clashes against the Italians in East Africa:

> The Jerries came over at about 1.20 am and the first bomb woke us all with a hell of a start. The wild Irish fellow who sleeps next to me reckons "the game is on" (also his first baptismal fire). We put on our steel helmets and lay flat where we were and watched the search lights and ack [anti-aircraft guns] giving old jerry a go. He dropped two big bombs and about five little ones and then pissed off.[8] Except for the fellows directly hit, nothing much was damaged. We all lay fascinated by the whole affair and hoped jerry didn't come any closer. It was only ½ hour later that I felt windup and realised what a bastard game we'd just watched. All the fellows reckoned, "so this is war eh?"

---

7   Gerard Gafney to Harden Gafney, 22 October 1941.
8   Gerard Gafney to Harden Gafney, 22 October 1941.

A blast clearing away somewhere near Halfaya Pass, 1941. (Photo: Guy Gafney)

From then on, Gerard was ready for anything. He remembered how, early in the mornings, the light would be in their favour to attack the Germans, and in the evening, the situation was turned around and the 8th Army would be on the receiving end.

One night, after surrounding a German garrison at Halfaya Pass and taking about 7,000 prisoners, Gerard remembered how:

> Some of our chaps went mad at that stage, they had come across some German and Italian hooch and great celebrations went on. I think the Germans if they had tried could have taken us prisoners at the end of that first night, however they'd had enough of war anyway, and so it went by quite peacefully. But during the night two of our chaps who were well oiled, decided that they would fight a duel, and armed with 38s or 45s they enacted a duel for our benefits, and it was only after they'd fired 2 or 3 shots that they realised it was dangerous and gave up the game.[9]

This was the same battle that the three brothers of the DMR referred to as the 'Hellfire business', also the one which De Villiers Graaff narrowly missed. As Gerard recalled, '…during this period S. A. troops suffered very badly, the Irish Brigade was just about wiped out, and the artillery suffered severely.'[10] It was also during that time that his brother Stewart was taken prisoner, and although Gerard only received

---

9 G. Gafney, Oral reminiscences.
10 G. Gafney, Oral reminiscences.

the news some time later, he knew then that the, 'war really started to look ugly for us.' Yet, luck also played a part in his survival.

The highlight of Gerard's desert experience was when, single-handedly, he almost ended the life of Hitler's favourite general at the time.[11] Remembering this event, Gerard said:

> We were on our forward reporting position of German columns and things, when out of the German column came a VW buggy, and in it there stood a man standing right up in his black desert jacket and his typical peaked cap with his glasses over the top of the cap, with a great big pair of binoculars observing the scene, and that was General Rommel himself. There was no mistaking him! When I saw this I ran across from my armoured car to Lt Richards who was our troop commander, and said to him "Sir, do you see Rommel?" and he said, "By God you're right!" "Can I have a go at him?" and he said, "Certainly", so I turned my armoured car around backwards because the anti-tank gun was bolted on the cars' behind and loaded the 47mm gun we had on there and trained it on Rommel's vehicle. I had him beautifully in my triangle but I'd misjudged the range, and I'd put him at 1500 yards and he must have been even closer, because my shell fell between his front wheels and skidded away into the distance, where we could see the tracer winding away. Needless to say I could only get 2 shots off, with the 1st one Rommel's vehicle spun around and ran back to the big column, and with the 2nd attempt the German mark 4 tanks opened up on us and we had to run for our lives once more and beat a hasty retreat, but that was something really worthwhile.[12]

Clearly, Gerard was fearless, courageous, and more than a little ruthless. However, his attitude towards the Germans was most probably a result of things he had seen in battle. Like many others who took the time to share their memories of the war, Gerard did not include every detail, but in some cases, conclusions can be drawn from what was left out.[13]

While out on patrol one night, Gerard saw two German trucks trying to find their way back to their base. Gerard's patrol quickly took aim and, in his words:

> It was like watching a greyhound racing. The first shell fell about 15 yards short of the Germans and they turned to run and the artillery dropped the next one in front of them. And so it went on back and forth, back and forth. Eventually they hit the truck and it burst into flames and the Gerries [Germans] in the truck piled out and started to run across the desert, with the artillery having a wonderful time dropping these big 5.5 shells on the chaps. When they started off there were about 7 or 8 of them running, but

---

11   Rommel was implicated in a plot to kill Hitler, and in 1944 became a victim of Hitler's revenge. Ian F. Beckett, *Rommel: A Reappraisal* (Barnsley: Pen & Sword, 2013), p.137.
12   G. Gafney, Oral reminiscences.
13   Gerard Gafney dictated his memoirs.

eventually there was only one poor bugger running, and he eventually disappeared. He had either fallen into a slip trench or he'd been killed as well. That was just by the by.[14]

It goes without saying that the 8th Army command had to know of every German movement, and Gerard's unit played a crucial role in this. After all, the 8th Army was there to stop the *Afrika Korps* and the Italians, and Britain was hell-bent on keeping Egypt and the Suez Canal, and thus prevent the Axis from gaining access to the oil they needed to fight the war.[15]

The terrain in North-Eastern Libya is marked by hills and the occasional rocky cliffs, and as Gerard's experience shows, the different forces could be creeping up the side of a dune only to come face to face with each other at the top. However, the patrols were necessary and Gerard became remarkably fearless while scanning the desert for Germans. Late in the afternoon of 26 May 1942, the beginning of the Battle of Gazala, Gerard's patrol became aware of movement from the North:

> A bloody great column of cloud and dust appeared, and a terrible noise … I thought, "Oooh what the hell's this?" At first we thought it was another of these Gypo [Egyptian] desert storms, but it was just this great column of tanks. Once more there were 3 little armoured cars sitting out there reporting this to the [defensive] box, … and a German armoured car, a 6 wheeler came charging out, very brave because of this mighty column of maybe 500 tanks behind them and once more Captain Richards said to me, "Give that bloke a go while the going's good", so once more we swung the cars around, [the first round struck under the front wheels and] we fired a second round and the German tanks opened up and we had to beat it.

They reached the Northumbrian Division defensive box through a gap in the minefields. With just enough time to fill up with ammunition, food and fuel, the Germans began their attack in earnest. By 11 p.m. Rommel's forces had broken through the defensive line and it was a case of 'each man for himself.' That was the night that Gerard earned his Military Medal.

Gerard's description of the events that led to his medal is vague, but his citation reads as follows:

> In the Gazala area, Trooper Gafney who was a crew commander of his car, forced a way through the enemy lines on the night of Sunday 14th June '42. Shortly after he had set out, he ran into enemy outposts which were cleared away by machine-gun fire from the cars. He was then faced by an anti-tank position containing two or three anti-tank weapons, which were firing at him and threatened to stop his advance. Trooper Gafney drove his car straight at this obstacle without hesitation and kept the enemy from firing

---

14 G. Gafney, Oral reminiscences.
15 S. Morewood. 'Protecting the jugular vein of empire: The Suez Canal in British defence strategy, 1919–1941', *War & Society* 10:1 (1992), pp.101–102.

Shaking out a blanket after a desert dust storm. (Photo: Guy Gafney)

with his machine-gun, finally over running the post and permanently putting it out of action. The promptness and disregard for consequences with which this action was carried out probably saved other vehicles from being hit.[16]

While retreating towards El Alamein, during the so-called 'Gazala Gallop,' Gerard's crew escaped German encirclements and death on more than one occasion. They were also ordered, twice, to turn back westwards towards the German line. Again they were called on to report the positions of the German forces, this allowed the British forces to prepare for the main battle while also attacking the German advance forces. On one occasion:

> …our 3 armoured cars were on patrol, Lt. Richards in charge again, when over the ridge at Tel el Eisa (the hell of Jesus) appeared 3 or 4 German tanks, the first of the leading attacking troops and later two 88s. We saw them turn around and unhitch their two 88s and dig them in, we reported this. They [8th Army] gave the Germans about 2 hours to get themselves dug in and unlimbered and then they put our artillery barrage onto them, and there were Huns [Germans] running around in all directions. They hitched up the 2 88s and they disappeared over the hills from where they'd come. That was the first of many such probes by German tanks.[17]

Tom Mitchell experienced the same barrage that signalled the beginning of the Battle of El Alamein. Just like Tom Mitchell, Gerard remembered the sights and sounds of that battle:

---

16 The National Archives, Kew. WO/373/21. July 1942.
17 G. Gafney, Oral reminiscences.

Christmas lunch in the desert, 1942. (Photo: Guy Gafney)

As you can imagine on our side all hell was let loose, the night sky was lit up as in daylight and there was no point in trying to hide because it was dangerous wherever you were [five days later] we were then told to follow through the cleared mine fields and decimate the remaining Germans, which we did with great glee after the number of times we'd been on the receiving end.[18]

The armoured cars spent the next week searching for Germans who were unfortunate to have missed the main retreat from El Alamein. The 6th Armoured Car Regiment, with whom Gerard was serving, ended the battle with 1 man killed in action, 14 wounded and 43 missing. Of their 40 armoured cars they lost 12, and 34 transport cars out of 68.[19]

Once the British 8th Army sent Rommel back towards the west, Gerard was sent off to tank training school in Cairo. Two months later, he found himself on leave in South Africa, his first visit home in three years.

It was then that his life changed dramatically when he crossed paths with a 'beautiful blonde'. Her name was Sheldine, and because there was no time to waste, they got married six weeks later. On board the ship that took him north, he had time to reflect on this recent experiences. Writing to Sheldine in September 1943, it was clear he had little patience with the,

> amazing restrictions and foolish parades … I think the person responsible for them must have a grudge against all mankind. However, 3½ years in the

---

18 G. Gafney, Oral reminiscences.
19 Harry Klein, *Springboks in Armour*, p.263.

army & one can endure most things … I find going up North when single & married are two very different things. I sit and think about & long for you all day long. I never thought it could be so hard…[20]

With the 6th South African Armoured Division getting ready for the Italian campaign, Gerard would have to find a way to focus on what was in front of him instead of what lay behind him in South Africa. A long training period in Cairo awaited him and the rest of the division, but for Gerard this was not something that interested him and he confessed to Sheldine that he was, 'tired of learning army rubbish & would almost prefer to be in the field again.'[21] Yet, his declarations of love and longing dwarfed his occasional complaints about life in the military.

By the end of 1943 Gerard was looking forward to going home and seeing Sheldine again, but by this time his longing for her was balanced by his sense of duty, writing on 31 December, 'May you & I be re–united as early as possible in the new year after the Jerries have been defeated.'[22] This feeling did not last long, and two weeks later Gerard admitted that his 'fondness' of her was preventing him from being a 'keen soldier.'[23]

In April 1944 the 6th Division was transferred to Italy, but Gerard's first letter to Sheldine only arrived in her post box in mid–May. He was now with B Company of the RNC and served under Major Thornhill. Apart from the Italian landscapes, there was nothing that appealed to Gerard.

Even before he arrived in Italy, he had made up his mind about the Italians, and he wrote to Sheldine, 'Jacko is funny. We were talking about malnutrition & the lack of vitamins causing rickets amongst the people of Europe. So he says "Yes, they need more vitamin .303, .792 & 75." i.e. kill the lot. Mind you, I wouldn't miss the Itis.'[24]

It was also in March 1944 that he felt optimistic about the war coming to an end soon, his Major estimated, 'the Jerries will crack up within six months. I hope he is right, though the Russians aren't leaving it to chance.'[25] Shortly before setting off to Italy, Gerard wrote that some of his men were to become riflemen, but as he had no infantry training, he would go on reserve. He was trying to put Sheldine's worries to rest, but the devastation left its mark on him and years later when he recalled the events of 1944, he said, 'everywhere buildings had been flattened by artillery fire, huge bomb craters were to be seen and we knew that we were in for a hard time.'[26]

During the first weeks in Italy, Gerard believed the Italians to be hardworking people, but that was the extent of their positive qualities. To his credit, he did realise that the Italians were the way he perceived them as a result of, 'the war & Musso & hunger.'[27] It was the first time he saw the consequences of war on civilians and the effect it had when it moved from the frontline to the home front.

---

20 Personal correspondence, Gerard Gafney to Sheldine Gafney, 16 September 1943.
21 Personal correspondence, Gerard Gafney to Sheldine Gafney, 8 October 1943.
22 Personal correspondence, Gerard Gafney to Sheldine Gafney, 31 December 1943.
23 Personal correspondence, Gerard Gafney to Sheldine Gafney, 14 January 1944.
24 Personal correspondence, Gerard Gafney to Sheldine Gafney, 31 March 1944.
25 Personal correspondence, Gerard Gafney to Sheldine Gafney, 31 March 1944
26 G. Gafney, Oral reminiscences.
27 Personal correspondence, Gerard Gafney to Sheldine Gafney, 11 May 1944.

The division began its journey from Taranto in the south and then went towards Matera and from there to Monte Cassino. Then it was Rome and Florence followed by six weeks' rest, much-needed after travelling about 840 kilometres.[28]

Although their first few days were quiet, the patrols would soon start again, this time over high mountains and deep valleys. This new terrain would prove a difficult obstacle in their way, and the mountains of Italy would stay in their memories for a long time afterwards. As the South Africans assessed their new environment, the British 8th Army and the American 5th Army had already seen heavy fighting in Sicily and Italy in September the year before.

When they moved north from Florence, it was under the American 5th Army command. At Pistoia, Gerard's regiment was ordered to push the Germans beyond their defensive Gothic Line. Lucca was the next rest area before they moved onwards to Bologna. They were in Italy a full year before the German forces began disintegrating with the final capitulation on 29 April 1945. The news only reached the South Africans on 2 May, when the surrender became effective.[29]

In what was probably Gerard's first patrol in Italy, his unit was ordered to find out more about the opposing troops. Gerard selected a few men, including his platoon sergeant, and set off towards where a German unit had settled in a farmhouse. Watching the enemy for about 30 minutes, Gerard and his sergeant decided that the Germans must have been, 'having a vino or two [and Gerard suggested] "What do you say we give those guys a crack?"' They moved forward with the intention to 'flatten whatever was in the house.'[30]

As they came within about 50 yards of the house, they had to climb up the bank of a donga, and for some reason, 'burst out laughing.' Obviously the Germans heard them, and all hell broke loose:

> I ran forward with my Tommy gun and the next thing a German jumped out of the scrub and ran, I let fly at him from the hip and down he went, but he got up and ran again out of my view. I followed and for morale's sake fired a burst of Thompson machine-gun fire and replaced the magazine. Just then from the other side of the house I heard two rifle shots and then another one. We ran forward and came across the German I'd hit in the first instance, with a very severe wound to his hip and no fight left in him. I then came across Corporal Shewan who was searching a dead German, and I said to him, "Oh good show Willie, wonderful shot", and he said to me "*Dis asof ons bokke geskiet het.*"[31] We'd done our job…

The first great battle site that Gerard and his fellow RNC members would have seen in Italy was Monte Cassino. The Allied forces had been trying to dislodge the Germans from the Abbey on the mountain since January 1944, and when the South Africans arrived the fourth battle at the site was about to commence. Although they

---

28 Ian van der Waag, *A Military History of Modern South Africa*, p.208.
29 Ian van der Waag, *A Military History of Modern South Africa*, p.209.
30 G. Gafney, Oral reminiscences.
31 It was as if we were shooting buck.

did not participate in this intense battle, Gerard and his friends were ordered to hold the line to the north-east of Cassino, along with the 12th South Africa Infantry Brigade.[32] Recently appointed as Rifle Platoon commander, Gerard watched from a nearby mountain what was happening at Monte Cassino. He was impressed by the huge German shells that landed in a valley below him, 'with a hell of a bang, and gave those base wallers [sic] behind us a hell of a time.'[33]

Watching the battle from afar did not hold his attention for long, and as he could not write to Sheldine in too much detail about where he was or what he was doing, he found something else with which to amuse himself during the long hours:

> While I was up in the cramped dugout of mine … I had nothing to do, apart from organising that we had sentries and so on … There were a lot of chameleons running up and down, and I decided that I would do some fishing so I found a little stick somewhere and I made a noose [with a string] at the end of the stick and I used to lasso these chameleons and once I'd had a look at them I'd let them go again, but there was one big chap there and he was a very shrewd guy. You know I couldn't catch him for days and I thought well you blighter, seeing I've got so much time here I'm going to catch you before we leave … I twiddled my fingers and made a big diversion and sure enough he looked that way at my fingers and I had the noose over his head. Boy was he cross, he wriggled and fought, anyway I put him down and let him go.[34]

More sinister was his memory of the steel wires set by the German forces across the roads. At night, the various units used Jeeps to carry messages from one base to another, and as they raced along, the wires would, in Gerard's recollection, decapitate those in the vehicle. They overcame that problem by fixing angled iron rods to the front bumpers to catch the wires before they could do any damage.

Not one for sticking to rules, his wish to write to Sheldine about his experiences got the better of him and on 7 May 1944 he wrote:

> I hope the old censor won't put me inside for writing this letter … sooner or later old Jannie or one of those ridiculous SG War Correspondents will short [sic] it all out so here goes … things are not too hot on our sector, just at the moment I can hear the most terrific artillery duel a few miles away. I say duel, but the jerries are getting the thin end of it … the jerries usually warms us up from 3 to 4 am each day just to let us know they are still there. Then we reply just twice as fiercely. One thing that is very noticeable here, the fact that there just aren't any jerry planes to worry us. We see the occasional Spitfire & of course tons of bombers going over to shake all the hun cities. Also here, no one moves about in daytime (to do so is asking for trouble) … I am writing this inside my dugout which is a very good one

---

32   James Holland, *Italy's Sorrow*, p.218.
33   G. Gafney, Oral reminiscences.
34   G. Gafney, Oral reminiscences.

GERARD GAFNEY AND THE ROYAL NATAL CARBINEERS   133

Gerard (left) and two friends in Rome. (Photo: Guy Gafney)

[it is] well hidden amongst oak & olive trees [I have] jam & biscuits inside it, my water bottle, webbing, binoculars, compass, maps & some hand grenades & my pistol which I keep next to me … You needn't worry about me as I 'aint' scared (yet)… [35]

---

35 Gerard included a drawing of his dugout in the letter. Personal correspondence, Gerard Gafney to Sheldine Gafney, 7 May 1944.

Gerard did not post the letter until he was 'allowed to', after all, he was responsible for censoring the letters of the men in his platoon.[36]

The victory at Monte Cassino was crucial as it paved the way towards Rome. The South Africans were at the forefront of the advance to Rome.[37] At 3 a.m. on 4 June, Gerard wrote to Sheldine that 'things are going well up here, but the jerries are using thousands of mines on the roads as they retreat & lifting & detecting these slows up our advance considerably … the news this morning says that the 5th Army is only 12 miles from Rome.'[38]

Three days later, Gerard wrote excitedly about Operation Overlord and the opening of the second front:

> It has taken so long to come that I wasn't surprised when I heard it. The same day I passed through Rome, one day after it had fallen & with some jerry snipers still in the city. As the jerries didn't make a real stand at Rome, it is almost undamaged. The Itis of Rome lined the streets on either side for miles on end & waved & threw flowers at the troops as we went through … we didn't waste any time there as we have a busy time catching up with the squareheads, they are retreating so fast … I am sorry that I am no longer in armoured cars or tanks as there are glorious opportunities of mowing down the retreating squareheads these days.[39]

Years later, Gerard's memories of Rome did not include the celebratory convoys through the streets of the city. He remembered how, 'A string of women probably about a mile long, ladies of easy virtue, lined up there waiting for the soldiers to come along. You could have cigarettes, or bully or a little slab of chocolate to trade for their favours.'[40]

Another memory that stayed with him was the children, begging for food at every chance they had. In Gerard's estimation, he never ate one of his ration issue chocolates, but gave them all away; 'It was absolutely amazing to see the joy with which these kids used to eat these chocolates.'[41]

From Rome, the next major objective was Florence, and the 6th Armoured Division reached this city a month after they had entered Rome. Writing to Sheldine on the eve of the liberation of Florence, he was optimistic about the placement of their guns around the city. With the seemingly smooth progress, Gerard was convinced that he would be home by Christmas and looking forward to his first 'romp' with his wife, especially since a 'fetching young [Italian] wench of about 20' was not doing him any good, as he admitted in a letter.[42]

A few days later he shared the news that he:

---

36 Personal correspondence, Gerard Gafney to Sheldine Gafney, 11 May 1944.
37 Ian van der Waag, *A Military History of Modern South Africa*, p.207.
38 Personal correspondence, Gerard Gafney to Sheldine Gafney, 4 June 1944.
39 Personal correspondence, Gerard Gafney to Sheldine Gafney, 7 June 1944.
40 G. Gafney, Oral reminiscences.
41 G. Gafney, Oral reminiscences.
42 Personal correspondence, Gerard Gafney to Sheldine Gafney, 31 July 1944.

Heard them say that the Kiwis were only 4 miles from Florence & today I know that the SAS are the first troops into Florence. Good show eh? … I'm afraid I had to dash off as two of my chaps trod on a German anti-personnel mine. What fiendish things they are. Full of nails, bits of iron etc…[43]

From Pistoia, 55 kilometres north of Florence, the South Africans moved out to drive the Germans over the Gothic Line. It was at this time that Gerard's colonel asked him to take a patrol to Monte Vigese. This mountain stood in their way to Monte Sole and further on to Bologna, an important city. North of Gerard and the rest of the South Africans was the German *16. SS-Panzergrenadier-Division*.

Veggio now lay before them, with various mountain tops encircling the small town like a protective barrier.[44] Veggio is tantalising close to Bologna, but the weather deteriorated as winter progressed, and the Apennine Mountain range made tank warfare almost impossible. So, Gerard and the rest of the Carbineers found themselves taking on infantry roles more often than not.[45]

The day before the South Africans received their orders, Gerard wrote to Sheldine that they had no shelter from wind or rain and that it had:

> …rained without a break for seven days now … the last 20 hours my platoon & I spent on the top of a peak 3,200ft high with no shelter from wind or rain. I've seldom spent a more miserable night … We had the nearest jerries only 200 yds from us, so you can imagine we stayed on the alert until we'd got rid of them. I had good fun directing our artillery onto these huns by means of my telephone.[46]

Following this letter there is a gap in the stream of letters of at least two weeks. Gerard had a cold, and the Germans still held most of the mountains in the area.

When new orders came through, they were told that four brigades would hold Mount Vigese, Stanco and Salvaro. D Company and Gerard's B Company of the RNC made their move on 10 October and reached their objective early in the morning. Soon after, however, the Germans began a counter-attack, which set off a tremendous fire from the Royal Durban Light Infantry. Despite their efforts to halt the German troops, one platoon of D Company was overrun. As the day progressed, and with a non–stop German assault, B and D Companies were ordered to withdraw.[47]

Among the most challenging objects for the Carbineers at this time was Hill 826. It was here that many UDF men would endure the worst experiences of the war. The South Africans were ordered to hold the hill.

---

43 Personal correspondence, Gerard Gafney to Sheldine Gafney, 4 August 1944.
44 James Holland, *Italy's Sorrow*, pp.404 & 411.
45 James Holland, *Italy's Sorrow*, p.372; Ian van der Waag, *A Military History of Modern South Africa*, p.207.
46 Personal correspondence, Gerard Gafney to Sheldine Gafney, 9 October 1944.
47 J. C. von Winterbach et al, '6th South African Armoured Division (part 3)', *Flames of War*, https://www.flamesofwar.com/Default.aspx?tabid=112&art_id=4402, accessed 17 January 2025.

One event that stood out for Gerard was a patrol day. At about 3 p.m., Gerard set off on a patrol. The misty weather was to their advantage and as long as they were silent, they could make their way up the mountain, laying low whenever the mist cleared. When Gerard could see the Germans, he decided to turn back and inform his colonel. As the actual attack took place, Gerard was not among his men, but was ordered to keep everyone informed of any movements by the Germans; Gerard heard the guns as A Company led the advance along three routes.

Later, Gerard learnt that:

> Tich Francis had got to the top of the hill and caught 20 Germans all asleep in that defensive position that I'd visited the afternoon before. The whole episode had been a fantastic success, so that was one job I'd done well. Tich collected an MC, the Colonel collected an MC and Joe Soap was said thank you for the information.[48]

Nine Germans were taken prisoner and the result was that the Germans withdrew from their stronghold.[49]

It was on Hill 826 that Gerard saw more than a few gruesome sights, one of which involved his OC. He was inspecting a map, along with Major Thornhill and a Corporal Clark, when, out of the blue, the corporal's forehead burst open, covering Gerard in blood and brain matter. It must have been a sniper's bullet or shrapnel, Gerard did not know, nor did he have time to find out. They got the body to the regimental aid post, but the stretcher bearers decided that from then on they would not go over the Hill again. It took some convincing from Gerard to get them to do their job.[50]

As if that was not enough, a mortar shell hit their headquarters. Gerard was very close to where the shell hit, and when he regained his senses, he saw that:

> Major Tomlinson was lying dead... Another young chap, I can't remember his name, he was dead, and the medical corporal, a chap called Holmes was sitting on a bank quite close by, and I went to this corporal and said, "For God's sake corporal why don't you do something about these chaps' injuries," and he did nothing and I gave him a little push and he fell over he was also dead, a piece of shrapnel had gone right through his chest. Well I then found myself as commander of B Co in a hell of a situation.[51]

On another occasion, Gerard recalled that A Company found themselves closer to Monte Sole itself. They were about to be relieved by another unit, but Kendall Brooke, the man in charge of the patrol, went further up the hill. It was cold and

---

48 G. Gafney, Oral reminiscences.
49 J.C. von Winterbach et al., '6th South African Armoured Division (part 3),' *Flames of War*, https://www.flamesofwar.com/Default.aspx?tabid=112&art_id=4402, accessed 17 January 2025.
50 G. Gafney, Oral reminiscences.
51 G. Gafney, Oral reminiscences.

dark, and the sounds of men moving around created confusion. Unfortunately for Kendall, he walked straight into a German patrol. A hand-to-hand fight for survival broke out and Kendall was shot in the face at close range, the bullet going straight through.[52]

Gerard heard the story the next day, and he was told that, 'because [Kendall] was yelling in terror at the time the bullet had gone right through his cheek and out the other side, and hadn't even damaged his teeth.'[53]

This was one more Carbineer put out of action. Kendall was taken prisoner and spent the rest of the war in a POW camp.

Getting closer to Bologna, near Cà di Cò, Gerard thanked his lucky stars for his excellent night vision, they were doing night patrols in an area where German land mines were especially plentiful. In general, the patrols began at 10 p.m. and ended at about 3 or 4 a.m. Gerard also remembered that some patrols never made it back to the headquarters, and on one occasion, he almost did not return either:

> there was a sunken road leading to Cà di Cò and I was walking along with my patrol behind me, when all of a sudden the bank under my feet collapsed and I fell about nine feet or so. As I landed on the path at the bottom the earth was still tumbling down the side of the bank. I thought I heard footsteps … my heart thumping loudly in my chest. It wasn't very long when I heard … the typical sound of German jack boots coming along. Not only that but I could hear a characteristic ta ting, ta ting ta ting. That perfectly identified who was coming along, because German troops always had gas masks on them [and they] knocked against their rifle barrels …
>
> The only thing I could do was crouch and hide myself and hope that they wouldn't see me and if they did, let them have it with everything I've got … However, the Germans were quite happily walking along the path and they tramped past me … When they were about half way past me I thought well now I have a chance, I could kill the lot of them … I had to make up my mind whether to be a hero, or maybe a dead hero. At the last minute I decided that a lot of these soldiers were only 18 years old and they were some mothers' precious sons and I let them go and they went on down the path, past me … While all this was happening my corporal was walking up and down the bank shouting, *"God waar is die blerrie lieutenant?"*[54]

In every letter home Gerard wrote optimistically about the war ending soon, before Christmas. By the end of October, however, he realised that it would take some time yet, writing to Sheldine:

> Just at the moment all life seems pretty futile & the realisation that I have another winter of bitter war in front of me doesn't help much. I wish to God you'd stop defending the blasted Navy. Because you have a soft spot for

---

52 Holland, *Italy's Sorrow*, p.436.
53 G. Gafney, Oral reminiscences.
54 God where is the bloody lieutenant? G. Gafney, Oral reminiscences.

that bunch of Tommies, I haven't & lets leave it at that … [I] sat by the fire & it didn't seem possible that a few days before we had been mixed up in a terrible battle.[55]

He concluded his letter the next day by apologising that she, 'caught the backwash of [his] frayed nerves.'[56] Over the past month, Gerard had been enduring a tough time with the German forces 'worrying' them. Most of his letters were written from a slit trench, somewhere on the Apennines, with him and his 'old fellows' holding their positions. By now he was thoroughly aware of the 'horror of war.'[57] On 27 October he wrote that he had just been,

…through a week of hell. I am glad it is all over and we are resting behind the line in a warm dry "casa" … I am quite well & by the grace of God unscathed, but I am feeling shaken & unhappy … the colonel left us this morning for the Union. He has had a health & nervous crack up & P. Frances is the new colonel.[58]

Hill 826 was indeed a hellish experience, and even into November Gerard was forced to interrupt his letters when his company was 'whipped off into a scrap.' By 14 November, however, he was able to write that he was on leave in Florence, 'safely perched on a lovely soft bed.'[59]

The Apennine Mountain range and the bad weather certainly slowed down the Allied advance through Italy, and the determined German resistance put paid to their plans to capture Bologna during 1944. By mid-December the Carbineers had set up a temporary base near Monte Sole, but Bologna would not come into their scope for at least another five months.[60] In the meantime, Gerard experienced his first white Christmas.

The Carbineers were settled into peasant houses for a few day's rest when Major Thornhill was ordered to report to an American brigadier. Gerard, Jack Wyatt Smith and Bill Bailey went with Thornhill, and while the two officers spoke, Gerard and his two friends waited outside. It was then that Jack spotted a roast fowl on a shelf, and the three men decided that this would be their Christmas Lunch.

Gerard distracted the American corporal who stood nearby, while Bill held the attention of a wireless operator. It was Jack's job to take the fowl and hide it somewhere safe. When Thornhill emerged from his meeting, he told the three fowl thieves that their rest days were over and that they had received instructions to help the Americans. The American brigadier then took them to the base troops, but on the way Gerard decided,

---

55   Personal correspondence, Gerard Gafney to Sheldine Gafney, 29 October 1944.
56   Personal correspondence, Gerard Gafney to Sheldine Gafney, 29 October 1944.
57   Personal correspondence, Gerard Gafney to Sheldine Gafney, 18 and 22 October 1944
58   Personal correspondence, Gerard Gafney to Sheldine Gafney, 27 October 1944.
59   Personal correspondence, Gerard Gafney to Sheldine Gafney, 14 November 1944.
60   Holland, *Italy's Sorrow*, pp.466, 468.

A defensive position somewhere in the Apennines (Photo: Marianne Cilliers)

...that there was no time better than now to eat this fowl. We pulled it out of Jack's bunny jacket and broke off a drumstick or 2, and we all proceeded to chomp this lot. Major Thornhill said, "You buggers never left me any." He could see in the rear view mirror that we were having roast chicken for lunch.[61]

The purpose of the meeting with the American brigadier, according to Gerard, was to 'stop the rot' among the American servicemen who were 'running away on the high ground.' Gerard was not impressed by the American forces and he told of another occasion when an American major tried desperately to stop his troops from running down a hill when they should have been holding the summit. Halfway up the hill, Gerard saw the Major with two revolvers in his hands, '...and as the Yanks ran down the hill, he'd beckon to them and say, "Get back up that hill or I'll blow your brains out." The Yanks then ran up the hill, until they were out of sight of the major and then they'd run down the other side to safety.'[62]

Perhaps Gerard's impression of the Americans was clouded by what he experienced just a few days before. Gerard was leading a platoon which had been reduced

---

61 G. Gafney, Oral reminiscences.
62 G. Gafney, Oral reminiscences.

from 28 men to 17, some had been killed in action, while others had been wounded. As they ascended yet another hill, they came across an American Sherman tank:

> There was a Yank in the turret, which was open, and the engine was running. I wanted to ask this Yank what was going on, what the positions were, but my little friend the American corporal was so frightened that he only stuck his head out every few minutes to see if he was safe , otherwise he kept his head well down in the tank and he didn't answer any questions.[63]

Leaving the American to his own devices, Gerard and his platoon moved on and it was not long before they heard mortars being fired, one after the other, in quick succession. Gerard assumed that it was,

> …one Yank doing his stuff, you can imagine my surprise when I got there and there were no Yanks there, but a little Italian boy of about 14 years old, who was manning the mortar. He could only just lift the mortar shells up and get them in the pipe and smash them down. He was saying "*Morte Tedeschi*" [German death], and he said that he was staying there until he'd used up all the shells. He was going to kill these Germans which was most encouraging.

A few days later, while still holding their position on the hill, the platoon lost one of their members, Charlie, when the Germans closed in around them. As they saw the German forces coming closer, Gerard told his men to let the Germans get as close as they thought was safe, and then to use their grenades on them. By all accounts Charlie was killed by a machine gunner.

A Brazilian brigade relieved them after this, and as they climbed down from the hill, Gerard was hit in the shoulder by shrapnel when,

> …some German chose to mortar us … It rather spun me round and gave me a bit of a fright and my left arm seemed to be a bit numb … I put my hand inside my bunny jacket, because we had a great coat and a leather jacket and a bunny jacket and there was just a mess in there and you get a bit panicky [the wound was] about 1–2 inches along. It turned out to be only a flesh wound, my shoulder seemed to work alright, and once I realised that I didn't worry any more, and we set off…[64]

New Year celebrations came and went, but the progress remained slow. It was only by April 1945 that the Carbineers, still at Monte Sole, began to see that the Germans' days were numbered on that mountain. In the end, it was the Cape Town Highlanders that took Monte Sole, perhaps leaving the Carbineers more than a bit frustrated as they could not claim victory where they had sacrificed so much.[65]

---

63   G. Gafney, Oral reminiscences.
64   G. Gafney, Oral reminiscences.
65   Holland, *Italy's Sorrow,* p.511.

Guy and Sheldine on their wedding day. (Photo: Guy Gafney)

After Monte Sole and the capture of Bologna in the same month, the Germans set off at full speed northwards. The men of the 6th Armoured Division were back in their tanks and pursued them towards Venice, covering more ground than they had in the past six months. By 2 May it was all over; the South Africans had taken 5,176 casualties in Italy, 753 of whom were killed in action.[66] Somewhere along the way, Gerard experienced a second close call when German gunners pinpointed them. Gerard's knee was hit by shrapnel, 'which has given me such hell all these years.'[67] In the greater scheme of things though, he still regarded himself as one of the lucky ones who fought in Italy.

Gerard was writing a letter to Sheldine when he heard of the German surrender in Italy. Unlike most others, Gerard was philosophical about the news, writing to Sheldine, 'I feel that my small contribution has not been in vain, most of the chaps are drunk, but I feel that it is better to sit back and take it all in quietly … we shall soon be together, that is the big thing, isn't it?'[68]

At the time he was staying in a 'casa' once again near the Po River, and they had a, 'couple of bottles of whisky, so even though we were only sitting in a lucerne field we all got a bit on our plonks, and it seemed to be alright.'[69]

As the news sank in, Gerard realised that he would never again receive an order to fight, and he wrote of his relief, because his 'tummy used to turn inside down on occasions.'[70] Yet, in one of his last letters from Italy, Gerard confessed to Sheldine that he could, '…have got out of the army because of my eyes years ago if I had felt so inclined.'[71]

---

66 Van der Waag, *A Military History of Modern South Africa*, pp.209–210.
67 G. Gafney, Oral reminiscences.
68 Personal correspondence, Gerard Gafney to Sheldine Gafney, 2 May 1945.
69 G. Gafney, Oral reminiscences.
70 Personal correspondence, Gerard Gafney to Sheldine Gafney, 7 May 1945.
71 Personal correspondence, Gerard Gafney to Sheldine Gafney, 13 May 1945.

10

Martin van Rooyen, the War Surveyor

Martin volunteered to fight with the UDF on 17 July 1940, but for him the war would only start two years later. It was only in March 1943 that he arrived in Egypt and was posted to the 46 Survey Company of the South Africa Engineer Corps (SAEC).[1] The SAEC field companies supported infantry brigades by securing water supply, making roads passable and building bridges.[2] As a surveyor, Martin's main job was to take photographs and produce maps.

At the age of 22, when he decided to go to war, he had already established himself in the Government's Forestry Department. In essence Martin was not a soldier, but from 1943 until the end of the war he would see the consequences of combat as 46 Survey Company traipsed from west to east along the coastline of Northern Africa.

Martin van Rooyen in uniform.
(Photo: Marianne Cilliers)

At his attestation he signed the oath to serve in Africa, but by 1943 things had changed, and those waiting to leave the Union had to sign an oath to fight anywhere. While signing an oath on paper is an easy matter, carrying out the duties attached to it is more complex. On 16 February 1943 Martin wrote:

> Got up this morning with a headache. Those of us waiting to go appear before the major about the new oath to serve everywhere. I am the first of us to sign, and as far as I know, the first minority in the entire company.[3]

---

1   DOD PF RS, Sgt V. Rooyen, M. F. (176938v) SAEC.
2   Ian van der Waag, 2012. 'The origin and establishment of the South African Engineer Corps (SAEC), 1918 – 1939', *Journal for Contemporary History* 37:2 (2012), pp.30–31.
3   Martin's diary extracts are all translated from Afrikaans. M. F. van Rooyen Diary, 16 February 1943.

For Martin and the others in his company, the future held many uncertainties. By the time he left the Union, the battles in Libya had come to overshadow those victories of the earlier East African campaign. The battles at Bardia, Sidi Rezegh, Tobruk and El Alamein, had been fought with great losses for the South Africans, most notably at Tobruk.

The company left Durban on board the *Selandia* on 28 February 1943. Passing by Aden, they arrived at Suez on 21 March.[4] The months following their arrival were punctuated by relocation after relocation, from one transit camp to the next. Moving between Tewfik, Cairo, Helwan and Amiriya, the men endured long days of lectures interspersed by sightseeing trips to various towns, watching films and swimming in the Mediterranean.

At the end of April, 46 Survey Company was on the move again as they boarded a ship bound for Tripoli where Martin first saw anti-aircraft fire, but he did not seem to realise the devastation that bombing from the air could wreak: 'Stay in camp while others go to town … British occupation point … Evening anti-aircraft fire over Tripoli; different colours of bullets show off beautifully. Someone calls it a super Guy Fawkes…'[5]

A few days later, Martin came closer to the front line as his company moved towards the capital of Tunisia, sleeping, 'in the open in a cornfield, about 4–5 miles behind the fighting line. All night cannon fire. Unique experience to listen to news from London and to actually see the fighting terrain as they describe it.'[6]

The next day fighting continued and Martin and a friend decided to make things more comfortable for themselves, they 'Pitch[ed] a tent of sorts and make ourselves at home. Continuous cannon fire all night over the lines in the mountains. Rumours that Jerry is very close to surrender…'[7]

The rumours were indeed correct as the Germans surrendered on 11 May, the same day that Martin had heard about the rumours. Between November 1942 and May 1943, British and American bombers were merciless as they destroyed cities beneath them. As the 8th Army, under command of General Montgomery entered Tunisia, their tanks laid waste to the last few towns that were still holding out. Two days later Martin wrote:

> News that hostilities ceased at 8 o clock last night. War in Africa is over. Wonder where we will go after this. Afternoon post but nothing for me. Also get 8th Army epaulettes, but do not really feel like wearing mine, because I have thus far not done anything for them … evening X-troop, which has been forbidden for us for a while, arrives with a load of gin and whisky that they had stored up to celebrate the victory. Drink to peace in 1943. Very friendly bunch of Tommies and we enjoy a pleasant evening with song and jokes. They only want to hear Afrikaans songs.[8]

---

4   DOD PF RS, Sgt V. Rooyen, M. F. (176938v) SAEC.
5   M. F. van Rooyen Diary, 5 May 1943.
6   M. F. van Rooyen Diary, 10 May 1943.
7   M. F. van Rooyen Diary, 11 May 1943.
8   MF van Rooyen Diary, 13 May 1943.

Martin and friends on a captured Italian desert reconnaissance car.
(Photo: Marianne Cilliers)

Martin van Rooyen somewhere in Tunisia. (Photo: Marianne Cilliers)

Martin posing next to a destroyed enemy tank. (Photo: Marianne Cilliers)

X-Troop was an inter-Allied Commando made up of volunteers who came from territories that had been occupied by the Axis.⁹ As most of these volunteers had had to flee their homes, they each had a personal motivation to fight Fascism. The primary goal was to rid the colony of German and Italian occupiers, and they achieved this. Tunis itself escaped much of the destruction because the harbour was some distance from the city centre.

Tunisia was the last of the African combat zones, and the Allies were eager to get things done and move on to the next target – in Europe. First in their sights was Sicily, followed swiftly by the invasion of the Italian mainland. The day after his celebrations with X-Troop, Martin went to investigate the fallen city:

> Our entire section [went] over to Tunis to go and see what it looks like. City larger than Tripoli and looks much more pleasant. Beautiful French ladies. Most shops still closed and I can't buy anything. Watch as a bunch of soldiers break into a wine store and carry away wine – later stopped by Redcaps. Bert gets hold of about 3 gallons of wine. See large POW camps along the way. First Germans that I see. Tunis full of troops of all nationalities. Area just outside Tunis looks like the Cape's green mountains. Afternoon back. Invite X-troop over to help us drink wine – about ½ mug each. Enjoy pleasant chat with some of them.¹⁰

---

9   N van der Bijl, *No.10 (Inter-Allied) Commando 1942 – 1945* (New York: Bloomsbury, 2006), passim.
10 M. F. van Rooyen Diary, 14 May 1943.

The Springbok Club in Tunisia. (Photo: Marianne Cilliers)

In the days that followed, Martin recorded how men from his company went into town on a regular basis to 'salvage' goods, including 'Tommy Guns', Italian Breda guns and odds and ends from other machine guns. Although the German forces destroyed much of their military equipment as they retreated, some of it was left behind and by Martin's judgement, the German materiel was no better than that of the 8th Army.

A few days later 46 Survey Company set off again, this time by road back towards Egypt. On the way, they passed Tobruk and El Alamein, where Martin wrote that they, 'Passed El Alamein where just a few months before heavy fighting took place. Burnt-out German tanks and cars and other armaments everywhere along the road.'[11]

When they reached Cairo, Martin noted that the city was full of 8th Army soldiers as well as members of the 6th South Africa Armoured Division, who were getting ready to go to Italy. Among their ranks were experienced men like Gerard Gafney, but also inexperienced volunteers who had joined the UDF just as the campaign in Africa came to an end.[12] They were the ones who signed up when Smuts launched the so-called 'Avenge Tobruk' recruitment campaign, calling for volunteers to replace those who were lost in the fall of Tobruk in June 1942.[13]

During this time, Martin's company moved mostly between Cairo and Alexandria, helping to get things ready for the move to Italy. Yet boredom remained

---

11   M. F. van Rooyen Diary, 4 June 1943.
12   Bourhill, *Come back to Portofino*, pp.31–32.
13   F. L. Monama, *Wartime Propaganda in the Union of South Africa, 1939–1945*, Dissertation presented for the degree of History, Stellenbosch University, 2014, p.141.

part of their daily existence and the men spent many hours reading and sleeping, getting frustrated at their inaction. However, with their training still incomplete, the South Africans would have to wait still longer before they could contribute to the war in Italy.

The invasion of Italy began on 11 June, first with British troops taking the islands of Pantelleria and Lampedusa, followed by Linosa. The Italian forces stationed at these places all surrendered without thinking twice. Sicily's turn came on 10 July when the Allies landed with 160,000 men and 600 tanks.[14] This momentous occasion did not enter Martin's diary, instead he wrote about lunches at Smuts House in Cairo and unloading and loading cargo ships in Alexandria.

On 24 June the South African forces could also vote in what would be called the 'Khaki Election,' which was the last election that Smuts would win. For Martin, the event passed without much fuss: 'Voted this morning for the general election that is to be held in the Union on 7 July. Afterwards [I] go to town to hand in my camera for a change…'[15]

D. F. Malan, Smuts's new rival, believed that South Africa would always play second fiddle to Britain's wishes as long as it remained a Dominion. He also wanted to dissuade those South Africans who felt an ancestral loyalty towards Germany, not to rely on the outcome of the war. When Germany invaded the Soviet Union in 1941, Malan realised that Germany was doomed, and this would put the pro-German Afrikaners in a position that would make it impossible for them to participate in the country's future. So, Malan thought it best that South Africa isolate itself from complex international conflicts and politics, and the only way to do that was to become a Republic. However, when the votes were counted, it seemed that the war had brought many of the doubters into the Smuts camp, and the ruling party counted 17 newly-won seats in their victory. Malan would have to wait until 1948 to try again.[16]

Like Malan, Smuts could also predict the future, and he brought in new electoral laws during 1941 and 1943, which allowed soldiers who were serving outside of the Union to participate in the election.[17] His critics were furious, but Smuts was sure that the volunteers in the UDF would support him. In his diary, Martin revealed their voting strategy: 'Same system as before – vote for party and not for individual candidates.'[18]

For those 'up north', politics at home was of less importance than the war, and there were things to be done, whether it was war-related or just plain sight seeing. As a surveyor Martin took many photographs as part of his work to produce maps. Strictly speaking, the authorities were supposed to store cameras as a security precaution, but Martin's huge collection of photos, not all related to surveying, shows his interest in the people and places he came across during the war.

In the meantime, the pace in Cairo remained one of work and boredom, and for Martin nothing much changed. He either worked day shift or night shift, slept, wrote

---

14 Gilbert, *Second World War*, pp.437, 442.
15 MF van Rooyen Diary, 24 June 1943.
16 Lindie Koorts, *D. F. Malan and the Rise of Afrikaner Nationalism* (Cape Town: Tafelberg, 2014), pp.361–363.
17 F. D. Tothill, 'The South African General Election of 1943', *Historia* 34:1 (1989), p.82.
18 M. F. van Rooyen Diary, 24 September 1943.

letters and went to the bioscope. Opportunities for leave were becoming scarce, and by the first week of September he set off towards Tripoli in a convoy of 80 vehicles. Once there, he attended lectures on photography, followed yet again by the familiar routine of sleeping, swimming and watching films.

In Italy things were moving considerably faster. Mussolini had been deposed in July, and with the Allied invasion of the mainland, Italy's new government felt they had no other choice but to join the Allies. Hitler was furious when he heard that Italy had changed sides, and when he was told of the Allied invasion at Salerno, he swore that Italy and its people would pay for their betrayal. The Germans set their sights on Rome where they set about taking prisoners, executing 'traitors' and rounding up Jewish inhabitants. Taking Rome also held strategic value for the Germans as they planned to send units south in an attempt to prevent an Allied landing on the coast of Italy.[19]

The Germans were correct in preparing to meet the Allies, even if they were not sure exactly where on the coast the landing would take place. Initially, the Allies planned to land at Naples, but in the end Salerno was deemed much more suitable for a seaborne invasion.

The American Fifth Army launched Operation Avalanche and landed at Salerno, but they were met with heavy German resistance. When the situation reached a near stalemate, Clark contemplated a retreat, he knew reinforcements from Sicily would not reach them in time as the Germans continued to put up heavy resistance. If it had not been for the 82nd Airborne Division landings on the night of 13 September, 14 September may well have been a victory for the German forces. Following this wobbly start, Naples, about 60 kilometres north, became Clark's next target.[20]

As the Americans set off towards Naples, Martin's leisurely days in Tripoli were coming to an end, and on 3 October 1943, 'In the afternoon an order came through to pack and be ready to leave within 1½ hours. To docks and we load our cars … we sleep on the upper deck just where we can find space between the cars.'[21]

On 8 October Martin's unit landed at Salerno and was met by the sights of the aftermath of battle left in the wake of Clark's invasion. Such sights of devastation would become very familiar to all surveyors who followed in the footsteps of the fighting units.

The contrast between the stunning Italian scenery and the people's poverty and hardship is evident in Martin's description of his first day in Italy:

> Salerno is squeezed in between the mountains and the sea. A monastery was built on cliffs on the side of the high mountain peak. Remnants of a castle and a fort. Buildings modern and high as space is limited. We sleep in our trucks across from the Pallazo de Governo. Women and children beg around us and crowd our kitchen. Bert and I go for a walk around town after lunch.[22]

---

19   Beevor, *The Second World War*, p.606.
20   Kenneth V. Smith, 'Naples – Foggia 1943–1944', https://www.history.army.mil/brochures/naples/72-17.htm, accessed 8 October 2024.
21   M. F. van Rooyen Diary, 3 October 1943.
22   M. F. van Rooyen Diary, 8 October 1943.

Italian orphans. (Photo: Marianne Cilliers)

A German field hospital in Italy. (Photo: Marianne Cilliers)

As the 5th Army made progress northwards, Martin's Company moved to their temporary camp at Castellammare di Stabia in the bay of Naples, and again he noted the plight of the people, 'Near Vesuvius and Pompey. Densely built-up areas and land intensively cultivated. Terraces against mountain slopes. Fruit and vegetables. People look hungry & lethargic and beg for food and biscuits. Struggle to talk to them and immediately I decide to learn to speak Italian.'[23]

A few days later, on 13 October, Martin made a small, but hugely significant note in his diary about the 'News that Italy declared war against Germany. Our departure postponed until tomorrow. Men in this section swopped out. I remain in section I.'[24]

On 15 October, 46 Survey Company left Castellammare for Cancello,[25] but Martin and his friend George Gordon were selected for other tasks; they were, 'isolated from the section and sent to C.I.W[26] at Pomigliano [d'Arco]. We work with Tommies and Yanks. Work very interesting. In the afternoon we walk around in town – later in conversation with 2 Yanks. Eat with Tommies.'[27]

Martin was clearly impressed by his new friends, commenting that 'Tommies & Yanks first class and we get along very well.'[28] One of the 'Yanks' who also found himself at the Pomigliano airfield described 'Pomig … as a home overseas.'[29] The airfield

---

23 M. F. van Rooyen Diary, 9 October 1943.
24 M. F. van Rooyen Diary, 13 October 1943.
25 Martin did not specify if it was Cancello Scalo or Cancello ed Arnone, both of which are near Naples.
26 Unfortunately, Martin did not elaborate on 'C.I.W.'
27 M. F. van Rooyen Diary, 16 October 1943.
28 M. F. van Rooyen Diary, 17 October 1943.
29 John C. L. Scriber, '111th Reconnaissance Squadron World War II Narrative History Part IX: Italy', *Texas Military Forces Museum,* https://www.texasmilitaryforcesmuseum.org/ang111p9.htm, accessed 7 October 2024.

Martin and two friends at the Trevi fountain in Rome, (Photo: Marianne Cilliers)

at Pomigliano d'Arco was established in 1938–1939 and was partially destroyed by Allied bombing during the Italian invasion. When the area around Naples, including Pomigliano, fell to the Allies, the RAF and the USAAF set up a base in the town. In 1944, while on his trip to Greece, Winston Churchill's Skymaster plane landed at the airfield, and did so again on his way back to London in December 1944.[30]

Martin and George began working night shifts when they were stationed at Pomigliano d'Arco, and as most bombing raids were conducted under cover of darkness, the two friends witnessed their fair share of them, the first of which they saw on 21 October: 'Sleep until midday. Early evening air raid over Naples. My first in Italy. Lasts about ½ hour. See a lot of anti-aircraft fire but not near us.'[31]

The bombing may have been a novelty for Martin, but for the inhabitants of the town and of nearby Naples it was a grim continuation of the war that had been raging around them since Hitler decided to wreak revenge on the country. As the Allies invaded the mainland, bombing raids were an all too frequent occurrence. Now, with Naples in Allied hands, they were yet again bombed, this time by the *Luftwaffe*.

To make matters worse, the Germans did not just retreat from Naples, they booby trapped everything of use in the city and left it with almost no infrastructure. When the Germans had gone, the Italian inhabitants, all 800,000 of them, saw the incoming Allied forces as a blessing. The Allies had food and medicine, commodities for which the Italians were desperate.[32]

---

30   Gilbert, *Road to Victory,* pp.1116 & 1133
31   M. F. van Rooyen Diary, 21 October 1943.
32   J. R. Hildebrand, 'The AACS Naples Detachment of the Army Air Corps, 1943–1947', *Air Power History* 60:2 (2013), p.8.

In the meantime, towns further north were still being blasted by Allied bombs as the Germans put up a fierce defence. Between Salerno and Rome there lay between four and six German defensive lines – depending on the chosen route. The immediate concern for the Allies was to cross the Winter Line, also known as the Gustav Line, but to do this, they would have to find a way to navigate the Mignano Gap. Clark and the American 5th Army decided to follow Route 6 to Rome, leading through the Gap. The British 8th Army, under command of General Montgomery took the route on the eastern side of Italy.[33]

Martin's work continued but the coming of winter in Italy made things difficult for him. As the weather began to cool down, it became more difficult to take photos, and as Martin's work could not be done without these, his days became drawn-out. The bad weather, however, did not stop the war, and on 9 November, 'An American artillery captain came to see how I plot positions [on the map]. Compliments from Captain Salt(?) and Americans on the results of my work.'[34]

It seemed that by this time Martin had also become used to the air raids and bombings as he nonchalantly wrote on 10 November, 'Weather still cold and overcast. Wake up early morning by the noise of anti-aircraft fire. Attack on Naples. Too cold to get up and I sleep on.'[35]

This attack was followed by an opportunistic raid two days later just as Martin returned from a night shift and a 'sudden short attack on the airfield next to us at 6am by a few enemy planes. They release two bombs and then they scatter. Anti-aircraft fire & fighter planes out. After breakfast go to bed and sleep until 5pm. Evening lots of work until 2:30am.'[36]

The winter was not conducive to a young man's need to spend his energy. Often, the overcast weather meant that no photos came in, however, it also put a stop to their walks around town. As the sun came out, so the photos came in, and Martin was desk bound to produce his maps. By 25 November he had had enough, and his diary reflected his frustration with, 'Rainy weather. Lie around all day and read. Sitting still and doing nothing is becoming very boring now.'[37]

He may have been exaggerating. The week before, he had been to see a concert performed by the Royal Tank Regiment. Two days after his 'boring' diary entry, he was on his way to the camp at Cancello to join a tour going to the isle of Capri.

At this time, the American 5th Army and the British X Corps were still in an almost standstill battle with the Germans as they struggled to move north beyond the Mignano Gap, which is about 140 kilometres south of Rome.[38]

Making no progress against the Germans, Clark decided to withdraw his men from the so-called 'murder mountain.'[39] It was now clear that the Allied forces had underestimated the German resolve, the Italian terrain and the freezing weather.

---

33 Antony Beevor, *The Second World War* (London: Weidenfeld & Nicolson, 2012), p.640.
34 M. F. van Rooyen Diary, 9 November 1943.
35 M. F. van Rooyen Diary, 10 November 1943.
36 M. F. van Rooyen Diary, 12 November 1943.
37 M. F. van Rooyen Diary, 25 November 1943.
38 Holland, *Italy's Sorrow*, p.xxxvii.
39 Beevor, *The Second World War*, p.641.

Clark and Montgomery now knew for sure that General Sir Harold Alexander's initial plan to reach Rome and Terni by 7 November and then to quickly move on to Lucca and Ravenna and to reach these towns by the end of the month was madness.[40] Both Lucca and Ravenna are about 350 kilometres north of Rome, with Lucca on the west coast of Italy and Ravenna on the east coast.[41]

With intense battles raging north of Martin's position, his daily routine remained more or less unchanged. November and December went by with night shifts interspersed with trips to town to see films, opera or theatre productions. A few nights of heavy drinking also helped to relieve the monotony:

> Day off and go to Naples. Meet McKenna and Johnston and together we go to the Arizona Club, which is almost as bad as Cairo's cabarets. In the afternoon we watched a 'Xmas show' in the Red Cross theatre, performed by Americans (?) Cognac from the Arizona Club helps me to enjoy it immensely.[42]

A few days later:

> We start to celebrate [Christmas] in the afternoon when my laundry lady offered me a few glasses of wine. After that drinking through town with about everyone I meet. Feel poisoned by Cognac. Evening to squadron to see 'Ziegfeld Girl.' Back here all the madness starts all over again. After midnight to bed.[43]

On Christmas day, Martin felt the effects of the previous day's 'madness', yet the combination of alcohol and the army was not unusual. It was generally accepted that alcohol was a reliable remedy for soldiers who experienced stress, and patients suffering from what was called 'battle exhaustion', known in the First World War as 'shell shock', were treated with a period of rest, good food and beer. On the battle front, British soldiers received a rum ration, although many servicemen used alcohol to calm their nerves, or to help them get some sleep when the enemy did not offer an immediate threat. Overall, the military authorities recognised that heavy drinking was the result of severe stress, but social drinking also boosted morale, which in turn had the potential to prevent nervous breakdowns.[44] It was a fine line between too much drinking and too little.

Christmas day started relatively calmly for Martin when he enjoyed coffee and doughnuts handed out by nurses in town. Later he attended a lunch where the rank and file were served by officers. From here things started to deteriorate. At the lunch, Martin was pleased to note that they had:

---

40   Alexander was Commander-in-Chief Allied Land Forces, 15th Army Group.
41   A. Bowlby, *Countdown to Cassino: The Battle of Mignano Gap, 1943* (London: Pen & Sword, 1995), p.12.
42   M. F. van Rooyen Diary, 22 December 1943.
43   M. F. van Rooyen Diary, 24 December 1943.
44   E. Jones and N. T. Fear, 'Alcohol use and misuse within the military: A review', *International Review of Psychiatry* 23: April (2011), p.168.

A soldiers' bar. (Photo: Marianne Cilliers)

Enough beer and wine. Happy that although most Yanks went back to their squadron, some stayed and ate with us … afternoon and evening one mad drinking party. Lost money on lotto game.[45] Sing songs obviously noisy. At about 9 o'clock I sober up. Annoyed with myself and go to sleep. Doubt if a drunk Christmas is best.[46]

The military authorities, having witnessed the rowdy celebrations, decided that a line had been crossed, and they decided to intervene before the New Year celebrations began in earnest. On 31 December an order was sent out that no soldiers would be allowed in Naples, Martin believed the reason was possibly:

because they were scared that [the soldiers'] behaviour would be too unrestrained. Americans all to a dance at San Anastasia. Most of them started drinking in the new year early in the afternoon. It is today a year ago that I was notified that I would be sent out of the Union. An entire year has gone by and I had the chance to see other countries and to experience all kinds of things. Yet it feels empty and worthless as if I never got the most out of it, and as if I really wasted most of my time. Or will 1943 stand out as one of the most important years of my life? What waits for me in 1944, and Rie[47] and all who are dear to me?[48]

---

45 Nowadays the Lotto game that Martin referred to is known as Bingo.
46 M. F. van Rooyen Diary, 25 December 1943.
47 Rie was Martin's girlfriend whom he married after the war.
48 M. F. van Rooyen Diary, 31 December 1943.

The first days of 1944 were largely uneventful for Martin. His shifts changed from night to day, but other than that, more films and operas were seen and more sleeping was done. At this time, however, the American 5th Army and the British X Corps, were facing a new obstacle. The Gustav Line and Monte Cassino would come to define the Italian campaign and would take immense effort and claim many lives.[49]

In the meantime, Martin had settled in and felt at home and at ease with his work routine. When he heard on 20 January 1944 that he and George Gordon were to be sent further north, he felt slightly distressed to be moved from the pleasant 'work group.' On 22 January George left, leaving Martin to show his replacement the ropes. Sometime after midnight, 'a bomber crashed into houses next to us. Huge fire, all occupants dead. Just missed our building.'[50]

On the same day, Allied forces landed at Anzio on the west coast of Italy, just 60 kilometres south of Rome. Those soldiers who stepped ashore did so with a sense of achievement which lifted their morale. Although the Anzio landings were seen as a success, with some historians describing the invasion as a surprise to the German forces, the personal recollection of one British soldier tells a different story.[51]

George Tewkesbury was a NCO who landed with the British 1st, 56th, and 5th Divisions and the 6th Corps of the US 5th Army, at Anzio in January 1944. He was also an avid diary keeper and as these extracts show, the Germans put up a determined fight and the Allies suffered continuous attacks as they tried to take the Anzio beachhead:

> 22 Jan Saw my first German tank since the landing...
> 24 Jan have been in action for three days and this morning things are picking up... our first casualties since the landing...
> 25 Jan Gerry is getting worse mortar fire is the regular thing now casualties are mounting up...
> 28 Jan 8 chaps taken out of our line with trench feet...
> 29 Jan off to widening the Bridge – head [sic] attack went in under heavy shell fire and mortar fire ... gain our position...
> 31 Jan Gerry putting up a counter attack have pushed us back 2 miles No.2 gun was hit killed 2 wounded 5...
> 2 Feb we can manage allright [sic] until reinforcement arrive...
> 3 Feb Gerry has been shelling us now for 4 hours ... Gerry put in a counter attack and is advancing he is just on our right...
> 4 Feb 4.10 AM starting shelling again 7.0 AM ... Gerry is pushing us back. Tanks were spotted this morning ... 7.30 German tanks have cut us of [sic] still fighting... 8.00 German tanks advancing ... ordered to fight our way out ... our only way out is backwards ... 8.20 AM My gun told to get out My no.1 is staying behind to destroy the gun ... 5.25 Our Gun

---

49 Beevor, *The Second World War*, p.640.
50 M. F. van Rooyen Diary, 22 January 1944.
51 L. Clark, *Anzio, the Friction of War* (London: Headline Publishing, 2007), pp.91–95.

An abandoned German half-track troop carrier. (Photo: Marianne Cilliers)

> hit No. 1 killed ... [I] have joined Coy Major Dill ... 9.40 Major Dill killed by tank fire. 10.45 Captured.[52]

Despite their losses, the Allies continued with efforts to take the beachhead at Anzio, but it was not until May 1944 that the Germans retreated. The idea behind the taking of Anzio was to aid those who were trying to cross the Gustav Line at Monte Cassino, almost 100 kilometres south from Anzio. With the taking of Anzio not going as smoothly as was hoped, Clark and the American 5th Army now had the added task of breaking through the Gustav Line to come to the aid of those at Anzio. Yet, between the two groups of Allies lay the mountains around Cassino, and *Generalfeldmarschall* Albert Kesselring, Commander-in-Chief of German forces in Italy, put up a fierce fight when the Allies made their initial advance on 20 January.

By this time the landscape held thousands of German mines, and the heavy mortar fire and difficult terrain caused the Allies to withdraw. Kesselring, however, did not become complacent, and prepared his battle plan for the fighting that he knew would come once the Allied forces had time to regroup.[53]

While the first battles raged in the mountains in the Cassino area, Martin was still in Naples, not doing much. Yet when word came for him to leave the city, he

---

52 George Tewkesbury, Soldier's Service Book, 22 January – 4 February 1944. George spent the rest of the war in a prisoner of war camp in Germany.
53 Beevor, *The Second World War*, p.647.

hardly had time to say goodbye to his friends. He was posted to Section I, and on his way to Sesto Campano, more than 100 kilometres north of Naples.[54]

Martin's new base was much closer to Cassino, and for the first time in his military career he was able to witness combat, albeit from afar. Still, the war now became more of a reality for him. On the other hand, Sesto Campano also offered a welcome change and a chance to become more active: 'Afternoon out to explore area. Not enough time to climb hill 1270. Area behind the front [line] very interesting. Astounded to see French women driving ambulances so close to the battle lines.'[55]

Hill 1270 was a rocky outcrop, which as with Monte Maio and Monte Vischiataro, lay south of Cassino. Monte Majo was taken by the American forces early in January, and by mid-January Monte Vischiataro had fallen into Allied hands.[56] On 27 January, with the battle scars still fresh on the mountains, Martin and his Survey Company arrived.

A day later, Martin climbed Hill 1270, 'to familiarise myself with the area ... for me it is familiar because I worked so many hours with the maps [of the area]. Dead Italian and Frenchman on the mountain.'[57]

Working in freezing temperatures, icy winds and deep snow, Martin's mapmaking work was draining, and with the dead not yet buried, the non–combatant surveyors now saw the human cost of war up close. On the days that the weather permitted him to work outdoors, Hill 1270 offered a good vantage point from which he could witness combat. On 8 February he wrote of another trip to Hill 1270, '…for observations. Watch as battle rages around Cassino. Heavy cannon fire and monastery above the town is also bombed. Bitterly cold on mountain and the summit under snow.'[58]

On that day, the Battle of Monte Cassino opened in earnest. The Germans had received an instruction from Hitler that they were to hold the Gustav Line at all costs. Threats such as these were nothing new to the German commanders nor to the rank and file, but while they would probably have accepted defeat, they could not afford to risk being blamed by Hitler – it could mean death.

Fierce fighting continued throughout the days ahead. Rain, snow and ice made the Allied advance almost an impossibility. Casualties were high and increased with each day. In some battalions, more than half of the men were lost. On 14 February, the two sides agreed that it was time to collect the dead, bringing the first phase of this battle to a close.[59]

The next day, the monastery was blown apart as tons of bombs were dropped. Unfortunately, the commanders on the ground failed to take advantage of the situation, and they left their attack too late after the bombers had left. Yet again progress was delayed.[60]

54　DOD PF RS, Sgt V. Rooyen, M. F. (176938v) SAEC.
55　M. F. van Rooyen Diary, 26 January 1944.
56　K. Finlayson, 'Wars should be fought in better country than this': The First Special Service Force in the Italian Mountains' *Veritas* 5:2 (2009), p.58.
57　M. F. van Rooyen Diary, 27 January 1944.
58　M. F. van Rooyen Diary, 8 February 1944.
59　Peter Caddick-Adams, *Monte Cassino Ten Armies in Hell* (Oxford: Oxford University Press, 2013), pp.122–125.
60　Beevor, *The Second World War*, p.655.

Relief from a relentless war; Marlene Dietrich performs for the men. (Photo: Marianne Cilliers)

Death was not limited to the battlefields, and on 21 February a young girl, who had been treated by a doctor of the medical corps, died. With his ambition to speak Italian, Martin had befriended an Italian woman, Louisa, and it is most likely that she was a friend of the girl who had died. As such, Martin became more intimately involved with the situation and consulted the attending doctor who believed it was stomach fever. Martin added, 'Lt R is getting better but wants to move as there is also typhus in Cesto C[ampano]. Many people come to see the body [of the girl] and it sounds as if everyone is taking part in the emotional outpouring.'[61]

---

61   M. F. van Rooyen Diary, 21 February 1944.

As Martin was a surveyor and not a combatant, his work allowed him experiences such as this that would have been out of reach to most in the military. When the funeral took place the next day, Louisa asked Martin to take a photograph of the body, but he, 'took two. Hysterical and crying women who kiss the body & general emotional atmosphere. Lt R gets new quarters at Filignano.'[62]

Martin also went to Filignano where the medical staff at the local CCS[63] inoculated everyone against Typhoid and Tetanus.

With the collapse of Italian infrastructure, the bad state of hygiene services in towns and cities, disease spread rapidly across the country. In Naples, for instance there were 2,020 cases of typhus reported between July 1943 and June 1944.[64] Martin recorded numerous instances of being vaccinated against tetanus, as were others from the British and American forces.

During the same period, the numbers of malaria cases began to increase. In the years before the war, draining pumps were installed to drain waterlogged areas to minimise mosquito numbers, but when the retreating Germans began to destroy the landscape to stop the Allied advance, they also destroyed the anti-malaria precautions that had led to a decline of the disease before the war. It was only in 1970 that the World Health Organisation finally declared Italy free of malaria.[65]

Early in March, Martin and George were separated when Martin was moved to section III, but it was not long before he met up with old friends from a division that had come over to Italy from North Africa. War events, however, remained the main topic of his diary entries, as 'German planes pass close by us and we see how one of them is shot down.'[66]

Even major natural events played second fiddle and when Vesuvius erupted on 17 March, Martin did not write about it until 24 March, granting the volcano one sentence; 'Very impressive with 500 (?) smoke columns.'[67]

Going to see Vesuvius again three days later, an American truck smashed into his car, sending two of his friends to hospital, one of whom was in a serious state. In April, Martin was himself admitted to a CCS when he jumped off a ridge and injured his knee. This period of rest was much-needed, as his diary entries of the weeks before almost all ended with 'very tired.'

Early in May he was well enough to return to work, doing mostly topographical work. On his next day off he went to back to his old haunting grounds in Naples:

---

62 M. F. van Rooyen Diary, 22 February 1944.
63 A CCS was typically used as a reception area for wounded soldiers. From the CCS, serious cases were sent to military hospitals while the less severe injuries were patched up so that the men could return to the front.
64 F. L. Soper, et al, 'Typhus fever in Italy, 1943–1945, and its control with louse powder', *The American Journal of Hygiene* 45:3 (1974), p.308.
65 Giancarlo Majori, 'Short History of Malaria and Its Eradication in Italy With Short Notes on the Fight Against the Infection in the Mediterranean Basin', Mediterranean Journal of Hematology and Infectious Disease 4/1 (2012), https://www.ncbi.nlm.nih.gov/pmc/articles/PMC3340992, accessed 11 October 2024.
66 M. F. van Rooyen Diary, 22 March 1944.
67 M. F. van Rooyen Diary, 24 March 1944.

'Buy nothing and just walk around. Go to see Aida in the afternoon. Evening at 11 o'clock an enormous artillery barrage over the front. Start of a new offensive.'[68]

By May a new offensive was underway in an attempt to take Monte Cassino. It was ill-timed, at exactly the time that the attack took place, the Germans forces were at double strength as it was the day that they relieved their forces. This time, the Poles, the American 36th Division, the Gurkhas and the French colonial troops all paid a high price for their attempts.[69]

The SAA, alongside the Poles, participated in the bombardment of the mountain. Among the Allies on the mountain slopes was Gerard Gafney with the Natal Carbineers.[70] The Gustav Line was broken and on 18 May the ruined monastery at last fell into Allied hands, at the cost of thousands of casualties.[71]

Martin's diary was silent until 4 June, when he recorded a move towards Artena where exhausted German troops experienced another devastating attack. The extra German troops ordered southwards by Kesselring had been marching for days to strengthen those forces already at Artena but before they were able to organise themselves an attack was launched that decimated their ranks. When the Americans moved into Artena, they were met with scenes of carnage.[72]

A few days later, Martin's unit arrived and 'Lt H. W. [went] ahead to seek out camp. Rest of us pack up. Move late afternoon. A lot of traffic on the way and it takes us 4 hours to go 20 miles. Nice camping site under oak trees beneath Artena which was taken over [from the Germans] about a week ago.'[73]

Artena is a mere 85 kilometres south of Rome and the success at Artena meant that the occupation of the capital was now a reality for Clark's forces. When Rome was taken, it seemed Martin did not realise the significance of the event, writing only that, 'News that Rome is taken. Pack up camp and do odd jobs. Evening walk through Artena … very few people back in their houses. Houses very little damage.'[74]

The next day more news came in, this time about events in France and the, '… invasion started in west of Europe. Everyone exited. Early afternoon back at camp. Les and I go for a walk in Artena in the evening. Dead Germans nearby.'[75]

The invasion of France, D-Day, codenamed Operation Overlord, created a new front in Europe. With Allied forces advancing from west to east in France, from south to north in Italy, and from east to west on the Russian front, Hitler began to feel the pressure. For Clark, who had been scrambling towards Rome to claim a victory ahead of his British comrades, D-Day came as a blow to his ambitions for recognition. He had been pushing his troops to their limit and each gain was hard won. Now he watched as the news correspondents raced from Rome to the French beaches, hardly a day after his triumphant march into Rome. However, if he felt

---

68   M. F. van Rooyen Diary, 11 May 1944.
69   Beevor, *The Second World War*, p.687.
70   Bourhill, *Come Back to Portofino*, pp.120–121.
71   Beevor, *The Second World War*, p.688.
72   Holland, *Italy's Sorrow*, pp.149–150.
73   M. F. van Rooyen Diary, 4 June 1944.
74   MF van Rooyen Diary, 5 June 1944.
75   MF van Rooyen Diary, 6 June 1944.

aggrieved, he did not say so. He stayed in Rome for a week, in the Excelsior Hotel, and then moved on with his troops.[76]

On 10 June Martin's unit also moved camp, but Martin and some friends remained behind and had a day off in Rome, 'No money so just walk around. City is still charming. End up in an Italian party with lunch & drink too much wine again. Meet American student who was caught up in Italy by the war. He tells me about many interesting events.'[77]

On 17 June they moved to yet another camp further north: 'Lt H Wood and I take Josef to his house near Foglino [Foligno] – 100 miles away. Interesting part. Foglino taken over by Italian partisans and without troops. Drop Josef off 1 kilometre from his house as bridges have been blown up.'[78]

Since Italy's declaration of war on Germany, the Italian partisans had been trying to make a contribution towards expelling their erstwhile allies from the country. From June 1944 their small operations gained limited support from the British and American forces.

It was also at this time that the numbers of partisans rose from around 9,000 to 50,000, yet many different groups among them remained largely disorganised. Among their contributions towards the Allied effort in Italy were sabotage operations, providing information on German locations and giving help to Allied POWs who had escaped at the time of the armistice the previous year.[79]

By 28 June Martin's camp was near Piancastagnaio while another part of the unit was stationed near Montalcino. Both towns are around 220 kilometres north of Rome. During July, however, they were moved around considerably as the front moved northwards. Martin and his fellow surveyors now had a much larger area in which they worked, and they moved back and forth between Rome, Sorrento and a number of smaller towns in central Italy. They often slept in tents but set up their working environments in houses and even empty factories.

By mid-July, Martin noted in his diary that it had been four years since he joined the UDF, and in that time he had witnessed air raids, made friends among soldiers from different nations, had managed to learn basic Italian and even met an escaped South African POW, who had re-joined the ranks. The survey work had become more demanding and they were expected to produce maps at an ever faster rate. The schedule did not allow for as many days off as in the first weeks of his Italian tour. Catching up on sleep became increasingly difficult. Swimming remained a favourite pastime, but in Italy it held its own dangers. Retreating Germans lay mines on the beaches, limiting the safe zones.

---

76 C. Anderson, 'Accidental tourists: Yanks in Rome, 1944–1945' *Journal of Tourism History* 11:1 (2019), pp.26, 28.
77 M. F. van Rooyen Diary, 14 June 1944.
78 M. F. van Rooyen Diary, 22 June 1944.
79 J. Le Gac, 'From Suspicious Observation to Ambiguous Collaboration: The Allies and Italian Partisans, 1943–1944', *Journal of Strategic Studies* 31:5 (2008), p.726.

On 22 July Martin wrote of the, 'Strong winds and stormy sea. Sea too dangerous for swimming and one American negro drowns in the afternoon. His body has not yet been found.'[80]

It is just as well that Martin did not go swimming on that day, as the next day the American troops went to clear the beach of mines: 'Americans clean mine field at the coast. S-Mine exploded and injured three. One dead.'[81]

Shrapnel mines were also known as S-Mines or Bouncing Bettys. When triggered the mine launched into the air and exploded at a height of about one metre. This, combined with the ball bearings and an amount of TNT explosive in the mine meant that the device caused maximum damage to a soldier's upper body. If an infantryman realised that he had stepped on a mine, he had about half a second to fall flat on the ground to prevent serious injury. However, with a foot on the mine, it was never possible to tell if it was a Bouncing Betty or a more widely used landmine. Most soldiers tried to run away because they assumed that most landmines exploded from the ground upwards, if it was a Bouncing Betty, running was useless.

When the war ended in 1945, great efforts were made to clear the battlefields of the mines, but in Libya, for instance, vast tracts of land are still unsafe as a result of minefields that had not been cleared.[82]

Martin's diary entries now increasingly began to contain descriptions of the effects of war. As someone who had been relatively safe working behind the lines, the space between Martin and the front line had been gradually narrowing for some time. However, there was still time for entertainment and on 19 August he attended an open air concert, recalling that it was the 'Best GI show I have seen so far ... a concert by men for men and as a result it became fairly vulgar at times.'[83]

A few days later he was transferred to a new section as his unit was sent to a new camp. His diary then remains empty for two weeks. The next entry recorded a dramatic event early in September. On a day off, Martin and some friends went to the town of Pisa, but it was on that day that he at last came face to face with combat:

> The Germans blasted the town with cannon fire and one bomb caught us near the L Tower [leaning tower of Pisa]. Joe Weitz (?) killed. Spikkey Holweins (?) and Bill Barbour critically wounded. We get the wounded away to the American hospital. We struggle to make arrangements for Joe's funeral. Sleep in Pisa ... Americans organise removal and care of [Joe's] body.[84]

After this the diary entries are vague, but it seems that the funeral took place on the same day, 7 September. The next day Martin's unit moved again, closer to Florence. Martin, however, returned to Pisa:

---

80 M. F. van Rooyen Diary, 22 July 1944.
81 M. F. van Rooyen Diary, 23 July 1944.
82 Jesse Becket, 'Bouncing Betty: The Story behind the scary 'Bouncing Betty' S-Mine', War History Online, April 2021, https://www.warhistoryonline.com/war-articles/bouncing-betty.html, accessed 1 Oct 2024.
83 M. F. van Rooyen Diary, 19 August 1944.
84 M. F. van Rooyen Diary, 7 September 1944.

> To see Joe's grave and to see if everything is in order. [?] comes along. We find section 2 near Pisa and sleep there. First to Pisa and then to the American funeral unit and after that to Joe's grave in British cemetery at Livorno. They did not have his details and he was buried as an unknown soldier. I bring everything in order. Sunday to hospital to see Bill and Spikey. Then to Castigliocello to say goodbye to all my friends whom I did not have time to greet before we left. Evening back in Florence.[85]

Back at work, he had to take over Joe's share of duties. Obviously, they had been working together for some time, yet Martin found his tasks had become a great effort for him. As they were both surveyors, it is unlikely that Martin found the technical aspects of the work difficult. He was obviously losing interest in keeping his diary up-to-date, and during the following week, Martin recorded two days simply as 'work.' Not even Florence, the city that gave birth to the Renaissance, inspired him to write more than, 'damaged a lot and did not make a big impression on me.'[86]

The next day he heard that they might get another period of rest, but he was held back to catch up on work when the others left to go on leave. Martin's last entry recorded, 'Rest of section except Herklaas and myself to Florence with leave. We must work in shifts from now on to finish all our work.'[87]

In October, Martin was admitted to hospital for an unknown condition. He did not write about this episode or, for that matter, anything else. The rest of his diary pages are empty and nothing is known about his experiences during 1945.

His personnel file shows that he embarked on his homeward journey from Suez on 13 September and on 26 September 1945, he arrived in South Africa.[88] The first thing he did was to send a telegram to his girlfriend Rie:

> Hooray I am back. Will call you as soon as the telephone line is open. Much love darling, see you soon. Love you, Martin.[89]

---

85 M. F. van Rooyen Diary, 9–10 September 1944.
86 M. F. van Rooyen Diary, 15 September 1944.
87 M. F. van Rooyen Diary, 18 September 1944.
88 DOD PF RS, Sgt V. Rooyen, M. F. (176938v) SAEC.
89 Personal correspondence, Martin van Rooyen to Rie, 28 September 1945. Martin died just 10 years later,

11

Amalia Snyman, Rescuer of POWs

The Allies and the Axis forces had been at each other's throats since September 1939 but Benito Mussolini, Italy's fascist dictator, waited nine months before he committed his country to the fray.[1] Mussolini declared war against France and Britain in an effort to gain control of the Suez Canal and Tunisia so that he could have unimpeded access to the Mediterranean and cement his control over the Italian colonies in Africa.[2]

From the start, things did not go well for the Italians. With relative ease, the colonies fell into the hands of the Allies. In North Africa, the Italian Army fought alongside their German allies, but had to adapt their strategy to fit in with that of *Generalleutnant* Erwin Rommel.

For the most part, the Italians favoured a sidestepping approach to avoid battles while Rommel preferred to lead from the front in fast-paced confrontations. In the end, however, the Allies were victorious in North Africa and in mid-1943 they began to plan the invasion of Italy. General Dwight D. Eisenhower was the Allied Commander for the invasion, with General George S. Patton commanding the US 7th Army and General Bernard Montgomery commanding the British 8th Army, among whom was the 6th South African Armoured Division.[3]

At the time Amalia Alaide Tasciotte, her sister Barbara, and her stepbrother, Lorenzo, lived at the family villa at Montemurlo with her stepfather, Erasmo, two servants Rita and Lena, the farm administrator with his family and numerous refugees from the province of Prato. Montemurlo is about 35 kilometres north-west of Florence and it would be almost a year before the liberating Allied armies arrived.

In July 1943, Mussolini was overthrown and the new Italian Government reached an armistice agreement with the Allies. This was not the end of the war for Italy, rather it was the beginning of a hostile struggle between retreating German forces and the Allies. To complicate matters, the Italian population was divided between those who refused to let go of Fascism, and those who joined the partisans, destroying infrastructure to obstruct German progress.

Luckily, Amalia's childhood had prepared her for conflict, for difficult choices, and most of all, for taking a stand. She had the courage of her convictions.

---

1   Moore and Fedorowich, *The British Empire and its Italian Prisoners of War*, p.1.
2   R. Mallett, *Mussolini and the Origins of the Second World War, 1933 – 1940.* (Hampshire: Palgrave Macmillan, 2003), pp.10, 14.
3   Holland, *Italy's Sorrow*, p.218.

Amalia was born in 1921, a year before Benito Mussolini took power in Italy and began strengthening his fascist regime.[4] It was a system that promised to restore the dignity of those humiliated by the peace treaty of the Great War – similar to what Adolf Hitler promised while he was gaining power in Germany in the 1930s. Fascist Italians saw the peace negotiations after the First World War as treacherous, and those willing to take up arms were regarded as heroic figures. The idea of militarism and war became the only way to rebuild Italy and to restore its dignity.[5]

When Mussolini declared war in 1940, his country was still struggling with the economic impact of the Great Depression. For the Italian people, the interwar era was one of food rationing, warnings from the new government to live frugally, while simultaneously producing more, whether it was on a farm or in a factory. In 1919, for instance, Italians protested against hardships and began to favour more conservative ideologies; fertile ground for the growth of Fascism. New tax laws were insignificant in effecting the much-needed changes and loans caused inflation to rise.[6]

Italy had been at war since 1935, fighting to expand its territory in Africa. Since Mussolini took power in 1922, he set out on a path of colonisation because, in his mind, an Italian Empire would restore the country's standing among other European Empires.[7] He forgot that the Italian people had been living in poverty for some time; they did not want more colonies, they wanted food on their tables. The only way Mussolini could muster up an army was by imposing conscription. To keep the population relatively quiet and obedient, he employed tactics of fear and threats.

Amalia's childhood, however, was not beset by poverty. She was born into a family that she considered to be 'quite well-off.' Her mother, Adriana, was only 18 when she married Emilio Tasciotti in 1920. A sheltered childhood did not prepare Adriana for a life with a husband who made the military his career. '[His] social life of an officer [the] horse racing with the inevitable betting, poker games and women', did not help, nor did the fact that the marriage was an arranged one. By 1926, she found her husband 'distasteful', and the couple separated.

Amalia and her sister Barbara were placed in La Quiete Convent near Florence. Amalia recalled that they felt at home in the convent as, 'many high society girls, often from broken homes, were sent to study at this exclusive convent.'[8] She and her sister enjoyed life at the convent, and they had opportunities that most Italians could only dream of. They studied English, French, history, Latin and embroidery among

---

4   G. Gori, 'Model of masculinity: Mussolini, the 'new Italian' of the Fascist Era' *The International Journal of the History of Sport*, 16:4 (1999), p.27.
5   A. Ponzio, *Shaping the New Man: Youth Training Regimes in Fascist Italy and Nazi Germany.* (Wisconsin, University of Wisconsin Press, 2015), p.27.
6   F. D. Esposito, 'Post-War Economies (Italy)', 1914–1918 International Encyclopedia of the First World War, http://encyclopedia.1914-1918-online.net/article/post-war_economies_italy, accessed 13 September 2016.
7   Jean-Guy Prévost, 'Statisticians, economists and the "new economic order" in wartime Italy (1940-1943)', *Journal of Modern Italian Studies*, 23:2 (2018), p.156.
8   Amalia Snyman and W. le Crerar. *A life on Two Continents in Two Centuries* (unpublished memoirs), p.81.

other subjects. Their mother was mostly absent at this time because, in Amalia's words, she was, 'working on her divorce' in Switzerland. This happy time came to an end when, out of the blue, their father, Emilio, arrived with a court order to take them away.

The two girls were left at their grandparents' farm at San Giovanni Incarico, in the south of Italy. Emilio left to join his regiment in Abyssinia. The two sisters spent almost three years on the farm, avoiding the local school as it was thought they would, 'never learn anything … only the dialect' – which was undesirable.[9] Although Italy was unified in 1861, the different regions remained unique, with widely different dialects, making it difficult for northerners and southerners to follow each other's conversations.

Another distinct difference between north and south was the pace of industrialisation and economic growth. With the levels of poverty higher in the south, the idea that the people of the south were also backward became widespread.[10]

Their grandfather was the mayor of the town, but this did not mean they had the same privileges they had at the convent. Amalia's experiences there led her to believe that her grandparents, 'didn't have much money and it seemed as if they had forgotten how to bring up children. Although we came to love them dearly, they never bought us anything and our clothes became all tattered.'[11]

Their lives changed again when their mother invited them to spend some time with her at the seaside. It was at this time that they got to know their stepfather, Erasmo, and their half-brother, Lorenzo. Living once again 'as befitted our family status', the two sisters decided not to return to their paternal grandparents. They were now 14 and 12, and were soon back in Florence, attending a private English School, this time to avoid the fascist propaganda espoused in Italian State Schools.

When the war began, food shortages compelled them to move away from the city to their family farm. It was on the farm that Amalia would see what war could do.

While Europe faced Hitler from 1939 onwards, Mussolini hesitated, giving Amalia time to go on skiing holidays and summers at the sea. But in 1941, the war caught up with Amalia's mother, and she 'started panicking and her anti-war and anti-fascist feelings became an obsession. Coping with rationing and many other restrictions on daily life became too much for her. This led to our move to Riva Bagnolo.'[12]

At the time, the war in the Western Desert generated events that would impact Amalia's life at Riva Bagnolo. In June 1942, the *Afrika Corps* launched an attack at Tobruk where the Allied garrison was under the command of General Klopper. Not wanting unnecessary deaths on his conscience, he surrendered and almost 30,000 British and Commonwealth soldiers were taken into captivity.

By 1943 most of these captives, among whom where almost 11,000 South Africans, found themselves in Italy. With prisoner of war camps across the country, and with

---

9   Amalia Snyman interview, 1 February 2016, Pretoria.
10   Holland, *Italy's Sorrow*, p.66; V. Daniele and P. Malanima. 2014. 'Falling disparities and persisting dualism: Regional development and industrialisation in Italy, 1891 – 2001', *Economic History Research* 10 (2014), pp.167–168.
11   Amalia Snyman and W. le Crerar. *A Life on Two Continents*, p.91.
12   Snyman and Le Crerar. *A Life on Two Continents*, p.99.

many Allied POWs working on farms, it was inevitable that they came into contact with local residents and for Amalia and Barbara their presence offered a chance for adventure. Her memoirs recorded the period thus:

> In the spring of 1943 about 100 allied prisoners of war were transferred from Laterina in the south of Italy to Montemurlo [Riva Bagnolo] near Prato where I was living on the family farm.
>
> Barbara and I, then in our early twenties, were very keen to meet these young foreigners and to be able to practise our English. We knew that they were billeted on our uncle's property not far from us, but we could not just pop in for a visit!
>
> A few days after their arrival they were put to work on the road between our house and our uncle's house. We saw then the opportunity to meet these chaps. We walked up the road and started chatting to the Italian guards, so bit by bit gaining their trust we eventually chatted to the prisoners as well and we came to know that they had been caught in Tobruk and were British and South Africans soldiers.
>
> To our surprise, we were allowed to visit them at their camp and talk to them across the fence. Their main interest of course (besides chatting up 2 young "*signorines*") was in the progress of the war and we passed whatever information we gathered from the clandestine radio broadcast from London.
>
> The police checked on us at different hours of the day, but eventually, maybe through lack of personnel or apathy they stopped. It wasn't until the 26 July 1943, with the fall of Mussolini's government that we considered ourselves out of danger.[13]

During an interview in 2016, she cast more light on the events:

> My sister and I were very curious, we couldn't wait to know who they were, can we speak English to them and so on and we saw that they were working on the roads during the day. They were filling up holes etc. so we passed them by a couple of times and then we said 'good morning, good afternoon', that's how we got to know them. And between, let's say July-August until September, yes, we had these little encounters, let's say, and the Italian guards were very careless, just left us to do what we wanted, but they were listening. And they heard us one day, we were mentioning names of places where there were battles and so on. They told us, 'yes, talk, but nothing about the war.' But we did and they reported us to the police, so the police came to fetch us and they interrogated us and they put us under house arrest.[14]

---

13   Amalia Snyman, *Memories of the War* (unpublished memoirs, nd.), p.1.
14   Amalia Snyman interview, 1 February 2016, Pretoria.

South African prisoners of war at Montemurlo, 1942/1943. (Photo: Amalia Snyman)

It was the rank-and-file prisoners who worked on farms, and being away from the larger POW camps, security was lax and the captives had a relatively high degree of freedom. While it would have been easy to escape from these working parties, many POWs decided against it, arguing that they did not know the language or the country and that they would not be able to get by on their own until the Allied forces had moved up north. Fear of reprisals and the chances of recapture also deterred many would-be escapers.[15]

Amalia and Barbara also thought, at first, that the 'police weren't very interested' in their conversations with the prisoners, and the two sisters continued see the prisoners, providing them with news of the war. However:

> One day, one of the Italian guards heard us mentioning a few place names in North Africa and got very nasty. He sent us away with a warning not to come back. Unfortunately, the matter did not rest there though. The guards reported us to the local police who came to fetch us for interrogation. They accused us of passing information to the enemy and placed us under house arrest at Riva Bagnolo, with the threat of being imprisoned later. Our mother, who by then was staying in Villa Paradisino in Florence, wrote a letter to us saying that she was very proud of us…
>
> When Mussolini's government fell the people including the partisans, took over the police stations and burnt all the files and records kept by the Fascists. The Italians had had enough of Mussolini and his gang.

---

15 Horn, *In Enemy Hands,* pp.151–154.

In the rest of Italy, the Italian population had lost hope; they could not envisage their country emerging from the war in any way other than in defeat. They were also hungry – the war had made deprivation a familiar companion. Mussolini's ministers were also despairing, and on 24 July they carried out a coup d'état. Mussolini's unpredictable and bombastic personality, however, was still a threat and one minister, Dino Grandi, who had been serving in the government since 1925, loaded his pockets with hand grenades as he left for the meeting, just in case things did not go according to plan.[16]

Mussolini on the other hand, seemed to think that the King of Italy, Victor Emmanuel III, would protect him against the usurpers. He did not, and the vote of no confidence in Mussolini gave the King the mandate throw him out.[17] *Maresciallo d'Italia* Badoglio was in charge of the new government and on 8 September 1943 he signed an armistice agreement with the Allies.[18]

In this way, Italy became a co-belligerent, but for the citizens a long road lay ahead as the German and Allied forces fought bitter battles on Italian soil. As the Allies moved up from the south, the Germans tried to maintain a foothold in the north of the country, using Mussolini as a puppet leader there.

For thousands of Italians who found themselves in no-man's-land, somewhere between the approaching Allies and the German occupied north of the country, life became a bitter struggle for survival. Amalia's family farm lay in the path of the retreating Germans.

By the time the Allies set their sights on the Italian mainland, the 6th South African Armoured Division was ready to join the British 8th Army under General Sir Alexander, who in turn fought alongside the American 5th Army under Lieutenant General Mark W. Clark.[19]

It would be almost another year before the fighting reached Riva Bagnolo, and in the meantime, Amalia had a lot on her hands. When the armistice was signed, the demoralised camp guards left the POWs to their own devices. As many as 50,000 POWs roamed around the Italian countryside, celebrating their freedom.[20]

It was short-lived. Nazi forces rounded up almost all of them and transported them to German occupied territory. Those POWs not caught up in the Nazi net relied on Italian peasants for food and shelter as they sought to reach neutral Switzerland or to take up the battle against the Germans once more either by joining up with the Allied forces or with one of the partisan groups.

In 2016, Amalia recalled the chaos of the days following the armistice in Italy:

> Our house overlooked a huge valley and we could see fires – bonfires all over and then we heard [on] Radio London ... that Mussolini had fallen and so on, then we heard the following day, yes, the police station is now [empty]... everybody is gone.

---

16 J. Whittam, *Fascist Italy* (Manchester: Manchester University Press, 1995), pp.106, 129–131.
17 M. Clark, *Mussolini Profiles in Power* (London: Routledge, 2014), pp.291–292.
18 Bourhill, *Come back to Portofino*, pp.48–49.
19 General Bernard Montgomery initially commanded the 8th Army, but by December 1943 Alexander took over. Bourhill, *Come back to Portofino*, p.44.
20 Holland, *Italy's Sorrow*, p.64.

Up there around the Prisoner of War camp, everybody's gone, the prisoners have been left alone and they started looking around for places to stay … but many of them were a bit worried about moving and so they went and asked the peasants if they could put them up…

[a South African POW] went to one of our peasants to ask to contact me and so they asked me to come over, he was waiting for me at the house. So I met him, you know we were very ignorant in a way about South Africa. When I met him I asked him, 'but where are you from, I have seen you along the road, but I've never asked you.' 'From South Africa.' So I said 'Aren't you black?' He of course thought it was very funny. So he explained to me the situation in South Africa.

[He] then said he had a place [to hide from the German forces], but he didn't know if he could stay there, and there were four others who were also staying there. He thought being five all together it was a bit too dangerous. So the following day I went to see the other peasants where they were staying, it was on the hill and it was a cave and they were in this cave. The peasants used to take food to them and so on.

So I said no, this can't go on like this, because too many of you and everybody will know about it, so you got to spread. So I told them look, I can't find a place for you, because I didn't dare, because I knew the danger. So I said 'if you can find a place then we can arrange that I can bring to the peasants like sugar and things that one can get with the rations' and help them in that way. In fact, he contacted me again and he told me yes, they found places, but they were all in this little place called Montemurlo … and now and again I used to go to this grotto, or to the peasants, it was quite a cold winter. Luckily not as cold as the following one, and so I took some blankets and so on.[21]

The risk to Amalia was indeed significant. The armistice initiated a civil war among the pro- and anti-fascist Italians. Those Italians who collaborated with the Nazis were likely to inform on their fellow citizens and trust between Italians became a scarce commodity. The Nazi forces regarded assistance to Allies, Italian partisans, former Italian soldiers and Allied POWs, as a capital crime.[22]

The fascist militia, known as the *Guardia Nazionale Republicana*, together with the Italian Military Police, or *Carabinieri*, took their orders from the Nazis. In an effort to maintain fascist control, they imprisoned, tortured and executed many Italian citizens who were found guilty of helping the enemy.[23]

As the war raged in Italy, the Wehrmacht at first went south to meet the Allies. To get to the Allied lines, they had to pass by Riva Bagnolo. Later, when the war began to turn against them, the Wehrmacht soldiers again passed by Amalia's villa. On one occasion, on a hot summer's day, her dog, Nero, began to bark viciously. By the time she went out to see what the commotion was about, two SS officers were already

---

21 Amalia Snyman interview, 1 February 2016, Pretoria.
22 Holland, *Italy's Sorrow*, pp.64–65.
23 Holland, *Italy's Sorrow*, p.265.

Amalia and her dog, Nero. (Photo: Amalia Snyman)

climbing the steps to the front door. Intending to make short work of the threat against them, one SS man took his revolver from its holster and took aim at Nero. In perfect German, Amalia shouted, '*Schießen nicht mein hund!*'[24] She recorded the day's events in her memoirs:

> I opened the door and then I saw how handsome and young these [German] boys were, one with black hair and the other blond, both tall, well-built and armed to the teeth, with gun, hand grenade and dagger, all draped around their body.
>
> My stepfather, Erasmo, joined us and they asked if we would give them some food as it was nearly lunchtime [sic] and they were a long way from their quarters. While I went to tell the cook to add something for our 'guests', Erasmo showed them to the dining room and there I found them talking about the beauty of Germany where Erasmo had been 2 years previously with an opera company and about skiing, a sport in which they seemed to excel and then [they spoke] about their experiences in the war.
>
> They still had their guns, hand grenades and daggers on them having removed only their caps and their gloves. Seeing them so handsome, so polite and friendly I could not imagine them committing any of the atrocities which were rumoured to have been perpetrated by the SS, but I soon revised my opinion as they started talking about their exploits in Poland.

---

24 Don't shoot my dog!

They were both in Warsaw at the time of the persecution and slaughter of the Jews. One of them told how he went to a block of flats. There was a grand piano in their [Jewish family] lounge. He snapped a cord with his knife, placed it around the neck of the father of the family, and cut his throat. In this manner, he killed all of them, throwing their bodies out of the window on a truck waiting below. He recounted all this with a smile on his face. Erasmo and I tried to keep our expression devoid of any emotion, but we could not help thinking that in the next room we also had a grand piano!

The other officer said that he had found a better way. A towel soaked in water and whipped at the back of their head would snap their necks with no mess at all. How did we finish the meal without getting sick and showing no emotion, I'll never know. I remember how relieved and how limp and exhausted we felt when the two SS said good-bye and left never to come back again.[25]

It was at this time of heightened stress that Amalia's stepfather agreed to help Mimma, the daughter of a Jewish friend, to reach Switzerland. Mimma would stay at the farm, with a false identity card, while plans were being made for her escape. During an interview in 2016, Amalia recalled how…

many plans were made for Jewish people and prisoners. You know the Italians are very brave that way. They don't like being soldiers. It's the only thing they don't like.[26]

At the same time, she also had to deal with the escaped POWs who were hiding out nearby and who were becoming restless:

Yes, at the same time these prisoners were getting a little bit too confident, because one of them [Victor Bell] came to my house, he knocked on the door and luckily I didn't let the maid and the cook open it, I realised the time, the evening 9 o'clock, I'm going to open and there he was, he said, "We're short of cigarettes." By the way, cigarettes were impossible to find, so we used to get black market tobacco leaves, we used to cut them very, very thinly…

So they prepared the cigarettes and then we shared, because I was smoking then. So he came to ask for tobacco, so I let him in immediately and I thought well, you know, now he's here, let's talk. So I told him it's very, very bad of you to come here, you must never come to my house, I'll come to you. If I have tobacco I'll bring it to you. So he said, "we were bored."[27]

At this point in the interview, Amalia laughed with a sense of disbelief, just as she must have done at the time of her conversation with Victor,

---

25 Snyman, *Memories*, p.3.
26 Amalia Snyman interview, 1 February 2016, Pretoria.
27 Amalia Snyman interview, 1 February 2016, Pretoria.

I said, "Okay, you were bored, but don't do it again." So I smuggled him out, in the meantime my Jewish friend and my sister and everybody else [were still there] and after this, my stepfather said. "It can't go on like this, you got to do something about it, don't get involved with them."

So for quite some time I didn't. In the meantime, they made the arrangements for the parents to meet my [Jewish] friend at the station in Prato. They told my stepfather, 'now take her to the station, sit at a little table until you see us. When you see us, walk out, leave her alone and then she can come and join us. Because otherwise they'll link [you to the escape]' – because they were already after the Jewish people. That's what happened and somehow or the other – they told me afterwards, they got to Switzerland.[28]

Victor Bell, the South African prisoner of war who took refuge with Amalia. (Photo: Amalia Snyman)

When her sister Barbara returned to Florence, Amalia remained where she was. She continued to provide food and other essentials to the POWs but, aware of the danger, she did not tell anyone, not even the cook, who,

> was like a mother to me, but I couldn't tell her what was happening with the prisoners of war, because I didn't want to involve anybody in case, you know, if they found out, they could have shot us all.[29]

It was Victor Bell who let the cat out of the bag. He was still in hiding with a number of fellow POWs nearby. When he knocked on the kitchen door one day, he was met by the cook's astonished expression. Trying, but failing to pose as a member of the partisans, Victor's South African accent betrayed him, and the cook ran upstairs to tell Amalia about the foreigner.

Victor was desperate; he was ill and needed help. Yet again, at great risk to herself and the others at the villa, Amalia decided to help and made him comfortable in an upstairs bedroom. In the meantime, the Germans were still occupying private homes as they deemed necessary. Amalia's family villa seemed to have been

---

28 Amalia Snyman interview, 1 February 2016, Pretoria.
29 Amalia Snyman interview, 1 February 2016, Pretoria.

Some of the prisoners of war who were given shelter at Amalia's villa. (Photo: Amalia Snyman)

a favourite location. More than once, with Victor silently tucked away upstairs, German soldiers feasted on Amalia's food supplies downstairs:

> One day I remember one of the Germans – because they always wanted something either to drink or to eat or what, and one of the Germans came up the stairs and the cook from downstairs started shouting – they called me Pupa. 'Pupa, Pupa, Pupa!' and I came out and I saw him and [Victor's] room was just around the corner.
>
> You know my legs gave in [with fear]. I went down on the steps and I said 'well, what do you want?' So he said something, I can't remember what he wanted, and he wanted to go up further so I said 'No, let's go downstairs, I'll give you something nice to eat.' But he said he didn't want anything to eat, so I said 'well, never mind, I'm going to give you something.' I stood up and, you know, my legs gone like this and I went down and I told the cook let's have something to eat now. So she made sandwiches and [the German] said 'well actually, I wanted wine.' So he's going to take the wine, I didn't mind what he took…[30]

With the shortage of food and poverty growing daily, especially among Italy's peasant population, the incidence of typhoid fever increased. This food-borne disease spread in unhygienic conditions and it was the most prevalent cause for the high mortality rate as a result of disease in Italy between 1941 and 1943, when the incidence went from 90 deaths per one million people to 163 deaths per one million people in 1943.[31]

A German field hospital had been set up in the Villa's storerooms. Her memoirs record, 'There was a continuous coming and going of ambulances bringing in the wounded from the nearby front line and I often saw the doctors operating outside under the trees. It was quite gruesome.'[32]

Because Amalia was able to speak German, the military doctor called on her services to assist him on his visits to the local population and it was there that Amalia realised that not all the medical staff were 'polite and pleasant'; the doctor 'never smiled [and] if we went to women who were in bed sick, he'd ask me to leave the room.'[33]

Despite the doctor's efforts, typhoid remained a problem in the area and when the South African forces arrived in there in 1944, Prato was one of the main centres of the disease.[34]

In the summer of 1944 Amalia had come to expect the unexpected. She knew that a knock on the door could come from Allied POWs hoping for food and shelter, or

---

30 Amalia Snyman interview, 1 February 2016, Pretoria.
31 V. Daniele and R. Ghezzi., 'The impact of World War II on nutrition and children's health in Italy' in *Economic History Research* 15 (2019), p.124.
32 Amalia Snyman and W. le Crerar, *A life on Two Continents in Two Centuries* (unpublished memoirs), p.120.
33 Amalia Snyman interview, 1 February 2016, Pretoria.
34 Bourhill, *Come back to Portofino*, p.347.

from Nazis retreating before the advancing Allied forces who were chasing them northwards. Fully aware of her precarious situation, she also realised that, despite the threat they presented, she had no choice but to welcome the uninvited Germans when they presented themselves at the villa.

> One such unwanted guest was a German colonel and his entourage. He arrived at the farm in a luxury car as long as a train, probably requisitioned in Rome from a wealthy family. It was followed by other more modest cars and as they stopped in the courtyard doors were flung open and a number of men in uniform spilled out, some taking position as if to guard the main car and others coming up the steps to our front door.
>
> As I opened the door a young captain saluted and informed me that his colonel wanted to spend the night in our house and required a bedroom and a sitting room and would I show him the house. Luckily I spoke German fluently, a fact which saved my life many times during the war and I showed him the rooms we could put at their disposal. It was no use refusing, as they could so easily have turned violent.
>
> After informing his colonel that the rooms available were suitable, the captain came back followed by a few soldiers carrying a portable drinks cabinet or bar, which I could see was fitted into the car in front of the back seat. Well, I thought, the colonel is treating himself very lavishly indeed. And then came the colonel himself, the most extraordinary figure I ever saw: he looked like a picture from an old family album. He was tall, thin, straight and immaculately dressed in the *Wehrmacht* uniform, with a lugubrious face and a monocle, which made his one eye look big and expressionless.
>
> He clicked his heels and kissed my hand, again clicked his heels to my stepfather and presented himself: Colonel Count von something or other, like in a Strauss operetta. I wish I could remember his name, but maybe I did not even register it so surprised and amused was I.
>
> After a short conference with his officers in the sitting room, his aide came to ask us to join the colonel for a drink. The drinks cabinet was standing on a table with an array of bottles of the best alcoholic beverages and the finest of glasses. The ex-owner had good taste and contacts that enabled him to obtain such quality drinks in ration times.
>
> Meanwhile some of the soldiers, evidently cooks, had taken over the kitchen after offloading chickens, vegetables and fruit. My stepfather and I wondered where they had stolen all that, maybe even from one of our peasants! They were decent enough to let our cook serve some of their food to us as well.
>
> The following morning, I heard a commotion in the courtyard. I looked out of the window and saw troops forming up facing the house and then in line with my window. I saw the colonel at his window, in pyjamas with the monocle on, very straight and marshall [sic] taking the salute, a strange sight indeed.

> On his departure, he again went through the ceremony of kissing my hand and clicking his heels and I felt as if I was saying good-bye to the last gentleman of the Austro-Hungarian Empire![35]

The next visit from the Germans was much more ominous. Erasmo had gone to Florence to escape being rounded up to fight on the Russian front. Amalia, Rita and Lena were left to manage the villa, and Amalia knew that when Germans arrived, she would have to 'do the talking':

> One morning a *Wehrmacht* car stopped in our courtyard and three uniformed men came to the door. The young officer asked to see the house as he was looking for accommodation for his superiors. It was amazing how they took it for granted that accommodation will be found and granted wherever they chose. When we got to the kitchen where Lena and Rita were, the officer insisted that he wanted to see the whole building … I explained that in the rest of the house were granaries, store rooms and the administrator's office. He demanded to see everything and when Lena and Rita started walking with us he said I must go alone with him and the two soldiers must remain with the two girls.
>
> I went with worry and trepidation. My heart was in my throat, my hands were sweaty, I did not know what to expect. We went up the stairs, along a corridor crossing the length of the house then down other stairs to the storerooms, all the time making conversation. He told me he was a university student, he did service in Africa then in Italy. So far so good, I thought, he seemed a decent young man. As we returned going up the stairs I was in front and suddenly he grabbed me by my shoulders, turned me around and pulled me towards him. I don't know how I got the presence of mind and the courage to push him with my knee. It was an instinctive reaction which left me absolutely drained. He went back a few steps. I turned around and carried on up the stairs thinking: now he is going to shoot me. I heard him walking behind me, not a word was spoken till we got to the top of the staircase. I looked at him and I said not to ever do that to decent girls. There were lots of prostitutes in Florence and that he'd better go there. To my surprise he answered that he was sorry. He was a nice man after all![36]

The 'last gentleman' and the 'nice man' did not change Amalia's negative view of the Germans, nor did it persuade her to lessen her efforts to assist those who held antifascist views. Years after the war, it is not possible to ascertain how reluctant or keen she was to take risks, however, in critical situations she seemed to act spontaneously.

> One day I heard excited women's voices at the kitchen door and Lena came to call me, I must quickly go with the women through the fields to the edge of the wood where there is a man badly hurt.

---

35   Snyman, *Memories*, p.4.
36   Snyman, *Memories*, p.6. It is unclear if Victor Bell was in the villa at this time.

> We ran as fast as we could and there on the edge of the stream there was a middle-aged man lying on the ground holding onto his side with his hand, full of blood and obviously in pain. With great effort he told he was shot by a German soldier. He was taking an escaped Allied prisoner of war to a new hiding place. Two German soldiers stopped them and pointing their guns at them they asked them for identity papers. The POW ran down a ravine and was shot. The man jumped over a wall, down into a gulley in the woods and was also shot, but he carried on running till he collapsed.
>
> A German doctor and an orderly, seeing the group of women running, followed us and when they arrived I told them the man had been shot by the partisans and needed help immediately. The doctor got 2 stretcher-bearers who took the man to their field hospital where they gave him first aid. I told the man to say that he was shot by the partisans. I saw him put in an ambulance and the doctor told me that he will be taken to the hospital in Prato.[37]

The Allied POW was South African, and the peasant family who had sheltered him buried him near their home. When the Allies liberated Italy, his grave was pointed out to them, and his personal documents, which the Italian family had kept, were also handed over and his family was informed of his death.

Although the partisans presented a convenient way out for Amalia in the case of the shooting of the Italian and the POW, she did not hold them in high regard. Just like the partisans, Amalia wanted to see Italy free of Nazi forces, but she did not agree with the partisans' ideologies or their methods. Talking in 2016, she was adamant that she never considered joining the partisans because she did not want to align herself with any political ideology. At the same time, she was aware that the partisans,

> …made life very difficult for all Italians… those who were not partisans, they didn't treat them very nicely, and in fact, with my peasants I had a lot of trouble, because they used to call me and say 'the partisans stole our chickens.' So eventually, through a link, I met up with the partisans of that region in one of the peasants' houses and I told them 'leave the peasants alone, if you want something, ask, they will give you something, but they're scared of you and we're not supposed to be scared of you. So that means you're doing something wrong.'[38]

In the meantime, the 6th South African Armoured Division, together with the 1st Canadian Corps, under command of Major General Evered Poole, were making slow but steady progress in Italy.[39] Each Allied victory in Italy demanded its pound of flesh, and the pace was slow. Arguably, the most critical battle took place at Monte Cassino. At this town, Allied forces became immersed in a battle that lasted four

---

37 Snyman, *Memories*, p.5.
38 Amalia Snyman interview, 1 February 2016, Pretoria.
39 Evert Kleynhans, 'The First South African Armoured Battle in Italy during the Second World War: The Battle of Celleno – 10 June 1944', *Scientia Militaria* 40:3 (2012), p.252.

months, through the coldest months of the year until early spring. In May, the battle reached a climax, and it was especially the RNC and the Witwatersrand Rifles/Regiment De La Ray that paid the price for this victory.[40] When it was over, the ancient abbey lay in ruins, littered with the bodies of 55 000 Allied soldiers and 20 000 Germans.

With bitter fighting behind them, the South Africans were hoping to be the first to enter Rome, and so gain recognition for their sacrifices in Italy. Unfortunately, just a few miles from their prize, they came across Americans who had landed at Anzio. After a strained discussion, Poole and his men watched from the side of the road as the Americans claimed victory in Rome. The next day, 6 June, the 6th South African Armoured Division skirted the outer suburbs of Rome.

Frustratingly for the Americans in Rome, the world's attention quickly deviated to France, as 6 June was also D-Day, the day of the Normandy Landings.[41] As it was, the Italian campaign remained of secondary importance when compared to the opening of a second front in France.

Perhaps realising that the fortunes of war were not in their favour, German forces reverted to ever more malicious tactics. Amalia clearly remembered how:

> …they terrorised the population, took hostages whenever the partisans blew up their vehicles or harassed them, and shot or hanged ten hostages for every German killed. They also hanged or shot those found to have aided escaped Allied prisoners of war.
>
> Many Italians went into hiding or joined the partisans, so it was left to the women to defend themselves and their property. Roads and bridges were systematically blown up by the Germans and the little bridge on the side of our house joining the road between Villa Barone and Prato, was to be the next to go. The peasants were frantic with fear and I realised that if it was blown up, part of our house would be blown up with it.[42]

Had it not been for the field hospital, and the German doctor's intervention at Amalia's insistence, the bridge would have been destroyed.

Sometime between 3 August 1944, when the South African forces reached Florence, and 12 September, when they arrived at Pistoia, the inhabitants at Amalia's villa at last saw the light at the end of the tunnel.[43] Since the first rumours about an Allied invasion of Italy started to surface in the POW camp, Victor had been looking forward to meeting his compatriots.

Then, at the beginning of September, the Germans were gone. Even the medics at the field hospital were packing and getting ready to leave. Then a few days later, they saw two men in khaki uniforms come up the road. Unsure of their identity, Amalia, Lena and Rita stayed inside, but Victor, seeing the red tabs on their uniforms, ran out of the house to meet them.

---

40   Bourhill, *Come back to Portofino*, pp.119–120.
41   Bourhill, *Come back to Portofino*, pp.136–137.
42   Snyman and Le Crerar, *A life on Two Continents*, pp.124–125.
43   Holland, *Italy's Sorrow*, p.347.

Amalia and the South African liberators. (Photo: Amalia Snyman)

For everyone in the villa, this moment signified liberation.[44] Talking about it in 2016, Amalia's voice still betrayed the emotion she felt on that day, for her it was:

> …like being saved from the fire, being saved from – I don't know, from the devil… we were standing at the window with the two – the cook and the maid, looking out one morning and we saw two khaki-dressed men coming up the road. Immediately [Victor] realised they were South Africans, because he saw the red tabs. I didn't know about it, because he didn't have red tabs, he had worn-out clothes. He ran like mad outside and I kept on shouting "come back! They'll shoot you!" and I saw him embracing them and they arrived – these two.
>
> Do you know it was the most emotional moment for all of us? All the peasants came out from their houses, all the refugees – you know, it was amazing. So they told us the South Africans are just down there in the village, but they're not coming up yet, they want to see where the Germans are. So I told them they're in my uncle's house [laughter]. So they said, "Oh well, we might have to bomb [them]." So I said, "No, you can't bomb that, it's a national monument that we love!"[45]

Obviously the South Africans wanted to flush out Nazis that may still have been in the vicinity, and they bombed the area around the house while Amalia, Rita and

---

44 Those in the northern parts of Italy remained under Nazi occupation until the end of the war in 1945.
45 Amalia Snyman interview, 1 February 2016, Pretoria.

Amalia and Ockert Snyman on their wedding day. (Photo: Amalia Snyman)

Lena took cover under the kitchen table. This nerve-wrecking event was followed by a day or two of uncertainty before the South Africans were satisfied.

Amalia recalled that the troops were from 22 Battery, 4th Field Artillery Regiment, and that their Commanding Officer was Captain Ian Ellis. The NMR were also in the vicinity, resting for a few days at Montemurlo before pursuing the Germans to the Setta River valley where they had gone into hiding. Taking advantage of Amalia's hospitality, the South Africans spent their days expanding their Italian vocabulary and consuming copious amounts of wine.[46] Amalia, Victor and the rest of the liberated POWs also celebrated, 'with the concertina and all…'[47]

Victor left with the South African troops, leaving Amalia with Barbara who had returned from Florence.

Amalia, however, was to play host to a number of Allied units. First the Americans arrived, with General Mark Clark taking the time to thank her for entertaining his troops with games of table tennis. Next, a British regiment of Ghurkhas arrived, and shortly afterwards, the 11 Field Punishment Centre, a South African Military Police Unit. Amalia was asked to interpret for them as they conducted their business, and in the process, she picked up a few Afrikaans words. The unit stayed at the Villa until the war in Europe came to an end. Moving their headquarters to Genoa, they asked Amalia to go with them as interpreter and clerk. She agreed.

It was early in 1946 that she met Warrant Officer Class 1 Ockert Snyman. Amalia described him as a 'real, raw *Boereseun*.'[48] By the time he began to appreciate Italian opera, they had fallen in love. They married in March 1947. Living in South Africa, Ockert continued with his military career and Amalia raised three children. Amalia received a certificate of appreciation from General Sir Harold Alexander for her efforts during the war. She never saw her mother again.

---

46   Bourhill, *Come back to Portofino*, p.270.
47   Amalia Snyman interview, 1 February 2016, Pretoria.
48   A real raw Afrikaner.

12

Constance Anne Nothard, Matron-in-Chief

When the Second World War ended in 1945, the Matron-in-Chief of the Medical Nursing Services received a four-page narrative, written by the Bureau of Information. It was a speech that she was to broadcast on 23 May 1945. It was written *for* her, not *by* her, and she had one day to prepare for the event.[1] She was not inclined to be dictated to, so naturally, as soon as the speech landed on her desk, she took out her pencil and made changes to the text.

If she was going to talk about the work of the wartime nurses, it would be in her own words. The opening lines of the speech, however, remained intact as these facts were indisputable:

> The Chief of the General Staff, Sir Pierre van Ryneveld, has told you in a national broadcast a few weeks ago, just how unprepared South Africa was for the task facing this young country. This South African Military Nursing Service, in common with other units, was just as unprepared. I recall the grave position at the time. We numbered one matron and 14 nursing sisters … I was then occupying a part-time position as Matron-in-Chief of the UDF…[2]

Constance Anne Nothard was not in the habit of standing back when circumstances demanded action. Born in 1889 in the Eastern Cape, she watched the South African War play out at a distance as a young girl. By 1915, when the blood-soaked trenches of the First World War demanded care for the young men, she joined a group of like-minded women and served in Europe. She returned to South Africa with the French *Croix de Recompense*, and with her name mentioned in despatches – twice.

After the war, she continued her work, but when she became part-time Matron-in-Chief of the South African Military Nursing Service (SAMNS) in 1935, she was dismayed to find the service on its last legs. With her war experience between 1914 and 1918, she must have had a good idea of what awaited those who chose to serve when Europe entered yet another war. However, at the time the military authorities decided that they would not call up more than 10 percent of the country's trained

---

1 DOD surgeon general (hereafter SG) GP2 Vol. 1. Box 11. Matron-in-Chief Personal MC 5/0/4. Bureau of Information to Matron Nothard. 22 May 1945.
2 DOD SG GP2 vol. 1. Box 11. Matron-in-Chief Personal MC 5/0/4. The South African Medical Nursing Services at War by Miss C.A. Nothard, Matron-in-Chief, UDF.

medical staff for war service. The home front, divisive as ever, needed care and attention to prevent outright riots, therefore, the politicians were adamant that the war would not disrupt the normal day to day functioning of civilian hospitals.[3]

The matron stood between the politics of the day and the medical needs of the war. Her task was to supply nurses for home front military hospitals, hospitals on the battle front as well as for hospital ships. As South African divisions moved from East Africa to North Africa, and later Italy, the demands on the nursing service grew in size and intensity.

Hospitals in Nairobi and Nyeri took in patients from different CCS and field ambulances during the East African campaign. While the hospitals remained stationary, the CCS and field ambulances were frequently relocated as the battle front moved.

When the South Africa 1st Division completed their task in the East of the Continent and joined the 2nd Division in the Western Desert, at least five new hospitals were established in Cairo, Suez, Helwan and Alexandria. Here, everything was different, dust and dryness marked each day, and the mobile nature of battle caused hospitals to be moved or amalgamated as needs dictated. New illnesses and heavy casualties confronted medical personnel who had no choice but to adapt, placing a heavy burden on the matrons who dealt with patient and staff issues.

In East Africa, battle casualties were less frequent, but diseases such as dysentery contributed significantly to casualty numbers. Already by February 1941, 60 percent of the 25 East Africa Infantry Brigade suffered from bowel conditions identified as bacillary dysentery, and 15 percent were diagnosed with malaria. At the time there were no battle casualties, but concern was expressed about the shortage of stretcher bearers.[4] The next month, the sick rate increased, and so did the casualties, with 4 percent among the 25 East Africa Infantry Brigade and 6 percent among the divisional troops, 2nd and 5th Brigades.[5] And so it went, each month the medical teams adapted to new circumstances and tests.

The geography and the climate of East Africa presented more challenges. Ulcers, which in the tropical areas were caused most often by flea infestations, affected the mobility and the ability of soldiers to carry out their duties. Tropical ulcers, in some cases, affected muscles, tendons and bone. Bacterial infections were also common as were infections from parasites.[6]

The Western Desert, on the other hand, presented problems associated with dry conditions. Sand-fly fever, for instance, became an irritating yet familiar condition that plagued soldiers and medical staff. In general, the dryer conditions presented fewer difficulties with regard to disease.

However, the open expanse of the terrain meant that hospitals had to be made safe against air raids. Large tents served as wards, and these were sunk a few feet below ground, almost like giant foxholes. In an attempt to minimise bombing raids

---

3 C. Searle, *The History of the Development of Nursing in South Africa* (Cape Town: Struik, 1965), p.362.
4 DOD CF Scheepers Collection. Box 4. Office of the ADMS 1SA Div. 14 February 1941.
5 DOD CF Scheepers Collection. Box 4. Health Report: 1SA Div. 19 March 1941.
6 J. F. P. Erasmus, 'Tropical Surgery in the East African Campaign', *South African Medical Journal* November (1942), pp.379–381.

at night, hospitals had to be able to black out any light at any given moment. This was the case for general wards, and more problematic, for operating theatres.[7] These conditions, combined with the dust storms and constant irritation of flies required patience from patients and commitment from nurses and doctors.

In both the East and North of Africa, however, malaria was a constant threat and doctors, nurses and patients were warned to be 'mosquito minded.'[8] With the South African 6th Division's move to Italy, some of the hospitals were relocated from the Middle East to Italy, while others stayed in Egypt and admitted patients who were flown in from Italy.

The requirements for Italy were initially set out as follows: one 12,000 bed hospital, one 600 bed hospital and one 2,000 bed convalescent depot.[9] However, the unpredictable progress of the war made planning for and establishment of hospitals exceedingly difficult. More often than not, medical staff were called upon to be ready for service in hospitals that were haphazardly set up in buildings not suited to the hygiene requirements of hospitals. Furthermore, the number of beds required could never be determined with any accuracy, as no one knew how many men would need treatment following a battle.

As military hospitals were set up, moved or closed down, the requirements for nurses changed, and Matron Nothard's task of recruitment and transferring of nurses became never-ending. For instance, in 1941, the South African Press Association (SAPA) proudly reported how:

> …a South African base hospital, which, during its first year, has increased nine times in size and has grown from a clearing station to a well-equipped hospital. The European staff is composed entirely of South Africans, and of the patients admitted, 77.5 percent have been South Africans. On July 25, 1940, the unit took over a converted school from a field ambulance. Almost immediately a programme of rapid expansion began and wards sprang up round the school.[10]

While articles such as this no doubt held positive propaganda value for those citizens who were anti-war or pro-German, the reality was that clearing stations do not equip themselves to become hospitals, nor do wards spring up by themselves. It took days of planning, many more hours of manual labour and as many hands to complete the tasks so proudly written about in a single newspaper article.

---

7   DOD SG, Box 29, No 106 S.A. General Hospital, Passive Air Defence for No. 106 (South African) General Hospital, Appendix VII.
8   DOD SG Diary: Box 25; No 101 NE S.A. General Hospital, Administrative Order 16 September 1942 by Lieut/Col. A. O. Dreosti, Commanding: No. 101 (S.A.) General Hospital.
9   DOD CF Scheepers Collection: Box 5. Scheme III: North. 17 April 1944.
10   DOD CF Scheepers Collection: Box 20. Sapa's War Correspondent, Mombassa. South Africa Medical Unit Expands to Hospital.

Nurses of the South African Military Nursing Corps. (Photo: Department of Defence Archives, Pretoria)

By the end of the war, Matron Nothard had increased the nursing contingent from 14 nurses in 1939, to 14,000 in 1945, all the while balancing the needs of civilian hospitals with military hospitals.[11]

Recruitment of suitably trained nurses created its share of headaches. As in other Commonwealth countries, nurses were not allowed to work once they got married, and with young nurses working alongside young servicemen, love and marriage was not unexpected. Nurses also became ill, and sometimes it was serious enough for them to return home. Others still realised that they could not stand the strain of battle front hospitals and requested to be returned home.[12]

The search for qualified nurses became an ongoing dilemma, for instance, between January 1941 and June 1941 between 20 and 25 nurses married and resigned.[13] During these months, casualties were escalating as battles in the East African campaign became increasingly demanding. At the same time, matrons and superintendents at hospitals in the Union appealed to Matron Nothard not to deprive them of the very few qualified nurses who were being tempted by military propaganda to volunteer and to serve in overseas hospitals.

---

11 DOD Director General Medical Services (hereafter DGMS): Box 31. Press clipping, *Protest by Nurses*.
12 DOD SG GP2 Vol. 2. Box 305. 154/351/4/0. Resignations – Members of the SAMNS. 8 July 1941.
13 DOD SG GP2 Vol. 2. Box 305. 154/351/4/0. Resignations – Members of the SAMNS. 8 July 1941.

In some cases, civilian hospitals had agreed to release a number of nurses each month so that they could serve with the SAMNS. The Johannesburg Hospital, for example, agreed to release three nurses each month, but when they realised they also had to fulfil their obligations to the Transvaal Memorial Hospital for Children, they wanted to opt out of the agreement. Their request was refused by the Director General Medical Services, Brigadier Orenstein, who reminded the hospital that, 'only 5 of the 18 [agreed upon nurses] have been supplied ... the alternative is resignations from the staff and direct recruitment which I am sure would leave your hospital in a worse position...'[14]

Desperate efforts to recruit nurses relied on more than threats to hospital authorities and the press was roped in to assist. Newspapers, radio and magazines played an important part in maintaining positive morale on the home front, and early on in the war *The Star* newspaper reported:

> as yet there are no patients [in South African military hospitals] apart from a few soldiers suffering from illness, but elaborate provision has been made to see that the South Africans receive every care and attention should they suffer casualties.[15]

First, the press assured the public that the sons and fathers of the nation were in good hands. Next, the press had to convince parents to let their daughters do their duty. This was no easy task, as the social structure of the country was based on stereotypes and hierarchical. When it came to war, there was never any doubt that white males would do their duty, at least in the pro-Smuts group. For white women in the same pro-war group, things were far more complex. Their job was still seen as that of a supporting role to their husbands and to bear children.[16]

In addition, for white women with ambitions to work or serve in the war, there was the issue of degeneration. White women were viewed, especially in Afrikaner society, as "shy, alienated, sensitive, poverty-stricken, sometimes backward and usually hopeless with neither initiative nor ambition."[17] No wonder mothers would not allow their daughters to nurse young men.

As battle casualties increased, especially after the clash at Sidi Rezegh, the shortage of nurses became a priority. Once again the liberal press offered their services and *The Star* reported on the, 'need for more nurses [and that it was] time that our young women of service age realised their duty to their country and joined the nursing staff.' The article also quoted Orenstein who stressed the importance

---

14 DOD SG GP2 Vol. 2. Box 305. DGMS to Superintend Johannesburg Hospital. 11 September 1941.
15 DOD UWH: Box 252. *The Star* S.A. Hospital in Egypt. 27 June 1941.
16 C. Walker, 'The Women's suffrage movement: The politics of gender, race and class' in Walker, C (ed.) *Women and Gender in Southern Africa to 1945* (Cape Town: David Philip, 1990), p.332.
17 *Vrou en Moeder,* June 1944 quoted in E. Brink, 'Man-made women: Gender, class and the ideology of the volksmoeder' in Walker, C (ed.) *Women and Gender*, p.287.

of, 'the essential oneness of mankind, and to break down the fear and distrust of foreigners to which so many are prone.'[18]

Beyond the supply of nurses to different hospitals in various theatres of war, Matron Nothard also dealt with all applications from qualified nurses, and those who wanted to volunteer to the Red Cross and the St John Ambulance.[19] She also had a hand in the appointment of matrons, seeing to the transfers of nurses between hospitals and from the battlefront to the Union. Unhappy nurses sent letters of grievances to the matron, while others sought advice and guidance. Unfortunately, they did not always get the answer they were hoping for. She did not suffer fools, but she was not heartless.

In a few cases, however, Matron Nothard believed she knew better than the regulations stated and enforced her will, disregarding any ill feeling from those who worked under her. One such case involved a large hospital in the Middle East. A decision was needed on whether to appoint a junior or senior matron to Hospital No. 101 in 1941. Initially, Matron Nothard appointed a junior matron, but the principal matron of the Middle East did not agree and she challenged Matron Nothard on her decision, pointing out that a 1,000 bed hospital, as was the case with Hospital No. 101, required the experience and authority of a senior matron.

Matron Nothard directed her subordinate's attention to the fact that most of the nursing was done by orderlies, European and non-European, and they in turn were supervised by qualified nurses. As such, Nothard pointed out that a senior matron would be redundant.[20]

More often than not, the matron tried to weigh up discipline and compassion as she dealt with each case, no doubt a time-consuming task. In 1941, for instance, she wrote to the UDF Matron of the East African Nursing Service about several troubling issues regarding nurses. Two probationary nurses were sent back to the Union, but the authorities in East Africa did not want to, 'interfere with the private life and associations of an individual…' In her reply, the matron stated in no uncertain terms that she was, 'sorry they are being returned to the Union without being informed why; I shall inform them of the reason when they report here, and I feel that I should have liked this co-operation from the north.'[21]

With regard to another nurse returning to the Union, she wrote, 'her case will be sympathetically considered with regard to her release…' In yet another example, the matron wrote of a nurse Douglas, 'who was sent down on compassionate leave [and she] will also remain in the Union.' With discipline and exactness never out of mind, she reminded the matron in East Africa of a few details:

---

18   DOD UWH: Box 252. *The Star*, 'Red Cross in Libya Care of South Africans Need for more nurses.' 20 December 1941.
19   DOD SG GP2 Vol. 2. Box 305. D.R 68/23. Recruiting: S.A. Military Nursing Service. 30 August 1941.
20   DOD C. F. Scheepers Collection. Box 5. Matron-in-Chief, SAMNS to Director General Medical Services. 27 December 1941.
21   DOD SG GP2 Vol. 1. Box 10. Matron Nothard to Miss Rees, Principal Matron, Nairobi. 25 April 1941.

> I am pleased that the nurses are behaving themselves and only need reminding on small points. I would however appreciate your reminding them that they are not allowed to wear the Springbok badge anywhere but on the front of their hats, and that when they are in public places without their tunics I do expect them to have their sleeves rolled down. All of this from the film of the landing of No. 5 CCS at Mogadiscio [sic] – Badges worn on their ties, and sleeves above their elbows. I was thrilled to see them, but disappointed that my nurses looked so untidy and undressed…[22]

Her words on a nurse who, in her opinion, 'was rather badly treated', held a warning for her own future. Saying that she, 'had hoped that [the nurse] would not press for anything further to be done on the matter, as these enquiries are always so unsavoury' may have been a sign of the pressure of the matron's work and that she was trying to smooth things out.[23]

Unfortunately, in not allowing the nurse to voice her objections, Matron Nothard inadvertently adhered to an approach towards nurses that the male dominated military structure applied passively towards female counterparts, including nurses, nursing sisters, principal matrons and ultimately towards the matron-in-chief.

It is not surprising that many nurses found working close to the battle front unnerving, but Matron Nothard had little sympathy. When nurses asked for a 'danger allowance' after they served at the Battle of El Alamein, she refused and reminded them that they were privileged as they were seeing the world at the Government's expense.[24]

The issue of pay remained a point of discussion and unhappiness throughout the war. In 1943, voluntary and probationary nurses wrote an appeal about not getting their field allowances. The matter was taken as far as the Prime Minister's office, as there was no agreement on a solution. The nurses wrote that:

> If we are officers, why do we not receive no field allowance – as we pay everywhere the rates for officers … We live in the desert under canvas, with various privations with no electric light, etc … The reason why we are treated so badly is because our Matron-in-Chief is a trained nurse first and an administrative officer second. For the whole of the three years I have been in the Army we have been continually up against her, with every bit of her trained nurse's dislike and distrust of the V.A.D. Now we find that all our letters of representation have evidently never gone further than her…[25]

---

22 DOD SG GP2 Vol. 1. Box 10. Matron Nothard to Miss Rees, Principal Matron, Nairobi. 25 April 1941.
23 DOD SG GP2 Vol. 1. Box 10. Matron Nothard to Miss Rees, Principal Matron, Nairobi. 25 April 1941.
24 O. Stratford and H.M. Collins, *Military Nursing in South Africa 1914 – 1994* (Pretoria: Chief of the National Defence Force, 1994), pp.78–79, 81 & 91.
25 DOD DGMS, Box 31. Extract of letter from S/P/N – V.A.D. NO.106 S.A. General Hospital UDF MEF 27/7/43.

Orenstein was aware of the nurses' grievances long before the letter reached him – military censors alerted him to similar messages in personal letters sent home by the nurses. He was not sympathetic to their plight, and was of the opinion that they should never have been given officer status. To make his decision clear, he concluded by declaring that their pay should be equal to that of the Women's Auxiliary Air Force and the Women's Auxiliary Army Services who were better trained than those probationary nurses. In addition, Orenstein expressed his concern that he was:

> Somewhat unhappy about the relations between some of the matrons, and particularly the matron-in-chief, and the nursing staff, as disclosed from censorship reports, and I am satisfied that a good deal of the agitation for higher pay arises out of discontent ... The latter matter will receive further consideration.[26]

Yet, when Matron Nothard believed she was right about a certain issue, she remained determined and committed to carry out her task to the point of self-sacrifice. Many, but obviously not all, colleagues and nurses respected her for this attitude and she also gained international recognition, in the form of a CB and CBE for her efforts during the war. However, some in the Union's military hierarchy viewed her grit and determination as obstinacy, an undesirable characteristic for women at the time, especially if they were part of the military chain of command which was dominated by men.

Military culture has long been dominated by masculine identities, and in the case of the matron, it would seem medical culture, also one characterised by discipline, clashed with military culture.

Conventionally, low ranking soldiers renounced their sense of individualism to fit in with the culture of obeying orders without question.[27] In civilian hospitals, nurses were not required to do this, although they were subject to a strict hierarchical structure. Whether the matron felt more at home in the military or the medical sphere, it was clear that most of her male UDF colleagues were unable to adapt to the idea of a woman in a position of authority.

The tense relationships between her and the top brass was again revealed when she applied for medals after the war. One document stated that there was no information on her attestation nor of her discharge.[28] Another terse statement indicates that matters were unpleasant, to say the least, during her last months in the UDF. However, the words 'Retired per instruction DGMS dd 10.12.45,' give a hint at the conflict of the last months of her service to the UDF as she officially retired six months later, in May 1946.[29]

---

26   DOD DGMS, Box 31. A. J. Orenstein to Private Secretary to the Prime Minister, 20 September 1943.
27   E. M. Kotze, 2021. *More than just pretty girls in uniform: A historical study of women's military roles during World War II, 1939 – 1945.* PhD Thesis, Stellenbosch University.
28   DOD SG Diary, SG GP2 Vol. II. *Aansoek vir Veldtogmedaljes (1939 tot 1945 en daarna).*
29   DOD SG Diary, SG GP2 Vol. II. Record of Services and particulars of discharge. 6.6.1946.

Her habit of signing her correspondence with the word CAN [Constance Anne Nothard] was perhaps a pun as it also implied something about her approach to her duties.

The war came to an end in May 1945, but the work of the medical personnel continued for some time. Patients were still arriving at military hospitals for treatment and others were in the process of recovery. In addition, the hospitals in overseas territories still had to be packed up and closed down before staff could return to the Union. In most cases medical personnel had to be evacuated systematically so as not to disrupt the normal hospital routine. Naturally, Matron Nothard intended to stay in her position until the last nurse stepped ashore.[30]

Brigadier Orenstein was known among some colleagues as a 'respected tyrant', and as Matron Nothard held a similar attitude to her duties, it is possible that the two of them enjoyed a professional, but tense, working relationship, especially when they both expressed opposing opinions in matters relating to medical matters. When Orenstein retired in August 1945, Nothard had to form a new relationship with his replacement, Brigadier W. H. du Plessis.[31]

The new DGMS and Matron Nothard did not see 'eye to eye', and she was promptly given 20 days to retire.[32] Her original part-time contract stated that she would retire at the age of 55, but that three months' notice would be given if her service was terminated.[33] While it would seem that there was some confusion as to her appointment, her pay and her retirement, comments made by Du Plessis added to her belief that she was being forced into retirement.

In a letter to Adjutant General Beyers, the new DGMS, Du Plessis, stated that Matron Nothard was obsessed with the idea that she had to fight for the interests of the nurses and was:

> …aggressive in her contacts with sections of the UDF and with members of the public, she insisted on regarding nurses as essentially different from other serving personnel… she was tactless and overbearing… the final incident that destroyed every possibility of collaboration arose over an attempt on my part to investigate the grievances of a certain nursing sister…[34]

Du Plessis was also of the opinion that Matron Nothard threatened to disobey his orders if he pursued the matter of the nursing sister.[35] In another instance, Du

---

30 DOD SG Diary: Box 29; No.102 S.A. Combined General Hospital, UDF, CMF. 1 September 1945 – 30 September 1945.
31 DOD SG GP2 Vol. 2 Box 305. PF: Brigadier Alexander Jeremiah Orenstein.
32 DOD DGMS: Box 31. South African Nursing Association (Marjorie Ross) to House of Assembly, 19 February 1946.
33 DOD DGMS: Box 31. Telex Px.364 JM Armour (A.A.G) to Secretary for Defence.
34 DOD DGMS: Box 31. Brigadier W. H. du Plessis to Major General Wakefield (AG) 23 February 1946, Retiral: Matron-in-Chief.
35 DOD DGMS: Box 31. Brigadier W. H. du Plessis to Major General Wakefield (AG) 23 February 1946, Retiral: Matron-in-Chief.

Plessis claimed that she 'was able to influence the future employment of members of the SAMNS and could thereby intimidate them.'[36]

By this time, Smuts was persuaded that Matron Nothard's time was up, but he instructed the Adjutant General that her retirement should be:

> ...on the ground of age only, and not because of any complaints against her service. She has done splendid service in a difficult time, and with staff which is tempermentally [sic] not easy. A nice appreciative letter from [the director] and another of thanks from me personally would put the whole matter on right footing.[37]

It would be interesting to know who Smuts regarded as 'temperamentally not easy', the nurses or Matron Nothard's colleagues in the higher ranks of the military hierarchy. Nevertheless, news of the matron's sudden retirement, which was set for 31 December 1945, spread quickly, and letters of objections, petitions and a few resignations from the Red Cross, the St John Ambulance Brigade and from nurses and matrons from all military hospitals arrived in quick succession at the office of the DGMS. The fact that she was given notice of only 20 days was a matter of concern for all nurses, as it gave the impression that they could also be dismissed on such short notice.

According to Beyers, Matron Nothard's letter of appointment indicated that she could be required to retire at 55. It also stated that her employment would be subject to three months' notice, 'from either side.'[38] On 18 December, official disapproval from the Chief of the General Staff reached the DGMS. They were informed, 'We seem to have aggravated the position unnecessarily. The P.M. thinks we have handled position tactlessly.'[39]

Despite Smuts's opinion that Nothard carried out her duties with great efficiency, controversy surrounded all attempts to bid a peaceful farewell to the matron. Late in January, Du Plessis was asked to explain in writing the reasons for Nothard's retirement. His carefully worded letter was rewritten at least three times before he sent it to the Secretary of Defence. While it is impossible to verify the statements of either Nothard or Du Plessis, it is clear that misunderstandings were in plentiful supply.

Yet, the end was nowhere in sight. Four days before her retirement, she was perplexed to hear that she was to, 'acquaint a Staff Officer "Q" with the routine and detailed duties of members of [her] Department to enable him to hand over to [her] successor when she is appointed.' Nothard was of the opinion that it would be more effective for her to hand over her duties to a matron, as such a person would have a better understanding of the demands of the position.[40]

The DGMS explained later that the officer in question had been given the task to confirm with Nothard the, 'routine and organisation of her office, in order to

---

36 DOD DGMS: Box 31. Brigadier W. H. du Plessis to Secretary of Defence, 5 February 1946.
37 DOD DGMS: Box 31. AG to DGMS, 8 December 1945.
38 DOD DGMS: Box 31. AG to Secretary of Defence, 18 March 1946.
39 DOD DGMS: Box 31. CGS to DGMS, 18 December 1945.
40 DOD DGMS: Box 31. Nothard to DGMS, 27 December 1945.

hand over to her successor.⁴¹ The animosity between the matron and the brigadier became clear when he referred to her as a:

> …rather forceful character, [who] has managed to gain control of everything regarding nursing in S. Africa – as Matron-in-Chief, President of the Nursing Council, President of the Nurses Association, and a member of the Medical Council, and yet she is continually on the defensive, and aggressively so, for fear that her dignity might be injured.⁴²

He also viewed her treatment of nurses as unreasonable, and cited Nothard's insistence of deducting pay when nurses in overseas territories took leave. According to Du Plessis, Nothard believed that nurses serving outside of the Union had to pay for their leave as they enjoyed benefits of international travel. Nothard set high standards for herself and her nurses, and it is likely that she believed that the military authorities had no idea of her workload, the nature or extent of it.

Driving home his point, Du Plessis also claimed that Nothard intimidated her would-be successors and that she encouraged matrons at military hospitals to protest against her retirement.

In turn, nurses were threatening mass resignations in protest of her treatment, apparently at the bidding of their matrons and Nothard. Mrs Cribb, the organising Secretary of the Nursing Association supported Nothard in her struggle, but Du Plessis believed that:

> members of the SAMNS are being incited to an action which will be an everlasting disgrace to the womanhood of S. Africa by this forced propaganda of the two women [Cribb and Nothard] – great friends as they happen to be – in whose hands the nurses of S. Africa had placed their destiny.⁴³

In another draught of his explanation, Du Plessis claimed that the level of control that Matron Nothard insisted on having over the nursing staff deprived them of certain benefits upon demobilisation, including that of pay and leave.

He went on to describe her as 'illogical and overbearing' and claimed that her irrational 'fear of allowing men any power in the handling of nursing affairs overshadowed all her actions.' By his account, not all nurses viewed Matron Nothard with respect. To illustrate his point, he gave this example:

> When I attempted to gain information from Miss Nothard in certain cases of dissatisfaction amongst members of the nursing staff, I met with considerable opposition. The climax was reached when I requested her to bring a certain sister before me to explain why she had gone to the BESL to have her

---

41 DOD DGMS: Box 31. DGMS to Secretary for Defence, no date.
42 DOD DGMS: Box 31. Secretary for Defence to the office of the Prime Minister, 21 January 1946.
43 DOD DGMS: Box 31. Secretary for Defence to the office of the Prime Minister, 1 February 1946.

grievances adjusted. I was told my Miss Nothard that such an action would undermine the discipline of the matron-in-chief. I asked Miss Nothard why, in view of the fact that there was so much dissatisfaction amongst members of the nursing staff, none of them had ever asked to interview me. Her reply was, "I consider that a bloody silly question. How can I know why they display no common sense?" When asked whether they had ever been informed regarding the procedure, she affirmed that they had. My summing up remark to this enquiry was: "Surely they cannot all be half-wits?" when Miss Nothard assured me with great confidence that they were. This incident when I wanted to see a certain Sister led from bad to worse, and Miss Nothard at one stage flatly refused to bring this Sister before me. It was only after I pointed out to her that such behaviour on her part would force me to recommend to the CGS that her services should be terminated, that she brought this girl before me. I asked the Sister one question only, and that was why she had gone to the BESL. Her reply was that she requested an interview with the matron-in-chief, and her request was refused by her own matron.

I then informed Miss Nothard that is was my intention to order a Court of Inquiry to get to the bottom of this whole affair regard the release of postponed release of this Sister Janse – the case in question. When about a week later the order went out for this Court of Inquiry to be convened, it was found that the principal witness had been posted away on the HS *Amra* by the matron-in-chief, and was then on the high seas.[44]

It is interesting to note that this extract is taken from a draught letter, when Du Plessis eventually sent his letter to the Secretary for Defence, he amended his wording to say, 'by virtue of her accumulate power she would brook no interference with her Department, with the result that I had a very serious quarrel with her owing to her obstructing every effort on my part to investigate the grievances of a certain nursing sister…'[45]

Perhaps he should also have replaced 'miss' with 'matron.' Clearly emotions ran high and Du Plessis took the time to find appropriate wording for his narrative of events, focussing on his version of events and forgetting his adversary's official title.

In the meantime, the objections to her treatment continued. Gradually, fellow matrons and nurses began to refer to her retirement as her dismissal, and the perception grew that authorities regarded her service during the war as second-rate. The South African Red Cross Society and the St John Ambulance Brigade stated their intention to launch an investigation on the reasons for Nothard's forced retirement.[46] The South African Nursing Council, for instance, wrote directly to Smuts,

---

44 DOD DGMS: Box 31. Secretary for Defence to the office of the Prime Minister, 1 February 1946.
45 DOD DGMS: Box 31. DGMS to Secretary of Defence, 5 February 1946.
46 DOD DGMS: Box 31. South African Red Cross and St John Ambulance. 28 January 1946.

expressing their, 'deep regret that our representations were of no avail in preventing what we consider a grave injustice [against] an able and loyal public servant.'[47]

Every military hospital wrote in support of the matron, but the military authorities would not reverse their decision, as it would be seen as an error of judgement, or as a weakness. In an effort to restore calm, the CGS instructed that the reply to the Nurses' Association should, 'correct the obvious imputation of dissatisfaction of Miss Nothard's services.'[48]

Then the newspapers got hold of the story, and ironically the silence from the military authorities seemed to support the one-sided articles. It was especially the headlines, which when read in isolation, created misapprehensions. The *Argus* announced 'Protest by nurses / summary dismissal of chief matron…' in February 1946. The content of many articles reflected the view of Nothard's supporters, and it is unlikely that the Department of Defence had any say in the opinions reflected in the various press articles:

> At a meeting held at Grey's Hospital, [Pieter]Martizburg, last night the secretary, Miss G Buttery, said it was an outrageous thing summarily to retire the matron-in-chief on 20 days' notice simply because the Director General of Medical Services did not see eye to eye with her. Miss Buttery read a circular letter issued by Mrs S. M. Cribb organising secretary of the [nursing] association, which set out details.

Another newspaper followed similar lines in its article, also emphasising the fact that Du Plessis obviously dominated the situation by exercising the authority of his rank:

> The circumstances of the retirement were that the newly appointed DGMS who stated that "he could not see eye to eye" with the matron-in-chief, decided to ask to have her removed. She was thereupon given 20 days' notice which "contrasts oddly with the more usual period of one month's notice of termination of service, and even more with the usual courtesy of at least three months' notice extended to senior personnel."

Others focussed on the shortage of nurses, which at the time of demobilisation was less of a problem than it had been throughout the war:

> Acute shortage
> While not questioning the legality of retiring the matron-in-chief, … it was beyond comprehension why, with the acute shortage of nurses, a woman of great experience, perfectly capable of continuing through the difficult demobilisation period, should be retired. There were women still in the SAMNS older than the matron-in-chief.

---

47   DOD DGMS: Box 31. South Africa Nursing Association to Smuts, 21 January 1946.
48   DOD DGMS: Box 31. CGS instruction regarding reply to South Africa Nursing Association, 29 January 1946.

The tone of these articles is very similar to the wording of many letters which were sent to object against Nothard's treatment, and it is possible that one or more of these letters found their way to the offices of sympathetic newspapers.

Although the date for her retirement was originally set at 31 December 1945, she nevertheless remained on the UDF payroll for some time.[49] On 28 December 1945 she was admitted to the military hospital at Voortrekker Hoogte, previously known as Roberts Heights. On 7 January 1946 she was granted sick leave for almost a month, being admitted to hospital again from 5 February until 17 February. In mid-April she was again granted sick leave which ended on 5 May. She was demobilised the next day, 6 May 1946.[50] She received the War Medal and the Africa Service Medal.[51]

Five years after the war, the SAMNS became part of the Permanent Force and military nurses were eligible for pensions.[52] In 1961, Matron Nothard was awarded the Florence Nightingale Medal for her work during the Second World War. The medal was awarded each year to 36 women who saw service as 'nurses and voluntary aids who have distinguished themselves exceptionally by their devotion to sick or wounded in the difficult and perilous situations which often prevail in times of war or public disasters.'[53]

---

49   DOD DGMS: Box 31. AG to Chief of Defence, 14 March 1946.
50   DOD SG GP2 Vol. 2 Box 305. PF: Constance Anne Nothard.
51   DOD SG Diary, SG GP2 Vol. II. Aansoek vir Veldtogmedaljes (1939 tot 1945 en daarna).
52   N. Gomm, 'Some notes on the South African Military Nursing Services' *Military History Journal* 1:2 (1968), Available http://samilitaryhistory.org/vol012gm.html, accessed 15 January 2020.
53   Central Committee of the National Red Cross, 'Eighteenth Award of the Florence Nightingale Medal, 12 May 1961', https://international-review.icrc.org/sites/default/files/S0020860400010366a.pdf, accessed 18 January 2021.

Bibliography

Archival Sources

Department of Defence Archive (DOD), Pretoria
Adjutant General, Prisoners of war:
Box 6. Italy Imperial Prisoners of War Alphabetical List. Section 5. South Africa. Union Defence Forces
Box 35. 1527 Vol. 1. *An airgraph received from the London Committee of the South African Red Cross Society.* 9 June 1943
Box 35. 1527/122. *Prisoners of war camp no. 122 visited 2nd October 1942 by Cap L. Trippi*
Box 35. 1527/122. *Prisoners of war camp no. 122 visited 14th October 1942 by Dr de Salis*
Box 35. 1527/122. *Prisoners of war camp no. 122 visited 6th March 1943 by Dr de Salis*
Box 35. 1527/122. *Prisoners of war camp no. 122 visited 11th April 1943 by Dr de Salis*
Box 128. Western Desert Campaign, Statement by No. 4448 L/Cpl Job Maseko alleging to have sunk a boat in Tobruk harbour
Box 130. Western Desert Campaign, Axis cruelty to native prisoners (Tobruk). Statement given on 11 September 1942

CF Scheepers Collection
Box 4. Health Report: 1SA Div. March 1941
Box 4. Office of the ADMS 1SA Div. 14 February 1941
Box 5. Matron-in-Chief, SAMNS to Director General Medical Services. 27 December 1941.
Box 5. Scheme III: North. 17 April 1944
Box 9: Diary of events from 18th Nov 41 to 30th Nov 41 By Capt P. M. Caldwell, 11th FD AMB
Box 9: GHQ., MEF ME/MEDITERRANEAN/3122: The Formation of Field Ambulances in Desert Warfare.
Box 9: Present state of Medical Services: 1SA Div. 21 January 1942
Box 9: Subject: Warfare in Mountainous Country.
Box 17: Die Suid-Afrikaanse Geneeskundige Diens [The South African Medical Service], JL Hartzenberg. 15 April 1995
Box 20. Sapa's War Correspondent, Mombassa. South Africa Medical Unit Expands To Hospital

Correspondence
CE 4/15. Union of South Africa Censorship. Correspondence suspected to require special attention

Director General Medical Service
Box 31. AG to Chief of Defence, 14 March 1946
Box 31. AG to DGMS, 8 December 1945
Box 31. AG to Secretary of Defence, 18 March 1946
Box 31. AJ Orenstein to Private Secretary to the Prime Minister, 20 September 1943
Box 31. Brigadier W. H. du Plessis to Major General Wakefield (AG) 23 February 1946, Retiral: Matron-in-Chief
Box 31. Brigadier W. H. du Plessis to Secretary of Defence, 5 February 1946
Box 31. CGS instruction regarding reply to South Africa Nursing Association, 29 January 1946
Box 31. CGS to DGMS, 18 December 1945
Box 31. DGMS to Secretary for Defence, no date
Box 31. DGMS to Secretary of Defence, 5 February 1946
Box 31. Extract of letter from S/P/N – V.A.D. NO.106 S.A. General Hospital UDF MEF 27/7/43
Box 31. Nothard to DGMS, 27 December 1945
Box 31. Press clipping, *Protest by Nurses*
Box 31. Secretary for Defence to the office of the Prime Minister, 1 February 1946
Box 31. Secretary for Defence to the office of the Prime Minister, 21 January 1946
Box 31. South Africa Nursing Association to Smuts, 21 January 1946
Box 31. South African Nursing Association (Marjorie Ross) to House of Assembly, 19 February 1946
Box 31. South African Red Cross and St John Ambulance. 28 January 1946
Box 31. Telex Px.364 JM Armour (A.A.G) to Secretary for Defence

Medical
Box 12. ADMS 142/1 Awards. May 1942

Personnel Files / Record of Service
Birch, John Vivian, DMR
Birch, Sydney, DMR
Birch, Walter Ernest, DMR.
Ernstzen, F. A. 274832 Private, *Application for Campaign Medals* (1939 – 1945 and onwards).
Ernstzen, F. A. Pte C274832. Form DD.293 (W.R.6)
Ernstzen, F. A. Pte C274832. Form DD.732
Ernstzen, F. A. 274832 Private, C274832. Pte Ernstzen, F. A. Form DD.293 (W.R.6)
Graaff, De Villiers, AG (1)736/55/48
Graaff, De Villiers, E4/110116, WS/Lieut Unit DMR
Graaff, De Villiers, Union of South Africa. DAG (P) 801/1/2889. Honours and Awards Sub-Section, 25 February 1947
Krige, M. U. Captain – GSC (V) ATT. SAPR. 29 March 1945

Krige, M. U. T/Capt. No. 558849V: GSC(V), 30 June 1945

Krige, M. U., *Aansoek om Veldtogmedaljes (Oorlog 1939–45)* [Application for war medals (War 1939–45)]

Krige, M. U. P1330/1: OI – SAPR1/3/1/21, DCS – DMI, 12 September 1944

Roux, C. L. M., Record of Service

Stuart, Sydney, 29338

V. Rooyen, M. F. Sgt (176938v) SAEC

Press and Propaganda

Box 39. *Appreciation on the prospects of attacking the enemy in Africa by means of propaganda* by JE Sacks 25 July 1940

Box 39. PR1/2/1 2nd January 1941

Box 39. PR1/5/2/ D.H.Q to E.A. Force Headquarters, 8 November 1940

Box 39. PR1/5/2 29 November 1941

Box 56. PR61. Stamping out the Saboteur (up to end of March 1942)

Box 63. Army publicity and propaganda. Nov. 26/40

Box 63. Bureau of Information Complaints, 22 Aug 1940 – 7 January 1941

Box 63. Weekly Newsletter No. 67. Week ending 22nd February 1941

Surgeon General

Box 25; No 101 NE S.A. General Hospital, Administrative Order 16 September 1942 by Lieut/Col. A. O. Dreosti, Commanding: No. 101 (S.A.) General Hospital

Box 29. No.102 S.A. Combined General Hospital, UDF, CMF. 1 September 1945 – 30 September 1945

Box 29. No. 106 S.A. General Hospital, Passive Air Defence for No. 106 (South African) General Hospital, Appendix VII

GP2 Vol. 1. Box 11. Matron-in-Chief Personal MC 5/0/4. Bureau of Information to Matron Nothard. 22 May 1945

GP2 Vol. 1. Box 11. Matron-in-Chief Personal MC 5/0/4. The South African Medical Nursing Services at War by Miss C.A. Nothard, Matron-in-Chief, UDF

GP2 Vol. 1. Box 10. Matron Nothard to Miss Rees, Principal Matron, Nairobi. 25 April 1941

GP2 Vol. 2 Box 305. PF: Brigadier Alexander Jeremiah Orenstein

GP2 Vol. 2 Box 305. PF: Constance Anne Nothard

GP2 Vol. 2. Box 305. 154/351/4/0. Resignations – Members of the SAMNS. 8 July 1941

GP2 Vol. 2. Box 305. DGMS to Superintend Johannesburg Hospital. 11 September 1941

GP2 Vol. 2. Box 305. D.R 68/23. Recruiting: S.A. Military Nursing Service. 30 August 1941

GP2 Vol. II. *Aansoek vir Veldtogmedaljes (1939 tot 1945 en daarna)*

GP2 Vol. II. Record of Services and particulars of discharge. 6.6.1946

Union War Histories

Box 252. *The Star* Red Cross in Libya Care of South Africans Need for more nurses. 20 December 1941

Box 252. *The Star* S.A. Hospital in Egypt. 27 June 1941

Union War Histories, Narrative Reports
Narep: ME/3. *Account of the adventures of the fellows taken at Sidi Rezegh. Statement by repatriated POW, 'Mr W.'*
Narep: ME/3. *Mr Whittaker Sidi Rezegh and captivity afterwards (Greece and Italy) related to Mrs G. R. de Wit by Mr Whittaker*

Stellenbosch University Special Collections, Uys Krige Collection
225.Fo.1.7: Photo: Uys Krige War Correspondent Italy
225.Fo.3.14: Photo: Uys, Lydia and Eulalia
225.Fo.4.20: Photo: Uys Krige and Vinecenzo Petrella (1940–1945)
225.NB.OC.7: 'Our Soldiers in Kenya'
225.RW.39: 'Towards Addis Ababa'
225.RW.14: Nazi Propaganda
225.RW.23: *'My werk as oorlogkorrespondent'* [My work as war correspondent].
225.RW.16: *'Kairo se eerste Lugaanval'* [Cairo's first air raid]
225.RW.12. *'n Generaal en 'n manskap.* [A General and a soldier]
225.RW: 'Die Slag van Sidi Rezegh' [The Battle of Sidi Rezegh]
225.KF. 15(10): Letter from Uys Krige to Lydia Krige, no date
225.KF. 15(12): Letter from 'George Kerr' to Lydia Krige, no date
225.RW.9: 'The Credit of POW life'
225.RW.5: 'Wat die Agtste Leer mee te kampe het' [What the 8th Army has to contend with]
225.KF. 15(1). Letter from Uys Krige to Lydia Krige, 30 April 1943
225.RW.6. No. 147. 10/5/1940. Nazi Propaganda
225.RO.6 (2): Uys Krige Interview with Noreen Purdon, 21 August 1944
225.RW. 40(3/2): Radio Trek No. 47. *Commanding Officer* by Capt Uys Krige. Transmission: Thursday, 8th February 1945
225.RW. 40(3/2): Radio Trek No. 54. *From a war correspondent's diary No. 9* by Capt Uys Krige. African Service: Thursday, 29 March 1945
225.RW. 40(3/3). *Uit 'n oorlogkorrespondent se dagboek – nommer drie – Uys Krige.* [From a war correspondent's diary – number 3 – Uys Krige] Transmission: Wednesday, 7th February 1945
225.NB.OC (4/1): Italian Soldiers!!
225.NB.OC (4/2): 'Italians!!'
225.NB.OC (4/3): 'Somali Soldiers'
225.NB.OC (6/1): Bureau of Information to Uys Krige, Nairobi

The National Archives, Kew
WO/373/21. July 1942

University of South Africa
United Party Papers: Sir De Villiers Graaff Collection. File 118: Sabotage; 118.1 General Acts, press cuttings, 1941 – 1943, 1964

Published Sources

South African Press Association – Reuter. 'Hitler announces new offensive', *Rand Daily Mail*, 6 June 1940

Interviews
Snyman, Amalia: interview with Karen Horn, Pretoria, 1 February 2016
Gafney, G. Oral reminiscences
Schwikkard, Bernard: interview with Karen Horn, Johannesburg, 17 March 2010

Personal Correspondence
C. L. M. Roux
David Graaff
De Villiers Graaff
Derrick Norton
Gerard Gafney
Peter Roux
Sydney Birch
Vyvyan Birch
Walter Birch

Personal Diaries
Tewkesbury, George, Soldier's Service Book
Roux, C. L. M., War Diary
Van Rooyen, M. F., War Diary

Memoirs
Snyman, A. and le Crerar, W., *A life on Two Continents in Two Centuries* (unpublished memoirs)
Snyman, A., *Memories of the War* (unpublished memoirs, nd)
Mortlock Jack, *The Endless Years Reminiscences of the Second World War* (Unpublished memoirs, 1956)
Hindshaw, William (Bill), *An account of my experience as a prisoner-of-war and escapee in the Italian Alps during the Second World War* (unpublished memoirs, nd)
Erntszen, Fred A., Memories of the war as told to Zane Boltman (grandson)

Secondary Sources

Books
Beaumont, Joan, 'Protecting Prisoners of War 1939–95' in Kent Fedorowich & Bob Moore, *Prisoners of War and their Captors in World War Two* (Oxford: Berg Publishers, 1996)
Beckett, Ian F., *Rommel: A Reappraisal* (Barnsley: Pen & Sword, 2013)
Beevor, Antony, *The Second World War* (London: Weidenfeld & Nicolson, 2012)

Bolloten, B., *The Spanish Civil War Revolution and Counterrevolution* (Chapel Hill: University of North Carolina Press, 1991)
Bourhill, James, *Come back to Portofino Through Italy with the 6th South African Armoured Division* (Johannesburg: 30o South Publishers, 2011)
Bowlby, A., *Countdown to Cassino: The Battle of Mignano Gap, 1943* (London: Pen & Sword, 1995)
Brink, E., 'Man-made women: Gender, class and the ideology of the volksmoeder' in Walker, C. (ed.) *Women and Gender in Southern Africa to 1945* (Cape Town: David Philip, 1990)
Brown, James Ambrose, *Retreat to victory A Springbok's Diary in North Africa: Gazala to El Alamein 1942* (Johannesburg: Ashanti, 1991)
Brown, James Ambrose, *The War of a Hundred Days Springboks in Somalia and Abyssinia* (Johannesburg: Ashanti, 1990)
Caddick-Adams, Peter, *Monte Cassino Ten Armies in Hell* (Oxford: Oxford University Press, 2013)
Chambers, J., *For You the War is Over: The story of H.R. (Aussie) Hammond* (Cape Town: HAUM, 1967)
Churchill, W. S., (ed.), *Never Give In! Winston Churchill's Speeches* (London: Bloomsbury, 2013)
Clark, L., *Anzio the Friction of War* (London: Headline Publishing, 2007)
Clark, M., *Mussolini Profiles in Power* (London: Routledge, 2014)
Crwys-Williams, J., *A Country at War 1939-1945 The Mood of a Nation* (Rivonia: Ashanti Publishing, 1992)
Davies, P., *France and the Second World War Occupation Collaboration and Resistance.* (London: Routledge, 2001)
Erwee, A. and Eksteen, Louis J. (eds), *The Second World War Experiences of Sydney Stuart: A South African soldier of the 2nd World War (1939-1945) who served in the 11th Field Ambulance of the SA Medical Corps* (Newcastle: Fort Amiel Museum, 2017)
Garcia, Antonio and van der Waag, Ian, *Botha, Smuts and the First World War* (Johannesburg: Jonathan Ball, 2024)
Gilbert, A., *POW Allied Prisoners in Europe 1939-1945* (London: John Murray, 2006), p.49
Gilbert, M., *Churchill and America* (New York: Free Press, 2005)
Gilbert, M., *Road to Victory Winston S Churchill 1941 – 1945* (London: Heinemann, 1986)
Gilbert, M., *Second World War* (London: Phoenix Giant, 1996)
Giliomee, H., *The Afrikaners Biography of a People* (Cape Town, Tafelberg, 2003)
Graaff, De Villiers, *Div Looks Back: The Memoirs of Sir De Villiers Graaff* (Cape Town: Human & Rousseau, 1993)
Hattersley, A. F., *Carbineer, The History of the Royal Natal Carbineers,* (Natal: Gale & Polden, 1950)
Holland, James, *Italy's Sorrow A year of war 1944 – 45* (London: Harper Press, 2009)
Holland, James, *Together We Stand: North Africa 1942-1943: Turning the Tide in the West* (London: Harper Collins, 2006)

Horn, Karen, *In Enemy Hands: South Africa's POWs in WWII* (Cape Town: Jonathan Ball Publishers, 2015)

Horn, Karen, *Prisoners of Jan Smuts Italian prisoners of war in South Africa in WWII* (Cape Town: Jonathan Ball Publishers, 2024)

Hoyt, E. P., *Backwater War: The Allied Campaign in Italy, 1943-1945* (Westport: Praeger, 2002).

Kannemeyer, J. C., *Die Goue Seun. Die Lewe en Werk van Uys Krige* (Cape Town: Tafelberg, 2002)

Katz, David B., *South Africans versus Rommel, the Untold Story of the Desert War in World War II* (Johannesburg: Delta Books, 2018)

Klein, Harry, *Springboks in Armour: The South African Armoured Cars in World War II* (Cape Town: Purnell & Sons, 1965)

Koorts, Lindie, *D. F. Malan and the Rise of Afrikaner Nationalism* (Cape Town: Tafelberg, 2014)

Krige, Uys, & Norton, Conrad, *Veldtog vir Vryheid 'n Kort Oorsig van die Oorwinning van die Afrikasoldate in Oos-Afrika, 1940-1941* (Pretoria: Bureau of Information, 1941)

Krige, Uys, *'Totensonntag', Sout van die Aarde* (Cape Town: HAUM, 1964)

Krige, Uys, *The Way Out* (Cape Town: Maskew Miller, 1955)

Leigh, M., *Captives Courageous: South African Prisoners of War World War II* (Johannesburg: Ashanti Publishing, 1992)

Mallett, R., *Mussolini and the Origins of the Second World War, 1933-1940.* (Hampshire: Palgrave Macmillan, 2003)

Mason, W. W., *Prisoners of War: Official History New Zealand in the Second World War 1939-45* (Wellington: Oxford University Press, 1954)

Mervis, J., *The Fourth Estate a Newspaper Story* (Johannesburg: Jonathan Ball Publishers, 1989)

Mitchell, C., *Tom's War* (Privately Published Memoir, 2018)

Moore, Bob, & Fedorowich, Kent, *The British Empire and its Italian Prisoners of War, 1940-1947* (London: Palgrave, 2002)

Nasson, B., *South Africa at War 1939-1945* (Johannesburg: Jacana, 2012)

Ogilvie, P., and N. Robinson., *In the bag* (Johannesburg: Macmillan, 1975)

Orpen, N., *The History of the Transvaal Horse Artillery 1904-1974* (Johannesburg: Speciality Press, 1975)

Orpen, N., *War in the Desert, South African Forces World War II, volume III* (Cape Town: Purnell, 1971)

Pimlott, John (ed.), *Rommel in His Own Words* (Barnsley: Greenhill Books, 1994)

Ponzio, A., *Shaping the new man Youth training regimes in Fascist Italy and Nazi Germany.* (Wisconsin, University of Wisconsin Press, 2015)

Pretorius, Fransjohan, *Life on Commando during the Anglo-Boer War 1899-1902* (Cape Town: Human & Rousseau, 1999)

Schamberger, Paul, *Interlude in Switzerland: The Story of the South African Refugee-Soldiers in the Alps* (Johannesburg: Maus Publishing, 2001)

Scheck, R., *French Colonial Soldiers in German Captivity during World War II* (New York: Cambridge University Press, 2014)

Searle, C., *The History of the Development of Nursing in South Africa* (Cape Town: Struik, 1965)
Somerville, C., *Our War How the British Commonwealth Fought the Second World War* (London: Weidenfeld & Nicolson, 1998)
Stewart, Andrew, *The Early Battles of Eighth Army: Crusader to the Alamein Line, 1941–42* (Mechanicsburg: Stackpole Books, 2002)
Stewart, Andrew, *The First Victory: The Second World War and the East African Campaign* (New Haven: Yale University Press, 2016)
Stratford, O. and Collins, H. M., *Military Nursing in South Africa 1914–1994* (Pretoria: Chief of the National Defence Force, 1994)
Todman, D., *Britain's War: Into Battle 1937–1941* (London: Penguin Random House, 2017)
Van der Bijl, N., *No.10 (Inter-Allied) Commando 1942–1945* (New York: Bloomsbury, 2006) passim.
Van der Waag, Ian, *A Military History of Modern South Africa* (Cape Town: Jonathan Ball Publishers, 2015)
Van Heyningen, C., & Berthoud, J., *Uys Krige* (New York: Twayne, 1966)
Whittam, J., *Fascist Italy* (Manchester: Manchester University Press, 1995)
Wing, S. K., *Our Longest Days: A People's History of the Second World War* (London: Profile Books, 2008)
Wolhuter, S. G., *The Melancholy State: The Story of a South African Prisoner-of-War* (Cape Town: Howard Timmins, nd)

Journal Articles and Book Chapters

Daniele, V. and Ghezzi, R., 'The impact of World War II on nutrition and children's health in Italy', *Economic History Research* 15 (2019), pp.119–131
Le Gac, J., 'From Suspicious Observation to Ambiguous Collaboration: The Allies and Italian Partisans, 1943–1944', *Journal of Strategic Studies* 31:5 (2008), pp.721–742
Monama, F. L., 'The Second World War and South African society, 1939–1945' in Potgieter, T. and I. Liebenberg (eds), *Reflections on War Preparedness and Consequences* (Stellenbosch, Sun Press, 2012)
Grundlingh, Albert, 'The King's Afrikaners? Enlistment and ethnic identity in the Union of South Africa's Defence Force during the Second World War', *Journal of African History* 40:1 (1999), pp.351–365
Hildebrand, J. R., 'The AACS Naples Detachment of the Army Air Corps, 1943–1947', *Air Power History* 60:2 (2013), pp.4–13
Horn, Karen, '"A sudden sickening sensation": South African prisoner-of-war experience on board the San Sebastian, December 1941', *Historia* 63:1 (2018), pp.112–129
Jones, E., & N. T. Fear, 'Alcohol use and misuse within the military: A review', *International Review of Psychiatry* 23: April (2011), pp.166–172

Kleynhans, Evert, '"Good Hunting": German Submarine Offensives and South African Countermeasures off the South African Coast during the Second World War, 1942-1945', *Scientia Militaria* 44:1 (2016), pp.168-189

Kleynhans, Evert, 'The First South African Armoured Battle in Italy during the Second World War: The Battle of Celleno – 10 June 1944', *Scientia Militaria* 40:3 (2012), pp.250-279

La Grange, Anna, 'The Smuts Government's justification of the emergency regulations and the impact thereof on the Ossewa-Brandwag, 1939 to 1945', *Scientia Militaria*, 48:2 (2020), pp.39-64

Linsenmeyer, W. S., 'Italian Peace Feelers before the Fall of Mussolini', *Journal of Contemporary History* 16:4 (1981), pp.649-662

Monama, F. L., 'Civil Defense and Protective Services in South Africa during World War Two, 1939-1945', *Historia* 64:2 (2019), pp.82-108

Monama, F. L., 'South African Propaganda Agencies and the Battle for Public Opinion during the Second World War, 1939-1945', *Scientia Militaria* 44:1 (2016), pp.145-167

Morewood, S., 'Protecting the jugular vein of empire: The Suez Canal in British defence strategy, 1919-1941', *War & Society* 10:1 (1992), pp.81-108

Petracarro, D., 'The Italian Army in Africa 1940-1943: An Attempt at Historical Perspective', *War & Society*, 9:2 (1991), pp.103-128

Prévost, Jean-Guy., 'Statisticians, economists and the "new economic order" in wartime Italy (1940-1943)', *Journal of Modern Italian Studies*, 23:2 (2018), pp.156-175

Scheck, R., '"They Are Just Savages": German Massacres of Black Soldiers from the French Army in 1940', *The Journal of Modern History*, 77:2 (2005), pp.325-344

Scianna, B. M., 'Forging an Italian Hero? The late commemoration of Amedeo Guillet (1909 – 2010)', *European Review of History*, (2018), pp.369-385

Soper, F. L., et al., 'Typhus fever in Italy, 1943-1945, and its control with louse powder', *The American Journal of Hygiene* 45:3 (1974), pp.305-334

Steimatsky, N., 'The Cinecitta Refugee Camp (1944-1950)', *October Magazine* (2009), pp.23-50

Stewart, Andrew, 'The "Atomic" Despatch: Field Marshal Auchinleck, the Fall of the Tobruk Garrison and Post-War Anglo-South African Relations', *Scientia Militaria: South African Journal of Military Studies*, 36:1 (2008), pp.78-94

Teer-Tomaselli, R., 'In Service of Empire: The South African Broadcasting Corporation during World War II', *Critical Arts South-North Cultural and Media Studies* 28:6 (2014), pp.879-904

Thomas, M. C., 'The Vichy Government and French Colonial Prisoners of War, 1940-1944', *French Historical Studies*, 25:4 (2002), pp.657-692

Tothill, F. D., 'The South African General Election of 1943', *Historia* 34:1 (1989), pp.77-94

Van der Waag, Ian, 2012. 'The origin and establishment of the South African Engineer Corps (SAEC), 1918-1939', *Journal for Contemporary History* 37:2 (2012), pp.1-31

Visser, G. E., 'Die Middellandse Regiment', *Scientia Militaria* 8:4 (1978), pp.13-18

Walker, C., 'The Women's Suffrage Movement: The politics of gender, race and class' in Walker, C. (ed.), *Women and Gender in Southern Africa to 1945* (Cape Town: David Philip, 1990)

Theses and Dissertations

Bentz, Gustav, 2013. *Fighting Springboks C Company, Royal Natal Carbineers: From Premier Mine to Po Valley, 1939–1945*. Master's dissertation. Stellenbosch University, pp.20–21

Fokkens, A. M., 2006. *The role and application of the Union Defence Force in the suppression of internal unrest, 1912–1945*. Thesis presented in partial fulfilment of the requirements for the degree of Master of Military Science (Military History), Faculty of Military Science, Stellenbosch University, p.105

Kotze, E. M., 2021. *More than just pretty girls in uniform: A historical study of women's military roles during World War II, 1939–1945*. PhD Thesis, Stellenbosch University.

Monama, F. L., *Wartime Propaganda in the Union of South Africa, 1939–1945* Dissertation presented for the degree of History, Stellenbosch University, 2014, p.141

Albertyn, Yolandi, 2014. *Upsetting the Applecart: Government and Food control in the Union of South Africa during World War II c.1939–1948*. Thesis in fulfilment of Master of Arts, Stellenbosch University

Electronic Resources

Anon, 'World War II Dates and Timeline', *United States Holocaust Memorial Museum*, https://encyclopedia.ushmm.org/content/en/article/world-war-ii-key-dates, accessed 22 August 2024

Becket, Jesse, 'Bouncing Betty: The Story behind the scary 'Bouncing Betty' S-Mine', *War History* Online, April 2021, https://www.warhistoryonline.com/war-articles/bouncing-betty.html, accessed 1 October 2024

Broch L., 'Colonial subjects and citizens in the French internal resistance, 1940–1944', French Politics, Culture and Society 37/1 (2019), https://go-gale-com.ez, accessed 7 April 2021

Central Committee of the National Red Cross, 'Eighteenth Award of the Florence Nightingale Medal, 12 May 1961', https://international-Review.icrc.org/sites/default/files/S0020860400010366a.pdf, accessed 18 January 2021

Coghlan Mark, 2005 The Natal Carbineers – 150th Anniversary. A glimpse of some new Battle Honours. *Military History Journal*, 13 (3). http://samilitaryhistory.org/vol133mc.html, accessed 12 November 2019

Delport Anri, 'South African Troops in Europe and the Middle East (Union of South Africa)', 1914–1918 International Encyclopedia of the First World War, (2017), https://encyclopedia.1914-1918-online.net/article/south-african-troops-in-europe-and-the-middle-east-union-of-south-africa/#toc_cape_corps_labour_battalion_cclb, accessed 22 August 2024.

Espositi F. D., 'Post-War Economies (Italy)', 1914-1918 International Encyclopedia of the First World War, http://encyclopedia.1914-1918-online.net/article/post-war_economies_italy, accessed 13 September 2016

Garland G., 'The Strange disappearance of Jan Christiaan Smuts and What it can teach Americans', American Diplomacy (2010), https://americandiplomacy.web.unc.edu, accessed 18 April 2021

Gomm, N., 'Some notes on the South African Military Nursing Services' *Military History* Journal 1:2 (1968), available http://samilitaryhistory.org/vol012gm.html, accessed 15 January 2020.

Hansard 1803–2005, *War Situation HC Deb 30 September 1941,* vol. 374 cc 509–51: *The* Prime Minister (Mr Churchill) https://api.parliament.uk/historic-hansard/commons/1941/sep/30/war-situation, accessed 15 October 2020

International Committee of the Red Cross, *Convention Relative to the Treatment of Prisoners of War. Geneva, 27 July 1929,* 305-IHL-GC-1929-2-EN PDF: https://ihl-databases.icrc.org/en/, accessed 22 August 2024

International Committee of the Red Cross, *Convention Relative to the Treatment of Prisoners* of War. Geneva, 12 August 1949, www.un.org/en/genocideprevention/documents/atrocity-cirmes/Doc.32_GC-III-EN.pdf, accessed 7 April 2024

Jacobs C., 'The War in North Africa, 1940–43. An Overview of the contribution of the Union of South Africa', South African Military History Society, http://samilitaryhistory.org/lectures/nafrica.html, accessed 21 August 2024

Majori Giancarlo, 'Short History of Malaria and Its Eradication in Italy With Short Notes on the Fight Against the Infection in the Mediterranean Basin', Mediterranean Journal of Hematology and Infectious Disease 4/1 (2012), https://www.ncbi.nlm.nih.gov/pmc/articles/PMC3340992, accessed 11 October2024

Merchiston Preparatory School, Our Story. https://www.merchiston.co.za/our-history/, accessed 12 November 2019

Mohlamme J. S., 'Soldiers without reward Africans in South Africa's Wars', Military History Journal 10/1 1995, http://samilitaryhistory.org/vol101jm.html, accessed 7 April 2021

Orpen Neil, 'East African and Abyssinian campaigns', South African Force World War II vol. 1 (1969), HyperWar: East African and Abyssinian Campaigns [Chapter 15] (ibiblio.org), accessed 9 February 2021

Owen R. E., (ed.) *Official History of New Zealand in the Second World War 1939–45,* http://nzetc.victoria.ac.nz/tm/scholarly/tei-WH2PMed-pt2-c4.html, accessed 19 November 2020

Red Cross Committee, *Frontstalag 133,* https://www.pegasusarchive.org/pow/FS133/cFS_133_RedCross18Jul44.htm, accessed 23 August 2024

Scriber John C. L., '111th Reconnaissance Squadron World War II Narrative History Part IX: Italy', *Texas Military Forces Museum,* https://www.texasmilitaryforces-museum.org/ang111p9.htm, accessed 7 October 2024

Sinclair A., 'Sidi Rezegh: Images of Death and Horror' Ditsong National Museum of Military History, https://ditsong.org.za/2020/07/23/sidi-rezegh-images-of-death-and-horror/, accessed 12 October 2020

Smith Kenneth V., 'Naples – Foggia 1943–1944', https://www.history.army.mil/brochures/naples/72-17.htm, accessed 8 October 2024

South African War Graves Project, Caserta War Cemetery, http://www.southafricawargraves.org/search/view-paginated.php?page=1&cemetery=480, accessed 17 November 2020

Staff writer, 'A hundred and ten not out for the Transvaal Horse Artillery', https://www.defenceweb.co.za/land/land-land/a-hundred-and-10-not-out-for-the-transvaal-horse-artillery, accessed 6 November 2020

Terblanche Erika, 'Uys Krige (1910–1987)', Litnet (2022), https://www.litnet.co.za/uys-krige-1910-1987/, accessed 22 January 2025

Von Winterbach, J. C. et al., '6th South African Armoured Division (part 3),' *Flames of War*, https://www.flamesofwar.com/Default.aspx?tabid=112&art_id=4402, accessed 17 January 2025

Wiesel Elie, 'Acceptance speech for Nobel Peace Prize', (10 December 1986), https://www.nobelprize.org/mediaplayer/?id=2028, accessed 1 October 2020

Wright K., 'Sebastiano Venier – Mediterranean 1942: Tribute to an Enemy', Naval Historical Society of Australia, https://navyhistory.au/sebastiano-venier-mediterranean-1942-tribute-to-an-enemy/, accessed 8 April 2021

Index

11th Field Ambulance, 45, 46, 47, 48, 49, 50, 57
12th South Africa Infantry Brigade, 132
17th Mechanical Transport Company, Cape Castle, 85
1st South Africa Division, 16, 18, 25, 52
1st South Africa Heavy Battery, 99
1st South Africa Infantry Brigade, 35, 56
4th Field Artillery Regiment, 183
4th Indian Division, 48
5th South Africa Brigade, 56
6th Field Regiment SAA, 101
7th Field Ambulance Unit, 45

Abyssinia, 32, 33, 46, 122, 167
Addis Ababa, 18, 19, 20
Aden, 144
Alem Hamza, 64
Alexander, General Sir Harold, 154, 170, 183
Alexandria, 76, 147, 148, 185
American 36th Division, 161
American 5th Army, 28, 31, 131, 134, 151, 153, 156, 157, 158, 170
Amiriya, 144
Anzio, 156, 157, 180
Aosta, *Duca di,* Viceroy of Italian East Africa, 20
Apennine Mountain Range, 135, 138, 139
Artena, 161
Auchinleck, General Sir Claude, 55, 56, 64, 65
Australia(ns), 43, 55, 60, 82, 83

Badoglio, *Maresciallo d'Italia* Pietro, 27, 170
Bagush, 55
Barcelona, 14
Bardia, 58, 59, 60, 61, 64, 80, 99, 115, 144
Beauvais, 94
Belgium, 85
Bell, Victor, 173, 174, 176, 180, 181, 183
Benghazi, 26, 50, 81, 88, 99
Beyers, Adjutant-General Leonard, 74, 192, 193
Bir El Gubi, 56
Bir Hakeim, 64, 105, 110, 113
Blitz, 23, 101
Bloemfontein, 97, 100

Blomeyer, Platoon Sergeant B, 38, 39
Bologna, xii, 31, 131, 135, 137, 138, 142
Brink, Lieutenant-General G.E., 56
Britain, 13, 17, 21, 32, 85, 96, 101, 127, 148, 165
British 8th Army, 28, 30, 55, 62, 64, 65, 66, 72, 81, 105, 106, 108, 110, 115, 125, 127, 128, 129, 131, 144, 147, 153, 165 170
Brits, Lieutenant Colonel E.G. (Papa), 32, 119

Cà di Cò, 137
Cairo, 23, 28, 41, 42, 43, 54, 56, 61, 78, 79, 80, 81, 82, 83, 101, 104, 113, 114, 129, 130, 144, 147, 148, 154, 185
Caldwell, Captain, 48
Cape Corps, 49, 85, 86, 88, 92, 94
Cape Town, 19, 72, 84, 85, 90, 96, 114, 140
Carabinieri, 171
Caserta military hospital, 67, 90
Caserta war cemetery, 69
Cassino mountains, 119
Churchill, Winston, xii, 23, 65, 79, 152
Cinecittà, *See* Prisoner-of-War Camp 122
Clark, Lieutenant General Mark, 28, 31, 149, 153, 154, 157, 161, 170, 183

De Villiers, General I.P., 77
Denmark, 85
Die Middellandse Regiment, 52, 53, 54, 55, 56, 57, 58, 59, 60, 61, 62, 65, 73, 75, 76, 80, 125
Dordrecht, 52, 68
Du Plessis, Brigadier W.H., 192
Dunkirk, 17, 18
Durban, 41, 45, 53, 74, 75, 76, 96, 101, 144

Egypt, xi, xii, 21, 36, 47, 53, 55, 62, 72, 76, 79, 81, 85, 105, 114, 116, 122, 123, 127, 143, 147, 186
Eisenhower, General Dwight D., 165
El Agheila, 80
El Alamein, 54, 77, 105, 111, 116, 121, 128, 129, 144, 147
  Battles of, 116, 119, 128, 190
El Buro Hachi, 36, 37
El Wak, 36, 37, 72
Ellis, Captain Ian, 183
Ethiopia, 19, 20

210

Filignano, 160
Florence, 131, 134, 135, 138, 163, 164, 165, 166, 167, 169, 174, 178, 180, 183, 197
Foligno, 162
Fort Mega, 46
France, 32, 85, 94, 95, 96, 161, 165, 180
Franco, Francisco, 15
French Cameroon(ian), 92
French Resistance
  Forces Françaises d'l'Interieur, 95
  Maquis, 94, 95

Gazala, 62, 64, 65, 102, 106, 127
  Battle of, 66, 109, 115, 127
  Gallop, 116, 128
  Line, 65, 81, 105, 107, 110
Gelib, 38, 40, 42
Geneva Convention, 26, 66, 86, 87, 91, 92, 96
Germany (Germans), 16, 17, 23, 25, 28, 30, 31, 44, 48, 49, 50, 59, 60, 64, 65, 79, 83, 84, 85, 87, 93, 94, 96, 111, 115, 116, 117, 118, 119, 120, 122, 125, 126, 127, 128, 129, 131, 135, 136, 137, 140, 142, 144, 146, 148, 149, 151, 152, 153, 156, 157, 158, 160, 161, 162, 163, 166, 170, 172, 174, 176, 177, 178, 180, 181, 183
Ghurkhas, 183
GilGil, 45
Graziani, *Maresciallo d'Italia* Rodolfo, 21
Greece, 85, 90, 152
Greyshirts, x
Guardia Nazionale Republicana, 171

Halfaya, 58, 59, 61, 64, 80, 99, 122, 125
Hartzenberg, Sergeant Major J.L., 46, 47
Havenga, N.C., 72, 73
Helwan, 144, 185
Hertzog, J.B.M., viii, 13, 15, 72, 73, 76
Hitler, Adolf, x, xii, 17, 28, 63, 77, 79, 81, 85, 126, 149, 152, 158, 161, 166, 167
Hobok, 46

Imperial Light Horse Regiment, 116
India, 82
Indian Corps, 86
Information Bureau, 13, 14, 16, 19, 20, 23, 26, 27, 28, 184
Italian partisans, 27, 162, 165, 169, 171, 174, 179, 180
Italy, 14, 21, 23, 26, 27, 28, 30, 31, 33, 36, 50, 66, 69, 85, 88, 91, 92, 93, 94, 110, 119, 120, 122, 130, 131, 138, 142, 147, 148, 149, 151, 152, 153, 154, 156, 157, 160, 161, 162, 165, 166, 167, 168, 170, 171, 176, 178, 179, 180, 185, 186

Japan(ese), 62, 79, 82, 83
Johannesburg, 19, 73, 188
Juba River, 37, 38

Kenya, 16, 17, 18, 38, 42, 45
Kesselring, *Generalfeldmarschall* Albert, 157
Kismayu, 37
Klopper, General H.B., xii, 43, 65, 66, 81, 167

Laterina, 91, 168
Lawrence, H.G., 75
Leibbrandt, Robey, 75
Libya, xi, 21, 22, 25, 36, 45, 47, 50, 56, 66, 87, 99, 127, 144, 163
London, 23, 28, 61, 91, 144, 152, 168, 170
Lucca, 131, 154
Luxembourg, 85

Madagascar, 83
Malan, D.F., 72, 76, 77, 148
Malan, Jacques, 28, 31
Maseko, Corporal Job, 87
McGillivray, Private, 50
Mediterranean Sea, 23, 54, 55, 65, 88, 112, 144, 165
Melzer, Major, 50
Mersa Matruh, 47, 55
Mogadishu, 18, 20, 22, 41, 190
Mombasa, 45
Monte Cassino, 119, 131, 132, 134, 156, 157, 158
  Battle of, 158, 161, 179
Monte Sole, 135, 136, 138, 140, 142
Montemurlo, 165, 168, 169, 171, 183
Montgomery, General Bernard Law, 28, 30, 31, 144, 153, 154, 165
Moosburg, 44
Mussolini, Benito, 27, 92, 93, 149, 165, 166, 167, 168, 169, 170

Nairobi, 18, 19, 185
Naples, 67, 149, 151, 152, 153, 154, 155, 157, 158, 160
Natal Mounted Rifles, 123, 124, 183
National Party, 72, 77
Native Military Corps, 86, 94
Netherlands (Dutch), 16, 32, 85
New Order, x
Northern Rhodesia, 100, 101
Norton, Conrad, 14, 16, 19, 25
Norway, 85
Nyasaland, 101

Operation Avalanche, 149
Operation Compass, 21, 99

Operation Crusader, 55, 56, 101
Operation Overlord, 134, 161
Orenstein, Brigadier A.J., 188, 191, 192
Ossewabrandwag, x, xi, 16, 74, 75, 77

Patton, General George S., 165
Pearl Harbour, 79
Philippines, 82
Pienaar, Major-General D.H. (Dan), 18, 19, 35, 56
Pietermaritzburg, 34, 35, 42, 44, 52, 114
Pisa, 163, 164
Pistoia, 131, 135, 180
Poland (Poles), 94, 161, 172
Pomigliano d'Arco, 151, 152
Poole, Major-General Evered, xii, 179, 180
Portugal, 80
Potchefstroom, 97, 98
Prato, 165, 168, 174, 176, 179, 180
Premier Mine, 35, 52
Prisoner–of–War Camp 122 Cinecittà, 92, 93

Ravenna, 154
Red Cross, 26, 48, 50, 66, 67, 68, 91, 92, 94, 96, 113, 154, 189, 193, 195
Regiment De La Ray, 180
Ritchie, Lieutenant General N.M., 64, 65, 66, 122
Roberts Heights, 70, 72, 73, 197
Rome, xii, 23, 31, 92, 119, 120, 121, 131, 133, 134, 149, 152, 153, 154, 156, 161, 162, 177, 180
Rommel, *Generalleutnant* Erwin, xii, 25, 39, 44, 47, 55, 56, 60, 63, 64, 65, 66, 72, 81, 83, 86, 99, 105, 109, 110, 115, 123, 126, 127, 129, 165
Roosevelt, Franklin D., 79
Royal Air Force, 23
Royal Durban Light Infantry, 135
Royal Natal Carbineers, 34, 35, 36, 37, 38, 123, 130, 131, 135, 180

Salerno, 27, 149, 153
Short, Arthur, 67
Sicily, 131, 146, 148, 149
Sidi Omar, 56, 58
Sidi Rezegh, 25, 48, 50, 51, 56, 144
    Battle of, 44, 56, 57, 59, 80, 86, 101, 106, 188
Singapore, 61, 62
Smuts, J.C., viii, ix, x, xi, 13, 14, 15, 16, 18, 52, 70, 74, 75, 76, 82, 102, 147, 148, 188, 190, 193, 195

Snyman, Warrant Officer Ockert, 182, 183
Sollum, 61, 64, 80, 99
Somalia, 22, 37, 38
Somaliland, 21, 22, 38
South African Air Force, 97
Spain, 14, 15, 25, 79
SS-Panzergrenadier-Division, 135
St John Ambulance Brigade, 189, 193, 195
Steyn, Colin, 77
Stormjaers, x, 16, 74, 77
Strijdom, J.G., 76
Suez, 53, 76, 85, 144, 164, 185
Suez Canal, 127, 165
Switzerland, 93, 167, 170, 173, 174

Terreurgroep, x, 16, 74
Theron, Lieutenant Colonel F., 77, 109
Tobruk, xii, 25, 43, 44, 47, 48, 55, 61, 64, 65, 66, 81, 83, 87, 105, 109, 110, 111, 112, 115, 116, 144, 147, 168
    Battle of, 44, 66, 83, 110, 167
    Siege of, 55, 56, 60, 64
Transvaal Horse Artillery, 99, 102, 111
Transvaal Scottish, 48, 86
Tripoli, 144, 146, 149
Tunis, 146
Tunisia(ns), xi, 92, 144, 145, 146, 147, 165

United States of America, 82
    America(n) / forces, 28, 31, 43, 79, 80, 82, 94, 131, 138, 139, 140, 144, 149, 153, 154, 155, 160, 161, 162, 163, 164, 170, 180, 183

Van Rensburg, H, 77
Van Ryneveld, Sir Pierre, 184
Verwoerd, Dr H.F., 76
Vichy Government, 95
Victor Emmanuel III, King, 27, 170
Vogel Vlei, 52, 53, 54, 55, 66, 69

Western Desert, 14, 45, 72, 104, 115, 122, 123, 167, 185
Witwatersrand Rifles, 180
Women's Auxiliary Air Force, 191
Women's Auxiliary Army Services, 191

Zonderwater, *See* Premier Mine
Zonderwater prisoner-of-war camp, 119